JEWISH LUDMIR
THE HISTORY AND TRAGEDY OF THE JEWISH COMMUNITY OF VOLODYMYR-VOLYNSKY

A REGIONAL HISTORY

VOLODYMYR MUZYCHENKO

Jews of Poland

Series editor—Antony Polonsky (Brandeis University)

JEWISH LUDMIR
THE HISTORY AND TRAGEDY OF THE JEWISH COMMUNITY OF VOLODYMYR-VOLYNSKY

A REGIONAL HISTORY

VOLODYMYR MUZYCHENKO

TRANSLATED FROM THE UKRAINIAN BY
MARTA DARIA OLYNYK

Boston
2016

Library of Congress Cataloging-in-Publication Data:
A catalog record for this book is available
from the Library of Congress.

Copyright © 2015 Academic Studies Press
All rights reserved

ISBN 978-1-61811-412-9 (hardback)
ISBN 978-1-61811-518-8 (paperback)
ISBN 978-1-61811-413-6 (electronic)

Cover design by Ivan Grave

Published by Academic Studies Press in 2015, paperback 2016.
28 Montfern Avenue
Brighton, MA 02135, USA
press@academicstudiespress.com
www.academicstudiespress.com

Dedicated to the memory of my mother, who survived all the horrors of the ghetto, and to her family, who perished at the hands of the Nazis.

Dedicated to the memory of the Righteous Among the Nations Fedosei and Uliana Karaschuk, who saved my mother, risking the lives of their own children.

For everything that I have, I thank you,
For everything that I have and will have.

Mykola Lukiv

Acknowledgments

The publication of this book was made possible through the generous support of the following individuals and organizations:

Dr. Harvey Budner
Moshe Margalit
Volodymyr Moiseievych Itkis
Iurii Mykolaiovych Havryliuk
Anatolii Ivanovych Kubliia
Serhii Stepanovych Sytnyk
Ievhenii Ievstakhiiovych Shylipina
Viktor Oleksandrovych Herasymchuk
Vitalii Stepanovych Tymchuk
Serhii Petrovych Yunak
Roza Moiseievna Zinkevych
Vitalii Myronovych Diachuk
Petro Stanislavovych Zhukovsky
Larysa Petrivna Ivanova
Ruslan Andriiovych Moroz

Lutsk Congregation for Progressive Judaism
The Jewish Joint Distribution Committee (JDC)

Contents

List of Illustrations x
How the English Edition Happened, *by Harvey Budner* xxiii
Introduction, *by Antony Polonsky* xxv
Author's Note xli
Foreword xliv

The History of the Jews of Volodymyr-Volynsky 1
    Introduction
    First Mentions
    Privileges
    The Kahal
    The Organization of Jewish Settlement, Fourteenth–
        Sixteenth Centuries
    Economic Conditions of the Community, Fourteenth–
        Sixteenth Centuries
    Va'ad Arba Aratsot
    Spiritual Leaders
    Shelomoh of Karlin (Karliner)
    Khane-Rokhl Werbermacher
    The Synagogue
    The Jewish Cemetery
    The Life of the Jewish Community in the Twentieth Century

The Tragedy of the Jews of Volodymyr-Volynsky 113
    From the Killing Fields: The Reminiscences of Zippora
        Weinstock-Zaar
    The Reminiscences of Yaacov Harari (Berger)
    The Reminiscences of Debora Interieur
    The Memoirs of Ann Kazimirski
    Moshe Krigser Recalls

The Reminiscences of Volodymyr Oksentiiovych Patuta
Oflag "Nord 365"

**The Catastrophe That Befell the Jews of
Volodymyr-Volynsky District** 195
    Moshe Margalit Recalls
    Mykhail (Motl) Bass's Account

Righteous among the Nations 223
    Kateryna Petrivna Lipińska
    Maria Otsaliuk's Account
    Franciszek and Hanna Strojvons
    Bronisława Ziental and Her Daughter Irena Yakira
    The Accounts of Liudmyla Stepanivna Yevtoshuk and Halyna
        Zinoviivna Nazaruk
    Oleksandr and Solomeia Diachuk

Jewish Natives of the Volodymyr-Volynsky Area Abroad 267
Memorial in the Village of Piatydni 279
Safeguarding Memory 289
Prominent Jews Born in Volodymyr-Volynsky 295
Addenda 301
Glossary of Terms 305
Bibliography 313
Index 321

List of Illustrations

Privilege granted to the Jews by Vytautas the Great
in 1388 (fragment of the Puławski manuscript) 9

Map of the city with Yiddish inscriptions prepared
by O. Tsynkalovsky 11

Defensive and religious structures in Volodymyr,
including a synagogue, fourteenth to sixteenth centuries 15

ha-Gaon Yitshak ben Bezalel 21

David ha-Levi Segal 23

Shema Shlomo (The Glory of Shlomo), the book written
by Shelomoh of Karlin. Petrokov, 1928 29

Contemporary editions of *Shema Shlomo*
by Shelomoh of Karlin 30

The *ohel* (burial vault) at the gravesite of Rabbi
Shelomoh Karliner 33

Matsevahs on the grave of Tsadik Shelomoh Karliner and
Yehudah (Yodl), son of Moshe 34

Map showing the Uniate women's monastery that
the Maiden of Ludmir may have visited 38

The *grünshtibl*, the Bet ha-Midrash of the Maiden
of Ludmir, early twentieth century 40

List of Illustrations

Diagram showing 1) the location of the Maiden of Ludmir's gravesite and 2) the plot where her grave is located 42

The grave of the Maiden of Ludmir 43

A group of pilgrims visiting the grave of the Maiden of Ludmir on the Mount of Olives 43

Rabbi Ruth Gan Kagan at the grave of Khane-Rokhl Werbermacher 45

Rachel Botchan playing the starring role in *The Maiden of Ludmir* 46

The foundation of a brick structure, probably a synagogue dating to the fourteenth to fifteenth centuries 49

Large choral synagogue built in 1801; photograph taken in 1901 49

Large choral synagogue; postcard from the early twentieth century. From the private collection of R. Mazurok 50

View of the synagogue 50

The synagogue in Volodymyr-Volynsky 51

Large choral synagogue. Illustration by an unknown artist 51

The interior of the synagogue: the *aron ha-kodesh** and the *bima** (amud), the pulpit used by the *khazan* (cantor) 52

The synagogue in Volodymyr-Volynsky; postcard from the early twentieth century 52

At left: the large choral synagogue 53

List of Illustrations

The spot on which the choral synagogue once stood; today: Roksoliana Street 53

The large choral synagogue built in 1801 54

The synagogue (aerial photograph) 54

The synagogue in the village of Porytsk 58

The Jewish cemetery in Volodymyr-Volynsky in an illustration by the artist Emil Weiss 73

The Jewish cemetery. Archival photo 73

Layout of the cemetery 74

The sidewalk on Vasylkivska Street 75

Matsevahs used for paving the sidewalk on Vasylkivska Street 75

Matsevahs discovered by the author in the yard of a private residence on Vasylkivska Street 76

A matsevah discovered by the author in a city courtyard 76

A grinding disk fashioned out of a matsevah 77

The Jewish cemetery 77

Jewish shops in Volodymyr-Volynsky; Austrian postcard, 1918 79

Volodymyr-Volynsky: a Jew wearing a tallit and holding a prayer book; photo dating to 1916–17 80

List of Illustrations

The Jewish quarter of Volodymyr-Volynsky in the early twentieth century 81

The Jewish quarter of the city 81

A water-pump near the synagogue in Volodymyr-Volynsky, 16 August 1925 82

Pupils of a Jewish school during the First World War, 1916–17 83

Teachers of the first Jewish school in Ludmir, period of the First World War 84

The building of the Talmud-Torah school on 2 Zelena Street 85

The pupils of the Talmud-Torah school and their teachers 86

The building housing the Talmud-Torah school, 2 Zelena Street 86

The administration of the Tarbut school and its pupils 88

The teachers and pupils of the Tarbut agricultural school 91

The building housing the Tarbut school, located at 24 Haidamatska Street 91

The Jewish scouting organization Ha-Shomer ha-Tsa'ir 92

The "People's Kitchen": members of its committee and the people whom it supported—mostly children, 1916 93

The members of the TOZ committee responsible for the care of orphans and their charges 93

The directors of the home for the elderly and its residents 94

Committee in aid of the poor and orphans, 1929 94

The TOZ organization 94

Summer camp for children, 1930 95

Children and their camp counselors 95

The directors of the summer camp for orphans, 1922 96

The new orphanage premises 96

Committee of Jewish civic, religious, and political organizations 97

Members of the branch of the Poalei-Zion Party 98

Souvenir photograph taken before the departure to Palestine
of Dr. Israelis's family 99

The first group of émigrés from Volodymyr-Volynsky
before their departure to Palestine, 1925 99

The Volodymyr-Volynsky committee of the Zionist Party 100

The Ha Halutz youth organization 101

Members of the city council 102

The Hebrew-language newspaper Ha-Khaver (Comrade), 1932 ... 103

The Yiddish-language weekly newspaper
Unzer lebn (Our Life), 1930 103

List of Illustrations

The ORT trade (technical) school, 1932 105

The members of the Betar organization 105

The members of the Betar organization 106

Building owned by Dr. Shekhter 107

Jewish shops located on the corner of Shevchenko and
Kovelska streets 108

The last Passover seder* celebrated at the orphanage, 1939 108

Rabbis Yaacov-David Morgenshtern (left) and
L. Goldshtern showing the city sights to a visiting rabbi 109

Leib Filarent, the *sofer* (Torah copyist), and his family 109

Large choral synagogue photographed between 1921-1924 111

The former prison, which was converted to a TB hospital
after the war 123

Mass grave uncovered by archaeologists in 2011 on the territory
of the former prison 124

Copy of the leaflet courtesy of the Lutsk Congregation
for Progressive Judaism 126

German occupiers abusing Rabbi Moshe Hagerman,
Olkusz, Poland 127

Area plan of the first ghetto 133

Text of E. Kumming's report 136

List of Illustrations

The building owned by the Golshtein family on
3 Soborna Street 142

Eliezer Reisfeld 149

Mass graves unearthed in Piatydni, spring 1943 151

Diagram of the third ghetto 152

Zippora Weinstock-Zaar 172

Yaacov Harari (Berger) 175

Debora Interieur (née Frimer) 177

Ann Kazimirski 181

Ann Kazimirski's identity card issued by the Judenrat of
Volodymyr-Volynsky 182

The Krigser family, Ustyluh 185

Moshe Krigser and General Roman Yagel 187

Arie-Leib Kam 192

Volodymyr Muzychenko by the gravestone, the only trace left of the
3,200 Jewish residents of Ustyluh 196

Nadia Lysiuk at the Jewish grave 201

Moshe Margalit. Photo dated 14 June 1939. From Moshe Margalit's
family archive 205

Volodymyr-Volynsky: The family of Moshe Margalit, 1938 207

List of Illustrations

Jewish child survivors after the city's liberation, 1945 217

Moshe Margalit.. 217

Mykhail Bass lives in the city of Holon (Israel). From
the Bass family archive.. 219

Mykola Mykhailovych Vavrysevych (1891–1978)
and his wife Maria Adamivna.. 227

Mykola Mykolaiovych Vavrysevych.. 228

Certificate of honor awarded to Mykola and Maria Vavrysevych
and their two sons Mykhailo and Mykola................................ 228

Article in the *New York Times* published on 28 November
1997 229

The reception held at the Ukrainian Consulate in New York City
in 1997.. 229

The medal awarded to Mykola Vavrysevych,
recognizing him as Righteous Among the Nations 230

Kateryna Lipińska and her daughter Iryna, Righteous
Among the Nations. Photo courtesy of A. Kupriichuk................ 233

Kateryna Lipińska's medal recognizing her as Righteous
Among the Nations 234

Memorial plaque near the tree planted in honor of Kateryna
Lipińska, Righteous Among the Nations, Jerusalem (Israel)........ 234

The cover of Henry Orenstein's book *I Shall Live* 235

Henry Orenstein and Matilda Topolia-Hertel............................235

Olha Pylypivna Miaskovska, her husband Serhii Tykhonovych,
and their daughter Halyna..239

Halyna Serhiivna Filatova (née Miaskovska) (b. 1928)................239

Pauline Kamm (née Cohen), who was saved
by the Miaskovsky family..240

Maria Oleksandrivna Otsaliuk (née Diachuk), Righteous
Among the Nations, lives in the USA..241

Oleksandr and Solomeia Diachuk...242

Franciszek and Hanna Strojvons with their son and daughter......243

Maria Fomivna Sheptytska...248

Stepan Antonovych Sheptytsky..248

Omelian Petrovych and Epistymiia Vakulivna Fisiuk...................249

Mordechai Mendelson's family with the grandchildren of
his rescuers 252

The synagogue next to Shulman's mill, 81 Lutska Street 259

The building housing the Akiba Jewish youth club and
the synagogue on Pidzamche Street 259

The *Etz chaim* (Tree of Life) after restoration 260

A building decorated with the *Etz chaim* symbol at 22 D.
Halytsky Street..260

List of Illustrations

The Jewish men's school at 17 Ustyluh Street 260

The Jewish school at 1 Soborna Street 261

The Beit-Yaacov Jewish women's school at 9 Drahomanov Street 261

Rabbi's house at 24 D. Halytsky Street 262

A copper cup used for *netilat yadayim* (ritual washing of the hands) found in the city 262

Fragment of a Torah scroll 263

A *matsevah* (gravestone) 264

A *matsevah* 264

A *hanukiah* (candelabrum with nine branches), which is lit for the feast of *Hanukah** 265

A box for storing *etrog**, a citrus fruit used in the rituals of the festival of Sukkot (lit. "booths") 265

Wall of Honor at Yad-Vashem, Jerusalem 266

Zippora (Feiga) Weinstock-Zaar 271

Commemorative marker on Mount Zion in Jerusalem 272

Stone on Mount Eshtaol, near Jerusalem, with a commemorative plaque 273

Inscription on the obelisk 273

List of Illustrations

The building of the Heichal Yahaduth Wolyn in
Givatayim, Israel 274

Monument to Soviet Jewish partisans of Volyn 274

A wall with the names of Wolyn towns and cities 275

Model of the Great Liuboml Synagogue in Beit Wolyn 275

Model of the monument to Holocaust victims in the
village of Piatydni 276

Photographic stands in the room dedicated to
Volodymyr-Volynsky 276

Moshe Krigser (at right), head of the committee of Jews from
Volodymyr-Volynsky 277

Menashe Kiper and Moshe Margalit 277

Soirée attended by members of the Federation of
Wolyn Jews in New York 278

Monument to the victims of the Holocaust in Piatydni 279

The first monument at the site of the mass shootings
in Piatydni, 1944 282

At the unveiling of the monument, 17 September 1989 283

The mass graves in the village of Piatydni 283

Grave no. 1 284

Grave no. 2 284

List of Illustrations

Grave no. 3 284

Memorial to the victims of fascism in Piatydni, mass
grave number 1 287

After installing the memorial plaques on the graves
of the Holocaust victims, August 27 2014 288

Meeting held at the monument in the village of Piatydni,
2006 292

At the unveiling of the information billboard in 2010 293

After the commemorative meeting in 2008 held at the
monument in Piatydni 293

Janusz Bardach 295

Abram Nuger in the role of Bobe Yakhne, the witch 298

Map of Volodymyr-Volynsky and surrounding villages,
published in the Russian Empire, 1867 303

Contemporary map of Ukraine 304

How the English Edition Happened

Harvey Budner

In 2010, a small group of us travelled to Ludmir (Ukrainian: Volodymyr Volynsky), a small western Ukrainian city from which my father and his family emigrated early in the twentieth century.

Volodymyr Muzychenko, the head of the Jewish community in Ludmir and our local guide, showed us the materials for a book he was writing in Ukrainian about the history of the Jewish community in Ludmir.

I was amazed at his seriousness of purpose and dedication to the project. He had spent several years searching in Ukrainian and Russian archives. He had also collected extensive personal reminiscences and many photos from both Jews and non-Jews in the region. What was most surprising was that he is not an historian but a classical guitarist and a teacher in the local music school. The culmination of that effort is the book you now have before you.

Volodymyr knows the community exceedingly well, even though he is not a native. Although I could provide only vague descriptions of the neighborhood from family stories, he promptly took us to a house in which it is highly likely my family lived. I did know that the family occupation was barrel-making, and that production was based in their home in Ludmir. (The name "Budner" is a version of "Bodnar" which in Ukrainian means barrel-maker).

The current, Christian occupant of the home, curious as to why there were people standing in the rain looking at her house, came out to speak with us. Volodymyr identified himself and explained to her our interest in her home. She said the original house was at least one hundred years old with several later additions. She welcomed us in and demonstrated unusual features such as the location of former rooftop windows, consistent with venting the steam and smoke produced in barrel-making. Volodymyr identifies strongly as Jewish, but as demonstrated by this example, he has a warm and accepting attitude toward his Christian neighbors, and they toward him.

After we returned, my extended family and I helped Volodymyr publish *Jewish Ludmir* in the original Ukrainian. I showed it to Professor Antony Polonsky, an expert on Eastern European Jewish History at Brandeis University. He was enthusiastic about the high quality of the scholarship and the historical significance of the photos, and he felt the work clearly deserved to be translated into English. He recommended Marta D. Olynyk to translate it. Marta accepted the assignment, and she did a most thorough and careful translation. She valued the book, in part, for its description of the centuries-long and usually harmonious relationship between Jews and Christians in Ukraine (unfortunately periodically punctuated by conflict). My extended family and I supported the translation and subsequent publication of this English edition of *Jewish Ludmir*.

I am enormously grateful to the extensive community of family and friends, unfortunately too numerous to name, who provided invaluable assistance with this project. However, I must acknowledge those who were absolutely essential in making this project possible by providing continuing explanation, support, and encouragement. Volodymyr Muzychenko, the author, worked tirelessly on the many details of translating and publishing his book into English. Professor Antony Polonsky was my guide through a process totally unfamiliar to me. Marta D. Olynyk not only produced a superb translation of the book itself but then assisted with translating the extensive follow-up communication between the publisher and the author. Debra Young (aided by husband Arnold) made the software understandable and manageable. The staff at Academic Studies Press was immediately responsive and very cooperative in the many decisions about editing and production.

I am thrilled with the result, and I hope you find it very enlightening reading.

Introduction

Antony Polonsky

In the introduction to his *Żydzi w Przemyslu do konca XVIII wieku* (The Jews in Przemyśl to the End of the Eighteenth Century), the historian Mojżesz Schorr wrote:

> The main failing of the method which has been employed up to the present in investigating the history of the Jews in Poland is that general questions have been approached before the detailed problems were resolved. Scholars have attempted to describe the history of Jews in the whole of Poland before research had been done on the history of individual towns. Attempts were similarly made to describe the general history of the Jews before the specifics of individual periods had been illuminated.[1]

His observation, dating back more than a century, applies to all of the lands of the Polish-Lithuanian Commonwealth and it is as true today as when it was first made. There is thus all the more reason to welcome this comprehensive and moving history of the Jews of Volodymyr-Volynsky (Polish, Włodzimierz Wołyński; Yiddish, Ludmir), based not only on books and documents but also on many interviews and conversations with people from the town, both Jewish and non-Jewish. Volodymyr-Volynsky, situated on the Luha River (a tributary of the western Buh river), is one of the oldest towns in Volhynia. It takes its name from Prince Volodymyr Sviatoslavovych of

---

1 Mojzesz Schorr, *Żydzi w Przemyslu do konca XVIII wieku* (L'viv, 1903).

Kyiv (ruled 980-1015 C.E.), who introduced Orthodox Christianity to Kyivan Rus' and established a stronghold here around 981. In 988, it became the capital of the Volodymyr Principality and the seat of an Orthodox bishopric, as is described in the Primary Chronicle. By 1300, the town had become the capital of the Principality of Galicia-Volhynia, one of the three principal states (along with Novgorod and Vladimir-Suzdal) which emerged from the collapse of Kyivan Rus'. In 1241, together with other Ruthenian principalities, it was conquered by the Tatars and incorporated into the Mongol Empire.

In 1349, the town was annexed by King Kazimierz the Great of Poland, but on his death in 1370 it was incorporated into the Grand Duchy of Lithuania, which had incorporated Volhynia, Podolia, and left-bank Ukraine after Grand Duke Algirdas defeated the Mongols in 1362 at the Battle of Blue Waters. In 1431, the city was granted municipal self-government in accordance with Magdeburg law by the Lithuanian Grand Duke Švitrigaila. After the constitutional union of the Kingdom of Poland and the Grand Duchy of Lithuania in 1569 (the two states had been dynastically linked since 1385), the town again became part of the Kingdom of Poland. It passed to the tsarist Empire after the second partition of Poland in 1792. In 1915, the town was occupied by the Austrians, and during the Russian Civil War it was disputed among Polish, Ukrainian, and Bolshevik forces, coming under Polish control in January 1919. In the interwar period, it was the seat of a *powiat* within the Polish province of Volhynia and an important army garrison.

Following the Nazi-Soviet Pact, the city became occupied by the Red Army on 19 September 1939 and became a part of the Ukrainian SSR. On 23 June 1941, it was seized by Germany, and during World War II a German concentration camp was located near the city. It was recaptured by the Red Army on 20 July 1944 and again became a part of the Ukrainian SSR. Today it is the district centre of the Volyn' oblast in independent Ukraine.

The Jewish community of Volodymyr-Volynsky is first mentioned in 1171 and was initially made up of Jews from Kyiv, the Khazar khanate, and other eastern communities. The town became an important way-station on the trade route between Spain and western Europe and the east, and among the merchants who took part in this were Jews from Ashkenaz (Northern France and Germany). In the last third of the thirteenth century, the community was led by Rabbi Chaim ben Yitshak (Maharah), author of *Or zaru'a,* and Rabbi Manoakh ben Ya'akov. According to Rus' chronicles, Jews participated in the funeral of Vladimir Vasil'kovich, Prince of Vladimir, in 1288. Tombstones from the fourteenth century are further proof of the Jewish presence in the town, as are the remains of a synagogue unearthed in 2009.

Organized Jewish life ceased to exist under Tatar rule but a small number of Jews were encouraged by Grand Duke Vytautas of Lithuania (ruled 1392-1430) to return to the town. Jews were expelled from the Grand Duchy by the Grand Duke Alexander Jagiellon in 1495. They soon returned, and in the early sixteenth century an organized community was re-established. Its growth was facilitated by the transfer, following the Union of Lublin, of the province of Volhynia to the Kingdom of Poland. It was now, in 1570, that King Zygmunt August II (ruled 1548-1572) granted a charter of privileges to the city, which came under his direct rule. According to it, the Jews, together with the Christians, were exempted from paying duties on trade apart from those on salt and beeswax. Jews now engaged in tax farming, the leasing of estates and mills, and the right to sell alcohol, and were active in trade, attending fairs at Lublin, Poznań, and Kraków, where they sold furs, woolen cloth, and wax. They also engaged in artisan trades, in spite of Christian attempts to limit this, above all shoemaking and leather processing. Ludmir was represented on regional and national Jewish councils, and one of its delegates was the well-known kabbalist and author Yom-Tov Lipmann Heller, who also served as community rabbi from 1634 to 1643. He was not the only distinguished figure to hold this office. Other important rabbis were Yitshak ben Bezalel, who served from 1547 to 1570, Ishaya ben Yitshak (Yitshak ben Shemu'el ha-Levi), who was rabbi until 1595 and later became rabbi of Kraków, and the talmudist Isaac ben Samuel ha-Levi (1580–1646), who was born in the town. There is much more to be found in the book on the spiritual leaders of the community at this time.

The Jewish quarter of Volodymir was located in the northeastern section of the town, along the defensive ramparts, not far from the Church of the Presentation of the Holy Virgin. The Jews of the town suffered greatly in the Khmel'nytskyi uprising. When it began, approximately 1,000 Jews lived there in 159 homes. During the uprising, Cossacks murdered or took captive many local Jews, and by the end of 1649, there were only thirty-nine Jewish homes in the town. In 1653 only twenty-five homes were subject to the poll tax. As a result, in 1653, and again in 1658, the leaders of the community were compelled to borrow considerable sums to assist its poorer members, and as a consequence the *kehila* became indebted to the royal treasury and private creditors.

These efforts to revive Jewish life do seem to have borne fruit. From 1653 the community's leaders once again began taking part in the Jewish regional council and also representing Volhynia in the Va'ad Arba Aratsot. A further sign of the revival of the community was the award in 1700 by King Augustus II of Poland-Lithuania (ruled 1699-1733) to a local Jew, Fishel Levkovych, the *parnas* of the regional council and the Crown Va'ad, of the title of "royal agent and purveyor and official secretary for the Council of the Four Lands." The 1764 census recorded 1,401 Jews living in Volodymyr-Volynsky, making it the second largest Jewish town (after Lutsk) in the Volyn region. According to the census of 1765, 1,327 Jews living in 159 houses paid the poll tax.

In 1795, the town was annexed by Russia; and in the following years, its population grew because of its importance as a center for trade and artisan crafts, close to the border of the Habsburg Empire. Jews traded in general goods, grain, and lumber; and the main artisan trades were tailoring, hat-making, and shoemaking. In 1805, there were 1,943 Jews and 673 Christians living in the town. According to the 1861 census, their number had now grown to 6,122, out of a total population of 8,636. The census of 1897, the first to be conducted using modern techniques, assessed the town's population as 9,883, of whom Jews comprised 59.3 percent (5,869 individuals). In addition, there were 1,735 Russians, 1,367 Ukrainians, 776 Poles, 14 Czechs, and 100 Germans. The fact that the Jewish population had fallen slightly since

1861 was probably the result of emigration. By 1912, the town's population had grown to 15,622 while the Jewish population was now 7,060.

At this time, there were two large synagogues in the city: one, elaborately decorated and made of wood, destroyed during the Nazi occupation; and the other, a brick choral synagogue, dismantled in the early 1950s. There were also two *Batei Midrash* and many smaller *shtiblach*, since the town had become an important Hasidic centre. In 1786, Rabbi Shelomoh Gotlieb ben-Yuta, a pupil of Aaron Perlov, founder of the Karliner hasidic dynasty, settled in the town and attracted a significant following. He was killed in 1792 by a Cossack involved in the repression of the Polish resistance to the second partition. In hasidic tradition, because of the circumstances of his death, Shelomoh of Karlin has been seen as the reincarnation of the first suffering Messiah, son of Joseph, who is reborn from generation to generation and is constantly present on Earth. His life and teachings are movingly described in this book. Today, Shlomo Wilhelm, one of his descendants, heads the Orthodox community in Zhytomyr and is Chief Rabbi of Central and Western Ukraine.

The town was also the home of the "Maiden of Ludmir" (Khane-Rokhl Werbermacher, born c. 1815), a popular miracle-working figure who was one of the few women to play an important role in hasidism and whose life and career is fully discussed in this volume. The Maiden of Ludmir established a reputation as a student of the Bible, Talmud, and other rabbinic literature. After the collapse of an engagement, the death of her mother, and a mysterious illness, she shut herself off from the world. She began to observe rituals usually reserved for men, using her inheritance to build a study house of her own and leading a weekly *tish* [gathering] for her followers, acquiring a following as a teacher and worker of miracles. At the same time, her behaviour aroused strong opposition, above all because of her refusal to marry, which was regarded as unnatural—although Jewish tradition legitimated on occasion male sexual abstinence, it deemed such behavior unacceptable for women.[2] The Maiden was thus forced to conclude two marriages, both

---

[2] See Ada Rapoport-Albert, *Female Bodies, Male Souls: Asceticism and Gender in the Jewish Tradition* (forthcoming).

of which were unconsummated. She died in Palestine in 1892. In 2004, a new tombstone was unveiled at what was believed to be her grave on the Mount of Olives. In the words of Ada Rapoport-Albert, author of a pioneering study of her career: "Had this tradition bestowed any legitimacy on the ascetic piety of women, the Maid might have found an outlet for it even within marriage as did men who managed to achieve it without altogether renouncing their ... obligation toward worldly existence."³

Jewish life in the town was affected by the new developments in the Pale of Settlement at the end of the nineteenth century. Modern medical and charitable facilities were created, including a mutual aid fund which offered Jews no-interest loans, and, in addition to the yeshiva in the town, a state Jewish school and Jewish technical school were founded. Modern Jewish political movements also established themselves in the town with branches of the Hovevei Zion Party, the Bund, and the Zionist Socialist Party.

Volodymyr-Volynsky was occupied by the Austrians in the summer of 1915 after part of the town had been destroyed by the retreating Russian army. It suffered further damage during the fighting in the latter part of World War I and during the Russian civil war and was occupied by the Ukrainian People's Republic (UNR), the Hetmanate of Pavlo Skoropadsky, and the Bolsheviks before it ultimately came under Polish rule in September 1920. All these forces attacked the local Jews, who were defended by a two-hundred-strong Jewish militia established during the Austrian occupation.

When peace returned in 1921, there were 5,917 Jews in the town, making up just over half of the total population. By 1931 the town's population had grown to 23,500, of whom 11,985 were Jews, comprising fifty-one percent of the total. Ukrainians constituted twenty-two percent. By 1934, the city's demographic face had changed, partly as a

---

3 Ada Rapoport-Albert, "On Women in Hasidism, S. A. Horodecky and the Maid of Ludmir Tradition," in *Jewish History: Essays in Honor of Chimen Abramsky*, ed. Ada Rapoport-Albert and Steven J. Zipperstein (London: Halban, 1988), 502–3, 508.

result of the incorporation of surrounding villages. According to the town records, it now had 27,117 inhabitants, of whom 10,406 were Jews.

Jews dominated the economic life of the town, and in 1926 eighty-four percent of the businesses were in their hands. The reconstruction of Jewish life was assisted by the the American Jewish Joint Distribution Committee ("the Joint"). Faced with anti-Jewish violence in May 1923, the tradition of self-defense established during the war was still effective. The most active of the Jewish political parties were the Zionists. The Zionist youth movements—*Ha-Shomer ha-Tsa'ir, Ha-Tsofim (scouts), Ha-Shomer ha-Leumi (National Guard), Ha-No'ar ha-Tsiyoni, and Betar* all operated in Volodymyr-Volynsky. In the municipal elections of 1929, Jewish groupings won twelve of the twenty-four seats. By the late 1930s, however, the rise in government and popular antisemitism made the situation of the Jews increasingly perilous, as is well-documented in this book by the memoirs of Juliusz Bardach, a native of the town who later became a leading Polish legal historian.

At the same time, Jewish cultural life was well-developed, with a large Sholem Aleichem Library of Jewish Literature and a Yiddish theatre. Several Yiddish-language periodicals were published there, including the non-party *Unzer lebn* and *Ha-Khaver*, published by the student union of the Zionist Tarbut school. Among the Jewish educational institutions were this Tarbut school and an agricultural school linked with it which offered theoretical and practical training for young people who intended to work the land in Palestine, separate Orthodox schools for boys and girls—part of the Yavneh and Beys Yankev networks—and a private Jewish gymnasium with Polish as the language of instruction. There was also an ORT technical school where students were trained as artisans.

After the Polish defeat in September 1939 and the incorporation of the town into the Soviet Union, large numbers of Jews fled eastward, and the Jewish population of the town rose to 25,000. The leaders of the Tarbut briefly obtained the consent of the new authorities to allow the school to continue to offer instruction in Hebrew, provided all study of religion was removed from the curriculum, but this lasted only two months; and sovietized Yiddish then became the language of instruction. As elsewhere in the newly incorporated areas of the Soviet Union, the initial hopes of many Jews that they would be able to live under Soviet rule were soon dispelled. Jewish businesses were nationalized, Zionist politicians were arrested, Jewish political parties were banned, and middle class Jews and refugees made up a significant proportion of those deported to the interior of the Soviet Union in the spring and summer of 1940.

The Germans entered Volodymyr-Volynsky on 25 June 1941, and the city became part of the administrative-territorial order of the *Generalkommissariat Wolhynia and Podolia* (Volyn and Podillia), which was part of the *Reichskommissariat Ukraine*. The account of the fate of the Jews of Volodymyr under Nazi rule is one of the most valuable and new aspects of this book. To Hitler and his closest associates, the myth of the Jewish conspiracy to destroy the German people provided a central motive which would unite the disparate elements making up Nazi doctrine. Though Nazi Germany had been slow to put into practice the more extreme elements of its antisemitism, by 1938 the regime was set in its deep-seated hatred of the Jews and its determination to root out Jewish influence wherever it could. In November of that year, a ferocious pogrom was unleashed over the whole of Germany in response to the assassination in Paris of a German diplomat by a desperate Jewish youth. As relations between Poland and Germany deteriorated, Hitler threatened the Jews with genocide: "If international Jewish power in Europe and beyond again succeeds in enmeshing the peoples in a world war, the result will not be the Bolshevization of the world and a victory for Jewry, but the annihilation of the Jewish race in Europe."

These genocidal threats were not immediately carried out after Hitler's occupation of Poland, but the twenty-one months that preceded the invasion of the Soviet Union saw Nazi policy towards the Jews grow increasingly harsh. It was this invasion by German forces on Sunday, 22 June 1941, supported by troops from Finland, Hungary, Italy, Romania, and Slovakia, that made genocide possible. The conflict that followed was seen by the Nazis as an ideological crusade and a war of extermination *(Vernichtungskrieg)*. Hitler and his circle saw the war as an opportunity to carry out an even more radical ethnic reshaping of the areas east of Germany than that attempted in the Polish areas directly incorporated into the Third Reich. *General Plan Ost*, formulated early in 1941, envisaged massive German settlement in the areas they hoped to conquer, which would be made possible by the expulsion or starvation of "thirty-one million Slavs" and, presumably, by the elimination of most of the local Jews. In addition, the awareness that Germany was fighting a war of attrition and the memory of the hardships created by the blockade during the First World War meant that Nazi planning was based on the rapid conquest of the Soviet Union and the seizure of its resources, above all grain and oil, which would be needed for the war with the British Empire and, in due course, the United States. The military requirement for a rapid campaign, combined with the Wehrmacht's logistical shortcomings, led to a decision to live off the land. That decision, plus the regime's determination to extract food for the home front, contributed to a policy of deliberate starvation by which the Germans expected to kill off a large portion of the Soviet population. Terror would be necessary to ensure the provision of food for the army and the German home front, and, because of the shortage of German personnel, to carry out the grandiose plans of the Third Reich. Moreover, German military strategy had long been based on the principle that pre-emptive action was necessary to forestall civilian resistance.

These considerations led to the adoption of a policy of genocide. By this time the policies adopted by the Nazis towards the congenitally ill and people with disabilities had resulted in the development of a technology of mass murder. The gas chamber, the iconic instrument of the Nazi anti-Jewish genocide, with its employment of assembly-line practices, its use of disinformation and deceit, and its avoidance of the need for the murderers to be personally involved in the shedding of blood, was first tried out in Germany in the "euthanasia" program in which 70,000 people with mental and physical disabilities were gassed between September 1939 and the summer of 1941. In September 1941, experiments with Zyklon B gas, an insecticide, were carried out on Soviet prisoners of war in Auschwitz. There was much interchange of personnel between those engaged in implementing these programmes and those later involved in the mass murder of the Jews.

Although such a policy was not part of the planning of Operation Barbarossa, its architects clearly envisaged mass killings of Jews and other civilians. In order to avoid such conflicts between the Wehrmacht, the SS, and the civilian authorities as had dogged the September campaign in Poland, agreement among these agencies was reached before the invasion on the abrogation of international norms in the conduct of war.[4] The ideological character of the war in the east meant that the commanders of the Wehrmacht were willing to cooperate with the Nazis' plans there. Thus, in accordance with Hitler's instructions, in March 1941 Reinhard Heydrich, the Head of the RSHA, and Kurt Daluege, the Chief of the German Order Police (*Ordnungspolizei*), were able to reach an accord with the Wehrmacht on their relative spheres of competence in the areas to be conquered.[5] This led to the promulgation of a series of orders, among them the Order Concerning the Exercise of Martial Jurisdiction and Procedure in Area "Barbarossa" (*Gerichtsbarkeitserlaß*), the Directives for the Behaviour of the Troops in Russia (*Richtlinien für die Truppe*), and the Commissar Order (*Kommissarbefehl*).

The first of these, issued by the Armed Forces High Command (*Oberkommando der Wehrmacht* [OKW]) on 13 May 1941, abolished the jurisdiction of courts martial in cases of "criminal activities undertaken by enemy civilians," authorizing officers to take "violent collective measures" against areas from which the Wehrmacht was attacked.[6]

---

4   A detailed account of the crimes of the Wehrmacht can be found in *Verbrechen der Wehrmacht* rev. ed. (Hamburg: Hamburger Institut für Sozialforschung, 2002), 16–36.

5   Helmuth Greiner and Percy Ernst Schramm (eds.), *Kriegstagebuch des Oberkommandos der Wehrmacht (Wehrmachtführungsstab) 1940-1945*, 4 volumes (Frankfurt am Main: Bernard & Graefe, 1961-65), vol. 1, 341; vol. 2, 336 ff; Götz Aly, *Endlösung: Völkerverschiebung und der Mord an den europäischen Juden* (Frankfurt am Main: Fischer, 1995), 270.

6   Erlaß uber die Ausübung der Kriegsgerichtsbarkeit im Gebiet 'Barbarossa' und über besondere Maßnahmen der Truppe, BA-MA, RW 4/v. 577, Bl. 72-74, cited in Christoph Dieckmann and Saulius Sužiedėlis, *The Persecution and Mass Murder of Lithuanian Jews during Summer and Fall of 1941* (Vilnius: Margi Raštai, 2006), 111–2.

The directives for the behavior of the army instructed soldiers "to take ruthless and decisive actions against the Bolshevik rabble-rousers, partisans, Jews and totally destroy any active or passive resistance."[7] The Commissar Order issued on 6 June 1941 laid down that the ideological functionaries of the Red Army (Commissars) and Jews in its ranks were not to be recognized as soldiers. On the battlefield, they were to be executed by the army, while behind the lines they were to be dealt with by the *Einsatzgruppen* of the Security Police and SS.[8]

These *Einsatzgruppen*, which had been used on a smaller scale in the Polish campaign of 1939, were to carry out the ideological tasks of the Nazi regime, above all in relation to Jews. In the spring of 1941, four battalion-size units of these special militarized police, numbering initially around 4,000 men, were set up and given special orders for the liquidation during the campaign of potentially hostile elements.[9] They were supplemented by several brigades of Waffen SS troops, directly subordinate to Himmler, and thirty to forty battalions of the German Order Police under the command of the Higher SS and Police Leaders. Their tasks were set out in two messages sent by Heydrich to the *Einsatzgruppen* and to the Higher SS and Police Leaders shortly after outbreak of the war.[10] On 29 June 1941, Heydrich wrote to the *Einsatzgruppen* commanders, drawing their attention to the "the

---

[7] Richtlinien für das Verhalten der Truppe in Russland, 19 May 1941, BA-MA, RW 4/v. 524, Bl. 13 ff, quoted in Dieckmann and Sužiedėlis, *The Persecution and Mass Murder of Lithuanian Jews*, 111-2.

[8] Richtlinien für die Behandlung politischer Kommissare, 6 June 1941, BA-MA, RW 4/v. 578, Bl. 42-44, quoted in Dieckmann and Sužiedėlis, *The Persecution and Mass Murder of Lithuanian Jews*, 111-2.

[9] On the *Einsatzgruppen*, see Helmut Krausnick and Hans-Heinrich Wilhelm, *Die Truppe des Weltanschauungskrieges: Die Einsatzgruppe n der Sicherheitspolizei und des SD* (Stuttgart: Dt. Verl.-Anst, 1981) and Peter Klein (ed.), *Die Einsatzgruppen in der besetzten Sowjetunion 1941/42. Die Tätigkeits- und Lageberichte des Chefs der Sicherheitspolizei und des SD* (Berlin: Hentrich, 1997). See also Alexander B. Rossino, *Hitler Strikes Poland: Blitzkrieg, Ideology, and Atrocity* (Lawrence, KS: University Press of Kansas, 2003) and Michael Wildt, *Generation des Unbedingten: Das Führungskorps des Reichssicherheitshauptamtes* (Hamburg: Hamburger Ed., 2002), 419-85.

[10] Orders Nr. 1 and 2 to the EG Commanders, 20 June and 2 July 1941, Klein, *Die Einsatzgruppen in der besetzten Sowjetunion 1941/42*, 318-21.

verbal instructions already issued in Berlin on 17 June" and reminding them that

> the self-cleansing attempts of local anti-Communist and anti-Jewish circles within the newly occupied territories should in no way be hindered. On the contrary, they must be encouraged, of course without leaving a trace, and even intensified, and when necessary, directed onto the right path, but in such a way that the local "self-defense units" could not later refer to orders or openly proclaimed political goals.... Initially the creation of permanent self-defence units under a centralized leadership must be avoided; instead it is advisable, as noted before, to encourage local pogroms.[11]

It was this incitement that led to anti-Jewish violence by some Ukrainians in Volodymyr in the first days of the occupation.

In a note of 2 July 1941 to senior SS and Police officers in the occupied Soviet Union, Heydrich repeated the terms of the Commissar Order of 6 June 1941, and singled out for execution "Jews holding certain positions in the Party and state institutions."[12] These orders were vague, calling for the liquidation of "other radical elements and the like," and they were almost certainly supplemented by an oral briefing to *Einsatzgruppen* and *Einsatzkommando* officers in Berlin on 17 June 1941,[13] as is suggested by the message of 6 August 1941 from Franz Walter Stahlecker, the commander of *Einsatzgruppe* A, which refers to the "basic orders of a higher institution to the Security Police not expressed in writing."[14] These probably involved the murder of

---

11 Heydrich to the EG Commanders, Einsatzbefehl Nr. 1, reproduced in Peter Longerich and Dieter Pohl (eds.), *Die Ermordung der europäischen Juden. Ein umfassende Dokumentation des Holocaust 1941-1945* (Munich: Piper, 1989), 118ff.
12 Heydrich to the HSSPF, 2 July 1941, BA, R 70 Sowjetunion 15, Bl. 6-10, also reproduced in Klein, *Die Einsatzgruppen in der besetzten Sowjetunion 1941/42*, 323-28.
13 There are no statements from that time about this meeting, only the testimonies of the postwar period. See Wildt, *Generation des Unbedingten*, 557.
14 Statement of *Einsatzgruppe* A Commander, 6 August 1941, Latvijas Valsts Vēstures Arhivs [Latvian State Historical Archive, LVVA], P 1026-1-3, Bl. 237-239; cited in

able-bodied Jewish men of military age. Other Jewish men, women, and children do not seem to have been singled out for murder at this point.[15]

What made possible the expansion of the policy of killing adult Jewish men and commissars during the first months of the war to include women and children? There is now general agreement that Hitler was primary in Nazi decision-making and that it was he who decided to "solve" the "Jewish problem" by a policy of mass murder.

Was the adoption of a policy of mass murder a result of the euphoria of victory? Or was it the consequence of the setback caused by the failure to take Moscow, the first check to the Blitzkrieg, and of the view that the Jews should be punished for the failure of the Nazi war? It does seem that Nazi policy was radicalized in quantum leaps in the first months of Operation Barbarossa, and that by August 1941 entire Jewish communities were being murdered, primarily in pre-1939 Ukraine. The most convincing explanation is provided by Christopher Browning, who argues that between 16 September, when the Germans completed the encirclement of Kyiv, and 18 October, when the last resistance ended in Bryansk, Hitler approved the deportation of Jews to the east, the first practical steps for the construction of the death camps of Bełżec and Chelmno were taken, the first Jewish transports departed for Łódź, and Jewish emigration from Europe was banned. These were clear signs that a policy of mass murder had been instated.[16]

The Jews of Volodymyr-Volynsky and of Volhynia as a whole were soon to feel the impact of these policies, as is graphically and movingly described in this book using many first-hand testimonies and interviews, which make it a major contribution to our understanding of

---

Dieckmann and Sužiedėlis, *The Persecution and Mass Murder of Lithuanian Jews*, 113.

15 Tilsit Gestapo to RSHA, 1 July 1941, ZStL, Sammlung UdSSR, Ordner 245 Ag, Nr. 254257, Bl. 2-5, cited in Dieckmann and Sužiedėlis, *The Persecution and Mass Murder of Lithuanian Jews*, 111–2.

16 Christopher Browning, "Hitler and the Euphoria of Victory: The Path to the Final Solution," in *The Final Solution: Origins and Implementation*, ed. David Cesarini (London: Routledge, 1994), 145.

what Father Patrick Desbois has called the "holocaust by bullets." On 5 July 1941, 150 Jews were rounded up by the Germans and their Ukrainian and Polish helpers and murdered in the prison courtyard. A twelve-man Jewish Council (*Judenrat*) was established, headed by Rabbi Morgenshtern. When he died two months later, his post was filled by a lawyer, Veiler. Veiler refused to hand over Jews as the Germans demanded and was shot. Between August and December 1941 the Germans continued to murder Jews, disposing of their victims in mass graves in the prison courtyard.

On 13 April 1942, a ghetto was established, fenced in by barbed wire rising to a height of three meters. In May, it was divided into two parts: one, described by the Jews as "the ghetto of life," for skilled craftsmen, and a second for the non-productive, nicknamed the "ghetto of the dead." They contained altogether about 22,000 Jews. In the summer of 1942, some young people succeeded in establishing links with partisans operating in the vicinity. On the night of 31 August 1942, the Germans began an *Aktion* that lasted two weeks, in which between 13,500 and 18,000 Jews were murdered. Some were killed in the prison courtyard, and the large majority in pits prepared near the village of Piatydni, located six kilometers from Volodymyr-Volynsky. Some Ukrainians were later also murdered there. On 17 September 1989, a twelve-meter-high obelisk was erected near the site of these mass graves, dominating the landscape. It is crowned with the figures of a mother and child and on it is inscribed a poem by Aleksandr Lizen (Isroel Lizenberg, 1911–2000). It reads:

> Let us pause, let us be silent for a moment.
> We solemnly, passionately swear
> That we shall never forget your torments.
> Inevitable punishment for all executioners.
>
> People, stop for a moment of silence,
> And make a solemn promise, devoted and strong as steel,
> That you will never ever forget our torments,
> And will never allow this to happen again.

Introduction

However, this has not prevented the grave site from being vandalized on several occasions, most recently in 2014.

After this *Aktion*, the ghetto, now reduced in size, contained only 4,000 persons. Leib Kudysh, who hoped to organize the Jews to work for the Germans to ensure their survival, was placed at the head of the Jewish Council. On 13 November 1942, another *Aktion* began, lasting several weeks, after which only 1,500 Jews registered and a smaller number of "illegals" survived. During this *Aktion* a group of young Jews attempted to resist, occupying a fortified position in a bunker near the brickworks. Their hiding place was discovered and thirteen were killed. The remaining Jews were murdered on 13-14 December 1943—many of those who attempted to escape were killed by the Ukrainian and Polish resistance movements, which were also engaged in a vicious inter-ethnic war, or by antisemitic individuals or those seeking to rob them. A few found shelter with sympathetic Ukrainians or Poles, thereby risking their lives and those of their families, since the Nazis made this a capital offense. A number of such noble actions are described in this book in the special section devoted to the Righteous among the Nations. In Muzychenko's words:

> Despite the prohibition and mortal risk to their lives, many Ukrainians and Poles hid Jews who were doomed to die. Without a doubt, they are the same kind of heroes as those who fought with weapons in hand, because every minute they were risking not only their own lives but the lives of their children and families. (p. 172)

The city was liberated by the Red Army on 22 July 1944. Of the total population of the town of 37,000, only 7,000 were still alive. Its devastated state is well described in this book. Some Jewish survivors returned, and soon there were approximately 140 Jews in the town. Most later emigrated to Poland, and from there to Israel and elsewhere. In the 1980s, about seventy Jews lived in the town; by 1999, there were no more than thirty. Even fewer are still living in the town today, one of whom is Volodymyr Muzychenko, author of this fine study and someone who has contributed greatly to the memorialization of the Jews of Volodymyr and to ensuring their memory is not forgotten. In his words:

> The Jews of Volodymyr-Volynsky have always loved their native land—the country of Ukraine. This is where their ancestors were born, raised, and worked and where they are buried. This is where their families perished. Those who managed to survive by immigrating to their historical Fatherland of Israel before the war still have an abiding love for their native city of Volodymyr-Volynsky, which they built together with the Ukrainians and Poles. They continue to love the Volynian land, where they left behind all their families and friends. (p. 201).

Author's Note

The city of Volodymyr-Volynsky has a centuries-old history, which was written not only by the representatives of the predominant peoples who lived in this land since time immemorial, but also by the representatives of the national minorities that settled there. Researchers have devoted little attention, if any, to the latter groups. Thus, my modest work is aimed at filling the gaps of historical memory.

Jews paid a terrible price for the experience gained by mankind during the Second World War so that various nations could coexist on Earth. Today, after the many episodes of bloodshed caused by national intolerance, we are simply obliged to safeguard the historical memory of the Jews of Volodymyr-Volynsky, their culture, traditions, daily life, religion, distinguished individuals, and the lives and tragic fate of these people and their contributions to the city's economic and social development. They left their traces, regardless of all attempts to eradicate them. That is why I would like to help recall the history of the Jewish community of the city of Volodymyr-Volynsky and not allow it to be forgotten. May this book be a kind of monument to these people.

I cherish the hope that this book will help us build a democratic society and strengthen understanding of one another. After all, we share one and the same fate and the same Fatherland.

I am certain that this book will be a useful tool for familiarizing readers who have an interest in both the rich history of this thousand-year-old city and Jewish culture in general.

Author's Note

The book is based on a large variety of available materials that I collected over several years in order to preserve the memory of one of the oldest Jewish communities in Europe. However, these materials are merely the tip of the iceberg, and there is still much work to be done. The study of this topic will help scholars rethink several events of our shared history for the sake of the future.

I realize how shocking some of the materials published here will be to many, but I am deeply convinced that this tragic history must be brought to people's attention, that their minds should not slumber and their souls should not become shallow. People should know the truth about the past. Only then will they be capable of correctly evaluating the phenomena that are taking place today.

During my conversations with residents of the city, I was often the recipient of "secret" revelations from individuals who revealed their Jewish background with some trepidation. Perhaps this book will instill in some of these people a sense of pride for their parents, grandparents, and other individuals—and the courage to stop concealing their origins, not to be ashamed of their parents, who deserve their admiration and respect, and to return to their roots.

Perhaps this book will serve as both a model for regional historians in other cities that had Jewish communities and a spur to the study of their history, since Jewish history and culture are inextricable parts of the history and culture of Ukraine.

I am profoundly grateful to everyone who assisted me in my work, all the more so because, when I first began researching this topic, precious little could be gleaned from the local regional history museum. Above all, I would like to thank those few Jewish natives of Volodymyr-Volynsky who managed to survive the horrors of the Holocaust and convey the truth of what they had witnessed: Moshe Margalit; Mykhail Bass, honorary resident of Volodymyr-Volynsky; Moshe Krigser; Zippora Weinstock, Eliezer Reisfeld (Israel); and the Righteous among the Nations Mykola Mykolaiovych Vavrysevych and Maria Oleksandrivna Otsaliuk. Unfortunately, Mr. Vavrysevych did not live long enough to see my book published, nor did Halyna Serhiivna Filatova, whose reminiscences are featured in the book.

Author's Note

I owe a debt of gratitude to Oleksandr Kovalchuk, with whose moral support I began working on this book; David Shkolnik (Rehovot, Israel), who translated the Hebrew-language materials for the Ukrainian edition; and Harry Feldman (Petah Tikva, Israel).

Foreword

The history of the Jews of Ludmir (Volodymyr-Volynsky) is a brilliant page not only from the history of the Jews, but also modern Ukrainian history as a whole. The roots of the Jewish presence in the Volyn region reach back all the way to the Old Rus' state.[1]

Anyone strolling through this city cannot fail to notice the considerable number of monuments of material culture that once belonged to the Jews. Nearly the entire contemporary center of the city was once Jewish, with its synagogues, market, Talmud-Torah, Tarbutt school, the grave of the righteous, and buildings owned by wealthy Jewish residents. It was not all that long ago—some seventy years—when Jews comprised more than seventy percent of the city's population. It goes without saying that Jews made a huge contribution to the development of the urban infrastructure and economy, and enriched it spiritually. In one fell swoop, all this Jewish potential, represented by tens of thousands of people, was brutally destroyed by the Nazis during the Second World War; and during the ensuing period of Soviet rule grave mounds arose on the spots where they were killed.

Of course, in view of this it would have been a just and fitting act to preserve the city's Jewish heritage as much as possible, starting with the publication of relevant literature, the inclusion of the history of the Jews of Volodymyr-Volynsky in local school textbooks, the marking of commemorative dates on the urban level, the erection of plaques on buildings recalling the Jewish historical presence in the city, and the

---

1   See *Narysy z istoriï ta kul'tury ievreïv Ukraïny*, ed. L. Finberg and V. Liubchenko (Kyiv: Dukh i Litera, 2005), 36–37.

rendering of care and assistance to the members of today's tiny Jewish community, which numbers no more than a couple of dozen people.

Unfortunately, practically no such measures seem to concern either the local or central administration. Neither does the rise of nationalistic—and in some areas, even extremist—moods foster the restoration of fairness vis-à-vis the role of national minorities (and in this case, of a particular majority, throughout a certain historical period) in the history of this region.

There is also a lack of a polyphonic and multicultural approach to the illumination and teaching of history in the academic sphere.[2] Ukrainian history is very nation-centric, in which all socioeconomic and sociocultural processes and phenomena are connected above all with the Ukrainian nation. As a rule, all other "parallel worlds" that coexisted with the Ukrainian one in the same lands are ignored and deemed unworthy of being incorporated into the national history. At issue here are deep cultural strata and multi-aspected national groups. How did a Jew suffer during the Khmelnytsky era, and how did he rejoice when he witnessed his son, having reached his thirteenth birthday, giving his first public reading of the Torah at the synagogue? It would be far more gratifying for Ukrainians of diverse ethnic backgrounds (not only Jews but Poles, Armenians, Greeks, Roma, etc.) to read about themselves from this kind of perspective in books, including history texts, in which each ethnic group could see itself as a hero in this history, a descendant of worthy people who developed their own unique culture, and thus take pride in this. In my view, the effect of such a multicultural approach would be far more proactive and would result in the practical unification of various people on the principles of equality in a single political nation.

---

2   A few years ago, this was the subject of a discussion that took place primarily between those historians who share the views of Professor Natalia Yakovenko, head of the history department at the National University of Kyiv-Mohyla Academy, and those who uphold the views of a history professor at this same academic institution, Rev.-Dr. Yurii Mytsyk. See Yurii Mytsyk, "Nove chy pryzabute stare?" *Dzerkalo tyzhnia*, no. 4 (2009); N. Iakovenko, "Liknep dlia profesora," *Dzerkalo tyzhnia*, no. 8 (2009).

Finally, I would like to say a few words about this book, which I am honored to introduce here, and about its author. Volodymyr Muzychenko is the founding member of the Jewish community of Volodymyr-Volynsky, and is well respected in the city for his sterling personal qualities and the many years he has devoted to teaching. He committed the last ten years of his life to gathering historical and data on the Jews of his city and the region. His work is thus the first and fullest narrative to date about the Jews of Volodymyr-Volynsky. The author drew on a wide array of sources, including scholarly and press articles, and unearthed a large number of illustrations, including rare photographs. He does not confine himself to a mere description of the city's Jewish history, but examines it contextually, placing it against the background of political, economic, and cultural processes that took place in the region. The book is noteworthy for its balanced material and the author's desire to avoid a purely lamentational type of exposition. Instead, he sought to show Jewish history as a variegated process marked by both tragic and distinguished pages.

I wish readers happy reading and new discoveries!

Vitalii Chernoivanenko,
scholarly associate and professor of history,
Omeljan Pritsak Research Center for Oriental Studies,
National University of Kyiv-Mohyla Academy (Kyiv, Ukraine)

The History of the Jews of Volodymyr-Volynsky

*Those who cannot remember the past are
condemned to repeat it.*
George Santayana

*History is ... witness for the past, example and counsel for the
present, and warning for the future.*
Miguel de Cervantes

INTRODUCTION[1]

The city of Volodymyr-Volynsky is mentioned under various but similar names: Lodomira, Lodmer, Ladmir, Ludmir; in Polish it was known as Wlodzimierz; in ancient documents it appeared as Volodymer; and in Jewish sources as Udmir or Ludmir. According to the Hungarian chronicle *Bele Regis Notarius* ("notary of Béla the King"), a city known as Ladomyr already existed in 884. The city is first mentioned under the name of Volodymyr in the *Tale of Bygone Years*, according to which the year 988 is considered the official date of its founding by Prince Volodymyr Sviatoslavovych. After the third partition of Poland in 1795, the city was absorbed into the Russian Empire and was thereafter called Volodymyr-Volynsky. From 1921 to 1939 the city was known as Włodzimierz.

Throughout its existence, the city belonged to various states and its status changed accordingly. In 1146–1300 it was the capital of the Volodymyr land; from 1300 it was the capital of the Galician-Volhynian

---
1 An asterisk appears next to words that are primarily of Hebrew origin. They are explained in the Glossary of Terms at the end of the book.

Principality; from 1393 it belonged to the Grand Duchy of Lithuania; and from 1569 it was the county center of the Włodzimierz Duchy within the Rzeczpospolita. In 1795 it became part of the Russian Empire, and in the nineteenth century and the early part of the twentieth it was a county city of Volhynia Gubernia. Between 1915 and 1920, the city was ruled successively by Austro-Hungary, the Ukrainian People's Republic (UNR), the Hetmanate of Pavlo Skoropadsky, and Russia. In 1920–1939 it was once again part of Poland, and from 1939 to 1991 it was part of the Ukrainian SSR. Today, Volodymyr-Volynsky is a district center in Volyn oblast, Ukraine.

෴ ෴ ෴

Jews are the oldest national and religious minority in Ukraine. The first Jews to appear in the territory of contemporary Ukraine arrived before the Christianization of Kyivan Rus', in the ninth and tenth centuries. Later, Jews from the Khazar Khanate settled in Kyiv.

Beginning in the late tenth to early eleventh centuries, with the strengthening of the Old Rus' state, its trade routes became more secure, and movement along them was eased by the construction of princely cities and fortresses in key places and between navigable rivers. Thanks to this, Jewish merchants traveling from Europe through Hungary, the Czech land, and Poland wound up in the cities of the Galician-Volhynian lands and from there they sailed on the Black Sea and the Dnipro River to Kyiv. From there, Jewish merchants and travelers could journey in other directions, including to Byzantium.

Owing to their wide-ranging economic ties, the Jews of Kyivan Rus' are mentioned in medieval Hebrew* sources of the eleventh and twelfth centuries. In particular, there are mentions in the text of responses, answers to questions, by the rabbis of Champagne and Prague. These mentions are mainly based on information provided by merchants who traveled on the Regensburg-Kyiv route, attesting to the fact that conditions for Jewish residence in Kyivan Rus' were quite favorable, and there were no serious conflicts, pogroms, or persecution there at the time. However, it should be noted that there were few Jews in Kyivan Rus', and their religious life was not marked by great activity: isolated from the main European centers, the Jewish communities of Kyivan Rus' lacked rabbis and cantors.[2]

FIRST MENTIONS

The history of the Jews of Volodymyr-Volynsky spans 800 years. If one considers the fact that since ancient times the city has always been called "Ludmir" in Jewish documents (derived from its ancient name Ladomyr), it may be presumed that the first Jews likely arrived there in the pre-Christian period. To this day, Jewish publications often refer to this city by its various names. In English it is known as "Ludmir." This name is also linked to the emergence of the rather widespread Jewish surname "Ludmirsky" (var. "Lyudmirsky"). The Ukrainian archaeologist Oleksander Tsynkalovsky wrote: "The Jewish colony in Volodymyr dates back to ancient times, when trade lured them to Volyn even before the princely period.... This colony was in the center of the town. The so-called 'Jewish Street' [*Zhydivska vulytsia*] was located here."[3]

The first written mentions of Jews in Volodymyr date to the twelfth century. These were Jews from Kyiv, Khazaria, and other eastern communities.[4]

In his book *Sefer Zekhirah* (Book of Remembrance), Ephraim ben Jacob of Bonn (1133–1196) recounts the persecution (blackmail) that a Jewish merchant from Volodymyr encountered during his journey to Cologne: "In [4]931 [1171 CE] two Jews arrived in Cologne: one of them was Rabbi Benjamin ha-Nadib (Benjamin the Generous) from Volodymyr, and the other was Rabbi Avraam Pysets from Carentan [France]."[5] The literary scholar and writer Dennis Sobolev, who teaches at the University of Haifa, also lists this source in his research on the origins of the European Jews.[6]

---

2 L. Finberg and V. Libchenko, eds., *Narysy z istoriï ta kul'tury ievreïv Ukraïny* (Kyiv, 2008), 35.
3 O. Tsynkalovs'kyi, *Kniazhyi horod Volodymyr; populiarno-naukovyi narys* (Lviv, 1935), 32.
4 *Rossiiskaia Ievreiskaia Entsiklopediia*, vol. 4, http://rujen.ru.
5 Aleksandr Kulik, "Evrei Drevnei Rusi: istochniki i istoricheskaia rekonstruktsiia," *RUTHENICA*, no. 7 (2008): 52.
6 D. Sobolev, "Vozvrashchenie v Khazariiu," http://www.sunround.com/club/22/return.htm.

It is worth noting that this is the first mention of Jews on the territory of Volhynia, based on which one may conclude that the settlement of Jews in this region began in Volodymyr-Volynsky.

Another mention dating to the twelfth century concerns the visit of Shlomo bar Yits[hak] (a later transcriber identified him as Rashi, the renowned author of the greatest commentaries in Jewish exegeses on the Talmud) to the Volodymyr community: "Rashi, may his memory be blessed, said: I, Shlomo bar Yits[hak] was in Rus', in Volodymyr, and on 9 Av* there was a circumcision, at which were present Rabbi David bar Khasdai, Rabbi Avraam and his son Rabbi Sinai, Rabbi Shimshon, and Rabbi Yosef from Hush Khalava. Citing the ancient sages, they declared that the rite of circumcision may not be conducted during the morning prayers, when mournful songs are pronounced." This is discussed by Alexander Kulik, citing the Paris manuscript.[7]

Jews flocked to the city of Volodymyr, where they settled down, because it was an important trading center. Thanks to the trading activities of Jewish merchants, this city located on the trade route between Eastern and Western Europe became an important place that was visited by Jewish merchants from Germany. Until the Second World War, the archive of the Hanseatic city of Stralsund, a German port on the Baltic Sea, held a letter dating to the eleventh to twelfth centuries, which the Jewish community of Volodymyr-Volynsky sent to the Stralsund community on the matter of exchanging goods.[8] Judging by this document, one may conclude that its authors were well-educated people.[9]

From Western Europe, Jewish merchants brought artisans' wares, bread, silk, broadcloth, and other goods. From the East they brought to Europe cinnamon and other spices, and camphor oil.[10] This fact was noted by Ignacy Schiper, a specialist in Jewish economic history: "Jewish merchants, in particular Eliezer ben Natan from Volodymyr,

---

7   Kulik, "Evrei Drevnei Rusi," 52.
8   *Rossiiskaia Ievreiskaia Entsiklopediia*, vol. 4, http://rujen.ru.
9   Ia. Isaievych and F. Martyniuk, *Volodymyr-Volyns'kyi* (Lviv: Kameniar, 1988), 9.
10 Aronius, *Regesten zur Geschichte der Juden in frankischen und deutsche Reiche bis zum Jahre 1273* (Berlin, 1902), 34.

Isaac ben Dubralo, and other coreligionists, shipped goods from France to Rus' through the lands of Subcarpathia and in the opposite direction—to the countries of Western Europe ... Jews participated very actively in this trade."[11] He also notes that, during this period, most Jews were engaged in farming.

Following the incursions of the Mongol hordes led by Batu (1241) and Burundai (1259), the princes of Rus' once again extended invitations to the Jews, anticipating the speediest possible revival of artisan trades and commerce, thanks to their connections. During this period the Volhynian lands were rather sparsely populated. The Volhynian princes Ihor Yaroslavych, Mstyslav Iziaslavych, and Roman Mstyslavych were favorably disposed toward the Jews, and they encouraged Jewish immigrants to settle there, offering them the opportunity to build synagogues, establish cemeteries, and found schools in prayer buildings, and helping them to conduct their trading affairs not only within the limits of the principality but also outside its boundaries. There were also quite a few Jews among the colonists whom Prince Danylo of Halych invited from Poland and Germany.

In the mid-thirteenth century, when Kyiv was in a state of decline after having forfeited its influence as the capital of Old Rus' and lost a considerable part of its population, the center of economic and cultural life in the Ukrainian lands shifted westward, to the territory of the Galician-Volhynian Principality. The existence of a Jewish community is also mentioned in documents from the late thirteenth century. The description in the Hypatian Chronicle of the death and funeral in 1288 of Prince Volodymyr Vasylkovych, the ruler of Volodymyr, mentions the presence of Jews: "The entire multitude of the Volodymyr populace wept over him [Prince Volodymyr]—men and women and children; Germans and the Surozh people and the Novgorodians; and the Jews wept, as though during the capture of Jerusalem, when they were being led into Babylonian captivity."[12] Interestingly, the description of the Jews' grief occupies as much space as the entire announcement; another

---

11 See I. Schiper, *Poczatki Zydow na ziemiach Polskich i Ruskich: Almanach Zydowski za rok 5678 (1917)* (Vienna, 1918).
12 *Povist' mynulykh lit*, trans. L. Makhnovets' (Kyiv: Dnipro, 1989).

similar entry in the traditionally laconic chronicle attests to the presence of a substantial Jewish community in the city in the late thirteenth century and its importance.[13] It is clear that, in addition to Germans and people from Surozh and Novgorod (Russia), Jewish merchants also engaged in trade in Volodymyr.[14]

An entry dating to the thirteenth century is also found in a book of responses by Rabbi Chaim ben Yitshak (Maharah). Part 157 of *Or Zarua* (Light Is Sown) discusses forcible divorce: "We sent for the wife and for an emissary to Volodymyr so that she would be divorced here; we compelled him to give her a divorce, but he refused, and we ordered that he be summoned from Kholm."[15]

In the thirteenth and fourteenth centuries, Jewish centers of habitation gradually shifted from Western to Eastern Europe. This migratory movement was determined by a number of economic, juridical, and ideological reasons: on the one hand, the conflict between Islam and Christianity, the supreme manifestations of which were the Christian reconquest of Spain (known as the Reconquista) and the Christian Crusades, and on the other, the emergence of numerous heretical movements in Western Europe and the struggle against them. All this created conditions for the ideological persecution of peoples who espoused different faiths in the Christian West, which was implemented by a policy of brutal isolation and assimilation. The majority of European countries adopted decisions to forcibly expel or Christianize Jews: in England (1290); France (1394); Spain (1492); etc. The eastward migration of Jews is also explained by the massive Jewish pogroms that took place in the West during the period of the Crusades.

The Jews practiced Judaism, the oldest monotheistic religion in the world, which later formed the basis of two subsequent religions: Christianity and Islam. The foundation of Christianity was laid by the holy book of the Jews, the Torah (the Five Books of Moses), which, together with the books of the Nevi'im (the Prophets) and the Ketuvim (Writings), comprise the Tanakh* (Old Testament).

---

13 Sobolev, "Vozvrashchenie v Khazariiu."
14 *Narysy*, 36–37.
15 Kulik, *Evrei Drevnei Rusi*.

Moving from the West, the Jews brought with them the language that they used in Germany, an amalgam of various German dialects enriched by the lexicon of various Slavic languages and Hebrew. Elements of the latter derived from Jewish theological literature, above all the Bible and the Talmud. This was how Yiddish, one of the languages spoken by European Jews, was formed. It became the basic language of communication of Eastern European Jewry in all spheres, and it was the language spoken by the Jews of Volodymyr-Volynsky.

PRIVILEGES

After the Tatar-Mongol invasions, the city fell into decline and experienced a demographic crisis. In order to revitalize the economy, the municipal authorities created all possible conditions so as to secure the influx of Jews to these lands. Jewish settlers were granted a number of privileges both of an economic nature (temporary exemption from paying taxes or permission to engage in certain types of activities), and of an ideological character (permission to maintain their ethnic and religious traditions). Throughout the thirteenth century, Polish kings granted Jews privileges that remained in force even after the city passed to the control of the Grand Duchy of Lithuania in 1393.

The majority of the privileges were granted to the Jews in accordance with the Vienna charter of privileges of 1244, which offered an internal justice system for Jewish communities, guaranteed inviolability of property and the person, and dictated punishment for violations of the latter right. This system remained in place in 1264, during the rule of King Bolesław the Pious, and in 1344, during the reign of Casimir the Great (1310–1370). In the Polish-ruled Ukrainian lands, these privileges came into force in 1367: "We, Casimir, by the grace of God [and the rest of his titles] ... inform both contemporaries and future arrivals, to which the given letter will reach, that we considered it necessary to announce to our Jews who live in Lviv and the entire Ruthenian [Ukrainian] land their statutes and privileges.... No matter where in our house a Jew comes, no one is to place some kind of obstacle before him or cause unpleasantness, and if he would bring some articles or goods, [and] a levy or customs duty would be gathered in all levying place, [but may he pay] solely the required duty that is paid by a resident of the city in which the Jew lives.... We also decree that Jews may sell and buy everything freely—bread and everything else that is essential—with his own money, like the Christians, and those who will impede [them] should pay a fine to us or to our *starosta* or a judge."[16] In the late fourteenth century, Vytautas, the Grand Duke of Lithuania, invited the Jews to his state, settling them not only in the Lithuanian lands but also in Ukrainian territories occupied by Lithuania. He granted the right of residence in his lands to the Jews of Lutsk and Volodymyr-Volynsky. During this period there were five large European communities in Lithuania: Volodymyr, Berestia (Brest), Grodno, Trokiv (Pol., Troki), and Lutsk.

Prince Vytautas granted the Jews privileges that safeguarded peaceful coexistence with the predominant population, as well as unimpeded economic development. In addition to regulating the Jewish community's rights and obligations, in 1388 he subordinated it to the royal, or great, princely court, removing it from the jurisdiction of lower instances, and in many cases of church law as well; for example, with respect to the widespread practice of accusing Jews of committing ritual crimes against Christians: "In accordance with the instructions of the Holy Father, we command most severely that in future no one is to accuse a single Jew who lives in our kingdom of consuming human blood, since according to the Law of Moses all Jews are supposed to refrain from consuming any kind of blood. Further, if any Jew is accused of killing a Christian child [by a] Christian and if a Jew is proved [to have done this] ... then that Jew will be punished only by the punishment that is due for the committed crime; if the crime is not proved, then he will purify his innocence with his own oath, and a Christian will accept the punishment."[17]

Of course, there were concrete economic goals behind the removal of Jews from the church's jurisdiction. Within the system of administrative and economic relations, the Jews were an ideal stratum for the state to manage its Christian subjects: restrictions existed that limited

---

16 *Narysy*, 39–40.
17 Ibid., 40–42.

the scope of activities of their Christian vassals within the framework of ecclesiastical law (for example, the formal, juridical absence of the possibility to compel people to work on fast days). Hence, the services of people of other faiths, who were exempt from such restrictions, were utilized.

In 1431 the city of Volodymyr-Volynsky became part of Poland, and in 1432 King Jagiello (1348–1434) confirmed the rights of the Jewish population of Western Volhynia on par with the rights of the Jewish community residing in the rest of the Polish lands.

In 1588 the bishop of Volodymyr-Volynsky leased the so-called tenth week in the city—the right to collect bridge, cart, and poll taxes (which belonged to the local church and its bishops)—to a Jew named Jakub Kleikhal.

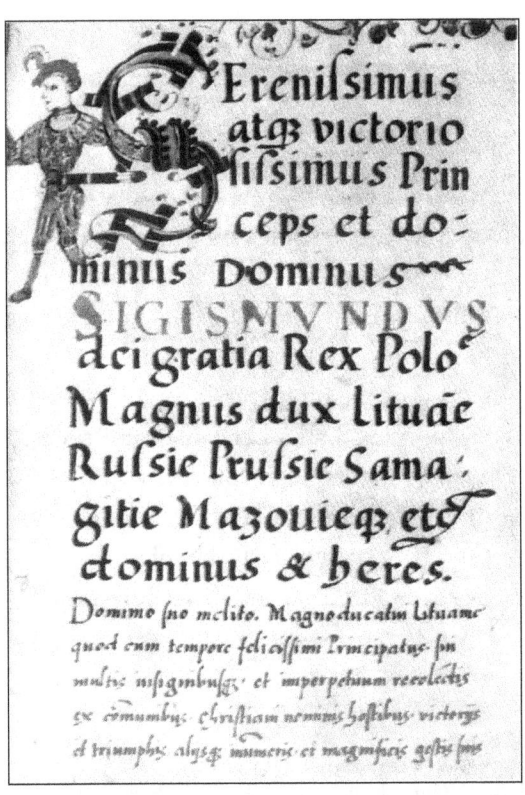

Privilege granted to the Jews by Vytautas the Great in 1388 (fragment of the Puławski manuscript). Eighteenth-century book cover.

Similar clauses are noted in the privilege granted by Casimir IV Jagiellon (1427–1492), Grand Duke of Lithuania, who acceded to the Polish throne in 1447: "If a Jew quarrels with a Christian... and they injure each other, neither a reeve nor burgomasters or anyone else but a palatine or his deputy may dare to judge Jews.... If someone... demands that a Jew appear before the court, then the Jewish defendant has the duty to appear only before the palatine, in whose district he resides. If a Jew is summoned to a Christian religious court, he is not obliged to answer to religious judges. The accused is to be invited to a court to his own palatine, who invites ... a *starosta*, and [the palatine] should defend, protect, and stand up for the Jew before the religious court." This tradition remained in force throughout the entire existence of Poland; later King Sigismund August (b. 1520, d. 1572) and King Stefan Batory (b. 1533, d. 1586) confirmed the granted privileges.[18]

In the privileges granted to the city by Sigismund August in 1570, Jews are mentioned several times on par with burghers; they were exempt from all customs duties, except for the tax on salt and wax.[19]

During the first half of the fifteenth century, Jews leased property in Volodymyr-Volynsky and even leased property from the king.

One of the reasons Jews settled in the Ukrainian lands was that, in the fifteenth century, Muscovy was the scene of a struggle against the "heresy of the Judaizers," and the Muscovite state had introduced a ban forbidding Jews to settle on its territory.

However, not all rulers had a benevolent attitude toward Jews. In 1495, Grand Duke Alexander Jagiellon, the son of Casimir, gave the order to "drive the Jews out of our land,"[20] as a result of which all Jews living in the Grand Duchy of Lithuania, including in Volodymyr-Volynsky, were expelled.[21] The Jewish community in the city

---

18 Ibid., 39–42.
19 *Evreiskaia Entsiklopediia Brokgauza-Efrona*, 1908–13, http://encyclopediya.ru/brockhaus-efron-jewish-encyclopedia/slovnik/03-5.htm.
20 M. Kuchynko, *Volodymyr seredn'ovichnyi* (Lutsk, 2006), 113–15.
21 V. P. Marochkin, *Ukraïns'ke misto vid XV do seredyny XVII st.: Zvychaievo-pravova atrybutyka iak istorychne dzherelo; Istorychna monohrafiia* (Toronto: Hypertext Plus, 1999), 37.

started to revive in the early sixteenth century, when, following the revocation of the document on the expulsion of the Jews (1503), their mass return began[22] and all their property was restored to them, with the exception of estates.

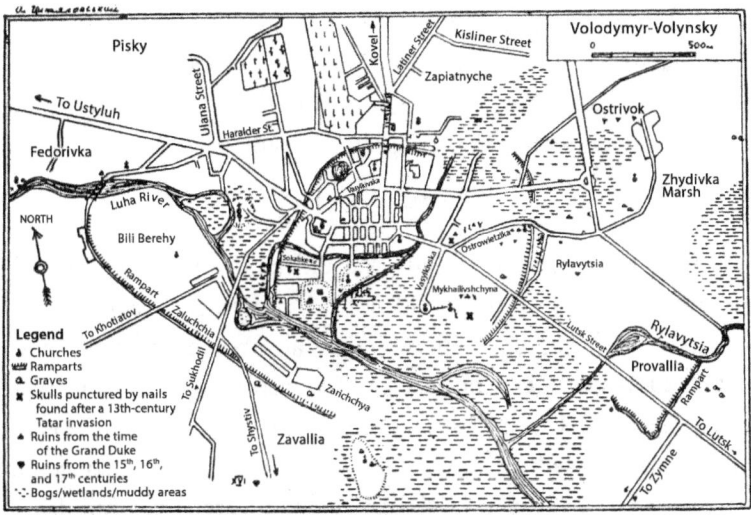

Map of the city with Yiddish inscriptions prepared by O. Tsynkalovsky.[23]

It is worth noting that decisions about certain economic restrictions (with an ideological subtext) were adopted in various years with respect to people of other faiths, above all Jews. These restrictions often made Jews targets of proselytization (conversion to another faith). Court registers dating to the late fifteenth and early sixteenth centuries prove that for the purpose of safeguarding property and economic positions there were cases where Jews adopted Christianity. Among them were Shania, a customs officer in Volodymyr-Volynsky, and his descendant, who converted during the rule of the grand princes Vytautas and Duke Svitrigaila and whose properties included two villages.[24]

---

22 Ibid.
23 *Wladimir Wolynsk: In Memory of the Jewish Community (Volodymyr-Volynskyy, Ukraine). Pinkas Ludmir; sefer zikaron le-kehilat Ludmir* (Tel Aviv: Irgun Yots'e Ludmir be Yiśra'el, 722, 1962), 13.
24 *Narysy*, 44.

After the signing of the Union of Lublin (1569) and the Church Union of Berestia (1596), as a result of which Volhynia became part of the Rzeczpospolita, a massive wave of Jewish settlers began moving from Poland to Volhynia, this migration attesting to the existence of economic and other conditions that were favorable to them.

In addition to the Ashkenazi, that is, European Jews who spoke a dialect based on Germanic and Slavic language groups (Yiddish), Sephardim—settlers from the Iberian Peninsula, who spoke a Spanish-Jewish dialect called Ladino—migrated to Volhynia.[25]

THE KAHAL

The Jewish population of the city was united in the *kahal**, an autonomous organization.[26] Kahals had not only executive (court, taxation) and legislative (religious) functions but also representative ones, and they served as mediators between the Jewish population and the local authorities. Until the mid-seventeenth century, the main revenue of the kahal was the *chazak*, a payment for the granting of a concession or the right to open stores and workshops and purchase a building. The chazak was one of the most important economic levers in the administration of the kahal and the migration of the Jewish population. Later, kahal administrations included commissions that oversaw the activities of hospitals and shelters for the elderly. The kahal was responsible for collecting taxes, resolved all problems within the community, and appealed to the government only in exceptional cases.

Community funds maintained the synagogue and its officials, religious courts, and educational institutions. The way of life of community members was regulated by *halakhah**, Jewish law based on the Torah, and by the halakhah codex called *Shulhan 'arukh**, daily adherence to which was ensured by learned rabbis, who were the chief authorities on all questions pertaining to the functioning of the kahal.[27] Underpinning

---

25 V. Nadol's'ka and L. Miroshnychenko, "Z istoriï ievreis'koï obshchyny Volyni," in *Mynule i suchasne Volyni: Oleksandr Tsynkalovs'kyi i krai; Materialy IX naukovoï istoryko-kraieznavchoï mizhnarodnoï konferentsiï* (Lutsk: Nadstyr'ia, 1998), 271.

26 Ibid., 271.

27 Marochkin, *Ukraïns'ke misto*, 44.

the kahal were general and special privileges granted to Jews by the royal government, as well as agreements concluded between the community and the palatines (the so-called *wojewódzki poriadok*, "palatine's code"). Common law, ethnic traditions, and Judaism regulated the life activities of every Jew and the community as a whole. They defined economic and family relations as well as daily life.

Property relations among the kahal's members were recorded in documents that were drawn up in Yiddish and notarized in a court. One such document, dated 27 May 1567, is the declaration of the Jewess Svietliba Tazhbuchevycheva about the sale by her husband Moshko of a house in the "fence" (within the limits) of the city of Volodymyr to his son-in-law Nachim Leizar and the drafting of a deed of sale in the Jewish language.[28] Such documents were legally equivalent to those drawn up in the state language.

The authority of the kahal in Volodymyr-Volynsky was not restricted to this city alone. So-called sub-kahals*, numerically smaller and less important communities, were also under its administration. One such sub-kahal was located in the large village of Lokachi, in which Jews had resided since at least 1588. In 1765, there were 907 Jews living in the small town of Lokachi and its "parishes." By 1847, the Jewish community had grown to 1,150, and in 1897, out of a population of 2,309 residents, 1,730 were Jews.[29] Also subordinated to the Volodymyr kahal were the synagogue and the leaders of the sub-kahal of Kovel (an independent kahal district since the eighteenth century), Kyselyn, and many others. The Volodymyr community also represented the interests of the sub-kahal communities. Evidence of this is "Ivan Kelemeta's Complaint from the Community of the City of Volodymyr against the Kovel Official, Prince Andrzej Kurbski, concerning the Illegal Imprisonment of the Kovel Jews Yusko Shmoilovych, Avram Yakovovych, and Bohdana Ahronova, the Sealing of Their Buildings, Cellars, and

---

28 *Volodymyrs'kyi Grods'kyi sud: Podokumentni opysy aktovykh knyh*, vyp. 1, ed. H. Boriak and L. Demchenko (Kyiv: Tsentral'nyi derzhavnyi istorychnyi arkhiv Ukraïny, 2002), 43.
29 *Evreiskaia Entsiklopediia*.

Granaries in the City of Kovel during the Sabbath Feast," dated 14 July 1569.³⁰

Gradually, communities were united in district *va'ads**—committees whose members consisted of representatives of local kahals.

The Volodymyr community played an important role in the fate and history of Jewry residing in Volhynia and Poland as a whole, as it was one of the four largest and most influential communities, along with the communities of Ostrih, Lutsk, and Kremianets.

In 1324, Volodymyr was granted the Magdeburg law, which was confirmed by King Sigismund I in 1509, according to which the city's leading elite obtained self-rule, the juridical basis of Jewish self-rule.

ORGANIZATION OF SETTLEMENT IN THE FOURTEENTH–SIXTEENTH CENTURIES

In the sixteenth century, the status of the city of Volodymyr was on par with such cities as Lutsk, Lviv, Cracow, and Lublin, among which there was a certain rivalry. Like the majority of cities with large Jewish communities during this period, there was a special quarter in the city that was known as the ghetto*. This was an area densely populated by Jews, with narrow streets on which stood buildings mostly of wood construction. The architecture of the Jewish quarter differed little from that of other neighborhoods in Volodymyr-Volynsky. Cheek-by-jowl with the Jews lived Ukrainians, Poles, and people of other nationalities. According to historical data, this district was situated in the northeastern part of the city. Jewish settlements occupied a significant part of the city center. Connected with them were such areas as Divycha Doroha, Korolivshchyna, Babyna Dolyna, the Smoch River (or Smochysko), Shkartani, Tukhivshchyna, Kylshchyna, and Jewish Street, where Jews had lived since ancient times.³¹ According to the 1552 census, out of 243 buildings situated in the "outer fortifications" (*okol'nyi horod*, the area surrounding a feudal castle), Jews owned 22 buildings on municipal lands, seven on priests' lands, and two families

---

30 *Volodymyrs'kyi Grods'kyi sud*, 122.
31 O. Tsynkalovs'kyi, *Stara Volyn' i Volyns'ke Polissia: Kraieznavchyi slovnyk vid naidavnishykh chasiv do 1914 r.*, vol. 1 (Winnipeg: T-vo "Volyn'," 1984), 226.

lived in rented accommodations. Jews living on municipal lands paid ordinary municipal taxes, except for the proportion of the general total of taxes of all Jews in Lithuania.[32] From the standpoint of historical and social topography, the structural design of the Jewish quarter greatly resembled other districts of Volodymyr. According to historical and literary sources, the Jewish quarter was situated in the northeastern part of the city's ancient outer fortifications, not far from the Church of the Presentation of the Holy Virgin, at the intersection of Lutska and Danylo Halytsky streets (the latter formerly known as Starolutska; see the illustration on this page). Most of the buildings in the quarter were constructed of wood, but some were made of stone. Tsynkalovsky mentions that several ancient brick buildings in this part of the city featured arches covered with red tiles.[33]

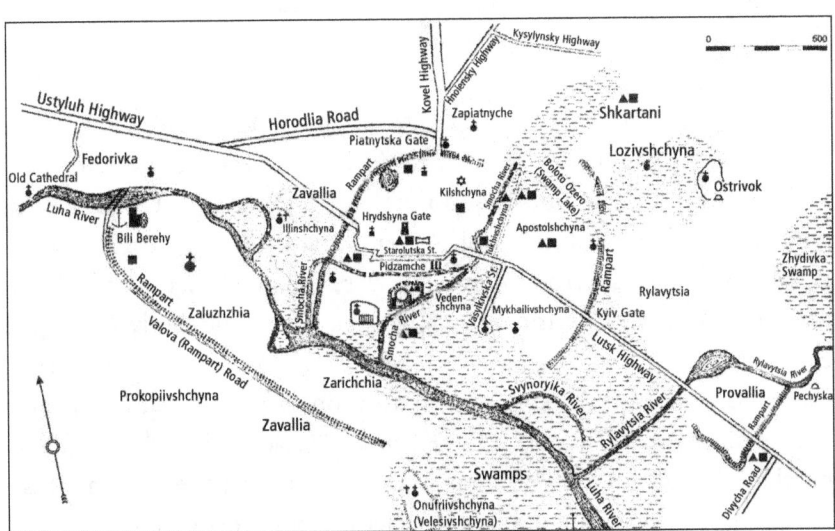

Defensive structures (triangles and squares), Christian religious structures (circles and squares with crosses), and a synagogue (Star of David), 14th to 16th centuries

As a rule, the streets of the Jewish quarter were marked by bustling trade, where petty tradesmen offered various services in an effort to

---

32 *Evreiskaia Entsiklopedia.*
33 Tsynkalovs'kyi, *Stara Volyn'.*

feed their families, since most of the residents here were not well-to-do.

ECONOMIC CONDITIONS OF THE COMMUNITY IN THE FOURTEENTH–SIXTEENTH CENTURIES

During the Late Medieval period the Rzeczpospolita—and therefore Western Ukraine with its cities—was the most auspicious country for Jewish residence. This is attested by the fact that in Ukrainian cities at the turn of the fourteenth century, Jews occupied strong economic positions. As Ukraine's premier historian Mykhailo Hrushevsky noted, beginning in the late fifteenth century the Polish Crown gradually became the vessel that gathered to it Jews from all over the world, who began to fill up cities and towns.[34]

Volodymyr-Volynsky continued to grow in importance during the fifteenth century. As various inspectors of the time noted, the main type of Jewish economic activity was trade.[35] During this period, trading stalls (twenty-four shops) in the "outer fortifications" belonged to Jews.

Markets were held in the city three times a year. Lively commerce took place with Lviv, Lutsk, and Kyiv. From the city of Ustyluh, situated on the banks of the Buh River, boats cast off bearing goods destined for Gdansk, from where they were shipped to Western Europe, and in the reverse direction. Vigorous economic activities were conducted in the city by Jewish traders, who brought goods to the Far East and back. In Volodymyr-Volynsky one could encounter Jewish businessmen from Turkey, Italy, Kyiv, and Cracow. Jewish merchants purchased goods in the Christian West and shipped them to the East, from where they brought silk and spices. Extant documents attest to the trade in lynx, beaver, marten, and fox furs, which were shipped

---

34 M. S. Hrushevs′kyi, *Istoriia Ukraïny-Rusy*, vol. 5 (Kyiv: Naukova Dumka, 1994), 225.

35 Michał Baliński and Tymoteusz Lipiński, *Starożytna Polska pod względem historycznym, jeograficznym i statystycznym*, 2nd rev. and exp. ed., 4 vols. (Warsaw: S. Olgerbrand, 1885–1886), 3:524. See also N. I. Teodorovich, *Gorod Vladimir Volynskoi gubernii v sviazi s istoriei Volynskoi ierarkhii; Istoricheskii ocherk* (Pochaiv: Tipografiia Polchaevo-Uspenskoi Lavry, 1893), 225.

from Kyiv.³⁶ Many Jewish tradesmen, including tailors, shoemakers, and bakers, settled in the city. A butcher's guild was one of the many associations that arose in the sixteenth century. In 1527, "Jewish servants," that is, princely vassals, paid a high tax of fifteen florins to the suzerain.

In the early part of the sixteenth century, and after Volhynia was annexed by Poland in 1569, the Jewish community continued its rapid development. During this period, Jews were already leasing tax collection in the city and the district (including in Poryts), and they plied various trades, mostly shoemaking and leather work. In 1569 a Jew named Zraïl Abramovych leased a mill from Prince Kostiantyn Ostrozky. At this time the lessee of a mill belonging to Bishop Feodosii of Volodymyr and Berestia, which was located in Bili Berehy, near the city of Volodymyr-Volynsky, was a Ukrainian named Vasyl Kaplia. Business rivalry emerged between the two men, as evidenced by a complaint lodged by Abramovych against Kaplia, whom he accused of "also serving burghers notwithstanding protection."³⁷

As a result of the conflicting interests between Jewish and other tradesmen, in 1582 the bootmakers' guild succeeded in obtaining a ban forbidding Jewish trade in leather products.³⁸

In Bishop Feodosii's dense forests, which were located in the Kupechiv district, Jewish merchants, such as Eska and Peisach Sachkovych, kept boats called *kom'iahy*, on which they transported grain purchased from episcopal farms and destined for Gdansk.³⁹

Until the mid-sixteenth century, when there were still only small numbers of Jews living in Poland, they leased the collection of customs duties from the state at border and domestic customs houses and took on leases for the salt, wax, and other trades, over time becoming monopolists. Beginning in the sixteenth century, they acquired leases to landowners' estates as well as other revenue-producing clauses, such as duties paid for the right to sell alcohol, the bridge tax, and other

---

36 *Volodymyrs' Grods'kyi sud*, 111.
37 Ibid., 127.
38 Benyamin Lukin, "Volodymyr Volyns'kyi," http://www.yivoencyclopedia.org.
39 *Volodymyrs'kyi Grods'kyi sud*, 80.

types of taxes. A large number of Jews were engaged in commerce. A record dated 1566 mentions the traders Isaac and Zelman, who used their own money to build and sell boats.[40] Practically all transit trade was in the hands of Jewish merchants.

In the fifteenth and sixteenth centuries, Volodymyr-Volynsky had many taverns and inns that served as hotels, and they were a distinctive feature of the architecture of tradesmen's districts. The taverns and inns resembled either ordinary houses divided by a vestibule into two halves or a prosperous burgher's building consisting of the tavern, a kitchen, guest accommodations, rooms on the second floor, and a fenced-in courtyard with various outbuildings: stables, huts, cellars, etc. Usually this depended on the proprietor's level of prosperity.

There was a steady stream of lodgers. The old inns and taverns of Volodymyr-Volynsky, which were still located in their traditional spots, were recorded in the 1930s by Tsynkalovsky. One inn was situated at the top of the Lutsk tract, near the eastern entrance to the city. Another stood on Biloberezka Street, near the southwestern entrance to the city. Among the taverns located in the city, one was on Lutska Street and another one—at the Pivnyk boundary line on Zymno road. Similar enterprises were situated on the Verbsky tract and in the village of Fedorivka, in the western part of the city.[41] It is likely that such inns and taverns existed in the mid-sixteenth century and were owned mostly by Jews. Documents indicate that there were a considerable number of Jewish-owned businesses in the city.[42]

VA'AD ARBA ARATSOT*

Va'ads, Jewish self-rule committees, which were formed in communities surrounding the largest centers of Jewish life, eventually formed the basis of regional councils and then a Jewish parliament after 1579, when Stefan Batory ordered the creation of a free representative body for the Jewish people throughout the Rzeczpospolita. This Jewish parliament

---

40 P. M. Sas, *Feodal'nye goroda Ukrainy v kontse XV–60-kh godakh XVI v.* (Kyiv: Naukova dumka, 1989).
41 Ibid., 198.
42 See Kuchynko, *Volodymyr seredn'ovichnyi.*

was called Va'ad Arba Aratsot (Council of Four Lands). Its other name was the Crown Va'ad, and it united the communities residing in Lesser Poland (Małopolska), Greater Poland (Wielkopolska), Red Ruthenia (*Chervona Rus'*, Eastern Galicia/Western Ukraine), and Volhynia. Until 1623 it included a special representative body for Jews residing in the Grand Duchy of Lithuania, which was in union with the Polish throne.

In the Va'ad Arba Aratsot, all of Volhynia was represented by the leadership of the Volodymyr-Volynsky kahal, an indication of the important role that this community played in the Rzeczpospolita.

The Va'ad Arba Aratsot, which consisted of two institutions—the Assembly of Regional Elders and the Assembly of Regional Dayanim (judges)—was overseen by an executive body headed by the *parnas*. This was the highest position to which a Jew could aspire at the time.

The heads of district and Crown va'ads were some of the rabbis of Volodymyr-Volynsky, Yitshak ben Bezalel (1547–70), Ishaya ben Yitshak (Yitshak ben Shemu'el ha-Levi; until 1595), Zanvil (from 1596), and Yom-Tov Lipmann Heller (in 1634–43).[43] For a time, the Va'ad Arba Aratsot was headed by Ephraim Fishel of Ludmir.[44]

Twice a year, during the great markets held in Lublin and Yaroslav, the members of the va'ad gathered to resolve urgent questions affecting all aspects of Jewish life.

In the minutes of the meetings we find an echo of problems that were emerging in the personal and community life of Polish-Lithuanian Jewry of that era. Among them were questions connected with religious legislation. For example, serfs were supposed to perform the *corvée* on estates leased by Jews on certain days, including the occasional Saturday. The va'ad sought to influence Jewish lessors to ensure that serfs did not work on their leased estates on the Sabbath. Community leaders avoided temptation and demanded that Jewish lessors and estate managers abide by the Sabbath rules, which forbid all work performed on that day on behalf not only of Jews but also of anyone staying in their homes and working for them.

---

43 Lukin, "Volodymyr Volyns′kyi."
44 See the family tree of Rabbi Naftali Ha-Cohen, http://www.loebtree.com/mahnl.html.

In 1602, the kahal of Volodymyr-Volynsky decided that serfs would be "fully exempted from work on the Sabbath and Jewish holidays. For when we were in exile and in Egyptian slavery, our forefathers chose the Sabbath as a day of peace; therefore, even in those places where people of other faiths are dependant on them [Jewish lessors], it is necessary to abide by the Torah's commandments."[45]

In 1700, King Augustus II of the Polish Rzeczpospolita granted the parnas of the regional council and the Crown Va'ad, Fishel Levkovych of Volodymyr-Volynsky, the right to bear the "title of royal representative, supplier, and official secretary of the Council of Four Lands."[46]

Among its other functions, the va'ad regulated relations between the state and taxpayers, settled quarrels, organized the collection of charitable donations, and oversaw the care of Jewish orphans: little boys were made to study the Torah and learn trades, while girls reaching the age of fifteen received dowries and assistance to marry.

The va'ad's autonomy was so great that it may be called without exaggeration *status in statu* ("a state within a state"). In medieval Poland, Jews possessed their own legislative, court, and executive authority.

The Va'ad Arba Aratsot was disbanded by the Warsaw Sejm (Diet) on the recommendation of King Stanisław August in 1764, because by this time it could no longer carry out its main function, the assignment to the kahals to collect the designated sum of taxes for the royal treasury and court. The Va'ad Arba Aratsot had existed for nearly 200 years, and throughout this period—from the last quarter of the sixteenth century to the mid-eighteenth century—it was recorded in the history of Polish Jews as a "Golden Age."

SPIRITUAL LEADERS

A key role in the life of the community was played by its spiritual leaders—rabbis, to whom since time immemorial Jews had turned with their problems, and not just those of a spiritual nature. The resolution of various disputes that arose among the members of the community

---

45 See http://alefsfarim.com/ettinger/ocherki__po__istorii__evreyskogo__naroda/1-22. htm.
46 *Encyclopaedia Judaica*, 1st ed., s.v. "Vladimir Volynski."

depended on their wisdom. The history of the Jewish community of Volodymyr-Volynsky is indissolubly linked to their activities. Therefore, it is crucial to discuss them in this book.

Until the thirteenth century, few Eastern European Jewish communities were in a position to support their own rabbis, and the rabbinical function was carried out mainly by parents and teachers. As noted by the Israeli archivist Benyamin Lukin, during the last third of the thirteenth century the community was led by the rabbis Yitshak, author of the manuscript *Or Zarua*, and Manoakh, son of Ya'akov,[47] even though the privileges granted to the Jews of Poland in the thirteenth through fifteenth centuries do not contain any direct mentions of rabbis or a rabbinate. During this period, the main centers of religious life were based in Western Europe.

ha-Gaon Yitshak ben Bezalel.[48]

---

47 "Yitshak ben Mosheh of Vienna," http://www.yivoencyclopedia.org/article.aspx/Yitshak__ben__Mosheh__of__Vienna.
48 *Wladimir Wolynsk*, 53.

From the mid-sixteenth century, several distinguished rabbis and scholars lived in Volodymyr-Volynsky; they were the leaders of the Jewish community. The first important rabbi in the city was Yitshak ben Bezalel, who was known as the Gaon* (sage) of Ludmir; he wielded immense authority and headed the community from 1542 to 1576 (1547–70).[49] He operated a *yeshiva** that was considered large at the time. Among the city's succeeding rabbis were his grandsons, the brothers David ben Shemu'el ha-Levi Segal and Isaac ben Samuel ha-Levi, who were also born in Volodymyr-Volynsky and enjoyed great authority.

For a certain period of time Yehoshua Ben Alexander ha-Kohen (b. 1555, Cracow, d. 1614), a scholar and halakhic authority, was the rabbi of Volodymyr-Volynsky. He is also known as Sema' (an acronym of the title of his book *Sefer me'irat 'enayim*, a commentary to the Hoshen mishpat portion of *Shulhan 'arukh*) and Yehoshua Falk.[50]

The halakhic authority and philologist Isaac ben Samuel ha-Levi (ca. 1580–1646) was also born in Volodymyr-Volynsky and was one of Falk's pupils. For some time he served as a rabbi in Kholm, and in 1627 he became the head of a yeshiva in Poznań. His responses were published in 1736. Some of his thoughts were recorded by his brother in the book *Ture zahav* (Rows of Gold). He was not afraid to express views that did not correspond to those espoused by other scholars and high-ranking officials. He was attentive to his pupils, and was loyal and sympathetic toward ordinary people. His intellectual range was extraordinary for that time and place. As head of the yeshiva, he was a researcher of halakhah; he also spoke German and studied geometry. Isaac ben Samuel composed a festive liturgical poem entitled "Shir Heulim," which was published in 1609 to mark the payment of a ransom to the Christians for the Lviv synagogue.[51] He was a scholar of Hebrew and an advocate of grammatical accuracy: he complained frequently that his contemporaries disregarded the rules of grammar, and railed at

---

49 *Encylopaedia Judaica*.
50 Meir Wunder, "Yehoshu'a ben Aleksander ha-Kohen," http://yivoencyclopedia.org/article.aspx/Yehosua_ben_Aleksander_Ha-Kohen.
51 Shalom Bar-Asher, "Yitshak ben Shemu'el ha-Levi," http://yivoencyclopedia.org.

examples of undignified style of the Hebrew language in their works. Isaac ben Samuel wrote many books, the most important of which was a Hebrew grammar, *Siah Yitshak*, published in 1627. His contemporary, the Talmudic scholar Yom-Tov Lipmann Heller, and the nineteenth-century Italian scholar Shemu'el David Luzzatto had a high opinion of this work. An abbreviated version of this grammar was published in Frankfurt in 1693.[52]

David ben Shemu'el ha-Levi Segal (b. 1586, d. 20 February 1667)[53] was also known by the acronym Taz, based on the title of his main work *Ture zahav*, a commentary to *Shulhan 'arukh*, which was first published in Lublin in 1646. His father was Shemu'el ha-Levi Segal, and his main teacher of the Torah was his older brother Isaac. David headed the synagogues in Ostrih (Ostroh) and Lviv, and was one of the most authoritative rabbis of his time.

David ha-Levi Segal.[54]

---

52 *Wladimir Wolynsk*, 25–26.
53 *Rossiiskaia Evreiskaia Entsiklopediia*.
54 *Wladimir Wolynsk*, 26.

For a certain period of time, the post of rabbi in the city was held by Meshulam Faivish (d. 1617), who was later a key figure in the yeshiva of Cracow. He introduced rules governing the celebration of the Sabbath in agriculture, which Jewish lessees were obliged to follow. Many of Poland's rabbis considered themselves his pupils.[55]

In 1590–1606 the head of the community was Rabbi Moshe, one of thirty rabbis who signed a law banning the purchase of rabbinical offices and other leading positions in Jewish communities. In keeping with the new law, a position could be obtained only if the candidate had the proper education and in accordance with the results of voting, evidence of the democratic system of Jewish communities. Rabbi Moshe was also the author of a book entitled *Jewish Life in Poland*.

From 1590–95, the other rabbis of Volodymyr-Volynsky were Isaac ben Isaac, known as Menahem Mendel (Mendel Avigdorish), and Rabbi Avigdor (d. 1599), who later served in Cracow.[56]

From 1634–42 (other sources state 1635–44[57]) the community was headed by the distinguished civic figure, Talmudist, and rabbi Yom-Tov Lipmann Heller (full name: Yom-Tov Lipmann ben Natan Heller, b. Wallerstein, Bavaria?, d. 19 August 1654, Cracow), whose influence extended far beyond the borders of Volodymyr-Volynsky, owing to the fact that at various times he headed communities in Vienna, Prague, Cracow, and Nemyriv. He was also famous for his commentary on the Mishnah (*Tosafot Yom-Tov*), which was published in three volumes in 1614–17 and is still in use today. Thanks to his efforts, in 1640 the Va'ad Arba Aratsot banned the purchase of rabbinical posts (as was done in the sixteenth century). Around 1645, Heller wrote a book of memoirs entitled *Megilat evah* (extant in two versions, Hebrew and Yiddish), which may have been designed for yearly family reading. The second part of Heller's account describes his activities as the head of the Volodymyr-Volynsky community in 1641.[58]

---

55 Elchanan Reiner, "Yeshiva: The Yeshiva before 1800," http://yivoencyclopedia.org/article.aspx/Yeshiva/The_Yeshiva_before_1800.
56 See http://www.iajgs.org/cemetery/ukraine/vladimir-volynskiy.html.
57 *Evreiskaia Entsiklopediia Brokgauza-Efrona*.
58 See http://www.yivoencyclopedia.org/search.aspx?query=ludmir.

Other rabbis included Yehudah-Leib Altshuler, a pupil of Yitshak ben Bezalel, who was succeeded in this position by his children, one of whom was Khainokh, who served as the rabbi of Volodymyr-Volynsky in 1603–12, Prague in 1659, and later in a Polish city.

From 1612, the rabbi of Volodymyr-Volynsky was Moshe Mendels ben Ishaya; in 1622 he was based in Prague; from there he left for Palestine.

Another rabbi from this period was Shemu'el from Ternopil. Jewish historiography also mentions Rabbi Yitshak from Ludmir, who was the teacher of Yehezekel ben Yehudah Landau (b. 8 October 1713, d. 29 April 1793), the Talmudist scholar and chief rabbi of Prague.[59]

For a certain period of time, Landau, who traced his lineage to Rashi, headed the local yeshiva.

There is a legend about a rabbi from Ludmir who, in the late nineteenth century, left his native city and made his way to the Holy Land. The Polish writer and journalist Hanna Krall recounts the following about him: "He settled in the mountains and became a water carrier. When he fell ill one day, some people came to find out what had happened to him. One of them noticed a sheet of paper lying on the floor. A book (that is written in Hebrew) is a holy object for the Jew, and not a single part of it may be found on the floor. They picked up the sheet and read it. It was a fragment from the Kabbalah. 'And you read this? You, a water carrier and ignoramus?' That is how they learned who he really was. Eventually he became a rabbi in the city of Tzfat."[60]

In the early nineteenth century, Volodymyr-Volynsky was home to Rabbi Noach, a pupil of Rabbi Ya'akov Yitshaak Horowitz ("the Seer of Lublin," b. 1740, d. 1815).

Beginning in the mid-eighteenth century, a movement known as Hasidism* emerged and spread through the lands of the Rzeczpospolita,

---

59 Ibid.
60 Khanna Kral', "Romelii," http://www.judaica.kiev.ua/eg9/eg913.htm.

including Volhynia. In 1804, by which time Poland was part of the Russian Empire, the Jewish Statute officially recognized Hasidism as a legitimate branch of Judaism. In the early part of the nineteenth century, many Jews from Volodymyr-Volynsky joined this branch, and eventually the city became one of the centers of Hasidism. There were sub-branches within the Hasidic movement, and their representatives also lived in the city.

Volodymyr-Volynsky enjoyed great Hasidic traditions (the Hasidim of Ludmir belonged to the Karlin-Stolin dynasty, whose name derived from the names of two populated areas now located in Belarus) and was well known among European Jews, above all because of such important figures as the *tsadeket** Khane-Rokhl Werbermacher and the *tsadik** Shelomoh Gotlieb of Karlin.

These two figures deserve separate discussion, as until recently very little was known about these extraordinary individuals.

SHELOMOH OF KARLIN (KARLINER)

A holy righteous man and philosopher, Tsadik Shelomoh Gotlieb ben-Yuta (b. 1740, d. 1792), known as Shelomoh of Karlin (Karliner indicates that he was from the city of Karlin, today a district of the Belarusian city of Pinsk; ben-Yuta means that he was the son of Yuta) was one of the most authoritative rabbis in the history of Hasidism and the head of the Hasidic community in Volodymyr-Volynsky.

The teacher of Shelomoh of Karlin was Aharon Perlov, also from Karlin, who, along with Shelomoh, studied with the Great Magid* Dov Ber from Mezhyrich. Aharon Perlov founded a Hasidic center in Karlin, where the movement that eventually came to be known as Karlin-Stolin Hasidism emerged. Shelomoh of Karlin was Perlov's ablest disciple, and after the latter's death he headed this movement, wielding great authority. The communities of Lithuania, Belarus, and Volhynia were under his influence. In 1786 he moved to Ludmir, where many of his disciples already resided.

During his lifetime, Shelomoh of Karlin was renowned for his large number of good works. He helped people regardless of their religious confession or nationality. It was said of him that the doors of his home, were always open to any person afflicted by troubles, anyone who came to him seeking his assistance or advice. Without hesitation he shared his last piece of bread. Legends and accounts of his good deeds were transmitted orally, and they have survived to the present day. His name stands alongside the legendary founder of Hasidism, the world-renowned figure Baʻal Shem Tov. Jews called Shelomoh of Karlin a righteous man during his lifetime.

Alter Rebe, one of the leaders of the Hasidic movement, held Shelomoh in great esteem, declaring that he was "a hand's length higher than the world." Since his youth, Rabbi Shelomoh's capacity for self-abnegation had made his prayers extraordinarily powerful. He spent the majority of his days worshiping and devoting himself fully to God. His prayers, which were marked by their prolonged nature and ecstatic form, became known as "Karliner prayers."

Accordig to his *Amud Hatefillah*, Baʻal Shem Tov had declared that before starting to pray, a person must be ready to die, because the very essence of prayer demands complete self-sacrifice of the individual. Wholeheartedly accepting this teaching, when Shelomoh of Karlin prayed, he gave himself up to prayer so intensively that Hasidim standing next to him would fall into a psychological state bordering on ecstasy.

Martin Buber, the distinguished researcher of Hasidism, edited a book of Hasidic legends, stories, and parables,[61] and later wrote a cycle of works dedicated to the eminent tsadik Shelomoh Karliner, whose death is described in the story "Armilus" as recorded by Buber:

> When Rabbi Shelomoh was already living in Ludmir, Russian troops were crushing the Polish uprising in that locality, and pursuing the routed rebels, they entered this city. The Russian general gave his people two hours to loot the city. This was the eve of Shavu'ot* [the Feast of Weeks, or Pentecost], which that year fell on Saturday, the seventeenth day of Tamuz according to the Jewish calendar [7 July 1792], and all the Jews

---

61 Martin Buber, *Khasidskie istorii: Pervye uchitelia* (Moscow: Mosty kul'tury; Jerusalem: Gesharim, 2006/5755).

had gathered in the synagogue. Rabbi Shelomoh devoted himself completely to prayer, and he was in such a state of ecstasy that he absolutely did not see or hear what was happening around him. Suddenly, in the window appeared the face of a limping Cossack, who glanced inside the synagogue and fired his rifle. At this time, he [Rabbi Shelomoh] was pronouncing in a booming voice the words "Yours is the kingdom, O Lord." The rabbi's little grandson, who was standing behind him, tugged at the hem of his grandfather's clothing and then fainted from fear. But at this moment a bullet hit Rabbi Shelomoh. "Why are you bothering me!?" the rabbi said. Ignoring his wound, he tried to continue the Sabbath service.

When he was carried home and put to bed, Rabbi Shelomoh requested that the book *Zohar** be opened at a certain place, and it was laid before him while his wound healed. He lay thus with the open book until the following Wednesday, the twenty-first of Tamuz 5552 [10 July 1792], the day that he died.

It is said that the limping Cossack was called Armilus. According to ancient tradition, this was the name of the malefactor who kills the Messiah, the son of Joseph.[62]

According to Hasidic tradition, Shelomoh of Karlin is regarded as the reincarnation of the first suffering Messiah, son of Joseph, who is reborn from generation to generation and is constantly present on Earth. Rabbi Shelomoh was killed while praying, but even after his death he continues his feat of praying.[63] Tsadik Yisroel from Ruzhyn, who lived during this period, said of him that he died because he was the *mashiach* (Messiah), son of Joseph.[64]

---

62 Ibid.
63 Ibid.
64 "Rabbi Shlomo of Karlin," http://www.nehora.com/pages/22%2A%2A%2A%2ARabbi-Shlomo-of-Karlin.html.

Shelomoh believed that performing miracles was not the main work of tsadiks. Their most important task was to teach the Jewish people how to serve God. He said: "The greatest of all miracles is to be able to inspire a Jew to the point that he can say a word before HaShem [a name for God]."[65]

One of the principal foundations of the life path of the Hasidim is joy. It is believed that a Hasid may be recognized by whether his life is filled with joy. The *admur*, the heads of the Hasidic movement, always emphasized the importance of joy, and they urged the faithful to eradicate all manifestations of sadness and depression. Shelomoh of Karlin said that *atsvut*, the Hebrew word for "sadness" or "depression," is the "entryway" for all types of evil, and he compared a person's depressed mood to sin.

Shema Shlomo (The Glory of Shlomo), the book written by Shelomoh of Karlin. Petrokov, 1928.

---

65 R. Shlomo of Karlin, *Shema Shlomo* (Jerusalem, 1956), 9.

Contemporary editions of Shema Shlomo by Shelomoh of Karlin.

Rabbi Shelomoh is often compared to the medieval Catholic monk St. Francis of Assisi, the founder of the Franciscan Order, because he was said to have the capacity to understand the language of birds and beasts. It is said that Rabbi Shelomoh was also able to see where human souls migrate.

Rabbi Shelomoh's extraordinary philosophical heritage has been preserved throughout the centuries thanks to the efforts of many generations of Jews. Books containing descriptions of his life, his commentaries on the Torah, and his discussions of feast days are still being published to this day, and they enjoy great popularity among the disciples and researchers of Hasidism. His works are available on the Internet, including the *midrash* Shema Shlomo*.[66]

His place and role in Hasidism is examined in greater detail in Wolf Rabinowitsch's history of Lithuanian Hasidism, which has been published in a number of languages.[67] Rabbi Shelomoh of Karlin requested God's grace in his prayers for Ludmir, where he lived and was buried, and predicted that no natural disaster would ever befall it. Unfortunately, few people in Ludmir today, including historians, are familiar with Rabbi Shelomoh of Karlin.

Below are several Hasidic parables that mention Rabbi Shelomoh, which were recorded by Martin Buber.[68]

Grievous Difficulties

One day, around the end of the feast of Yom Kippur, when Rabbi Shlomo was in a fine mood, he said that he could tell what requests every person had addressed to Heaven during these holy days and what answer he or she had received. The rabbi told one of his disciples: "You asked the Almighty to ease your life and send easy work so as not to offend service to Him. And they replied to you that the Almighty desires from you not simply learning or prayer but heartfelt regret that difficult labors for the sake of feeding yourself are distracting you from serving God."

Showing and Concealing

Rabbi Asher from Stolin [Ukr., Stolyn], a pupil of Rabbi Shlomo, gave this description of his Hasidic contemporaries: "They are dirty peasants and straw Cossacks! When they come to the rabbi, they show him only that which is nice, but they conceal the bad from him. When I would come to my sweetest, holy, and dearest rabbi (saying this, he kissed the tips of his fingers), I would conceal everything fine from him, but showed him the bad. For it is said, 'The priest shall make atonement for him' [Lev 5:13]."

---

66 Ibid.
67 Wolf Zeev Rabinowitsch, *Lithuanian Hasidism* (New York: Schocken Books, 1971).
68 Buber, *Khasidskie istorii*, 313–323.

The Worst

Rabbi Shlomo asked: "What is the worst of the acts of Evil?" And he himself replied: "To compel a person to forget that he is the son of the King."

How the Lord God Loves

Rabbi Shlomo said: "If I could love the most sublime of the tsadiks as the Lord God loves the lowliest sinner!"

Horses

During their peregrinations two brothers, Rabbi Zusia and Rabbi Elimelekh, frequently visited the city of Ludmir, where they always stayed at the home of a pious, poor man. Years later, after becoming famous, they visited this city again, not on foot but by carriage. They were met by the wealthiest man in this city, who before this time had never wanted to communicate with them, and he began pleading with them to stay in his home. But they told him: "Where we are concerned, nothing has changed that could compel you to change your attitude to us so markedly. The horse and carriage are the only novelty. Therefore, let them be your guests, and we will stay where we usually do."

Rabbi Shelomoh was buried in the Jewish cemetery, on the very spot where Gagarin Park is located today. Thanks to the investigative work of the American Association of Jews from the Former Soviet Union and the Union of Jewish Religious Organizations of Ukraine, who researched aerial photography archives dating to the Second World War, it was possible to locate the foundation of the *ohel (burial vault) at the gravesite of Shelomoh of Karlin. The ohel was rebuilt through the efforts of Jewish organizations.

Orthodox Jews regard Rabbi Shelomoh as a saint. Devout Jews, including pilgrims from all over the world, constantly come to say prayers at his grave, where they leave kvitl (notes) from family members and friends with requests for the holy rabbi Shelomoh of Karlin to help them with their problems.

Unfortunately, the ohel is now in a dilapidated state, and its walls are daubed with obscene graffiti. To the people who come here to pray, its besmirched walls represent the image of the city. Perhaps, this situation is caused by the city residents' lack of information about this sacred place and those who are buried here.

The ohel (burial vault) at the gravesite of Rabbi Shelomoh Karliner. Photo: Volodymyr Muzychenko.

The inscriptions of the epitaphs read: 1 (left): "The highly respected, holy righteous man, my Rabbi Shelomoh ha-Levi Segal of Karlin, holy righteous man of blessed memory, is buried here. Killed for the holy faith on the twenty-first day of Tamuz 5552" (1792, according to the secular calendar); 2: "The highly respected genius, righteous man of the Kabbalah, my teacher and spiritual father Yehudah (Yodl), son of the famous genius, teacher, and spiritual father Rabbi Moshe, righteous man of blessed memory and blessed saint, chief judge of the religious community of Kovel, co-author of the book *Ba-ketuvim*, is buried here: 'The voice of Yehudah on the tract *Shulhan 'arukh*, the "Light of Life" part.'" (Tombstone restored in 5760 [1999]; translation by D. Shkolnik and the Habad organization in Israel).

Matsevahs on the grave of Tsadik Shelomoh Karliner and Yehudah (Yodl), son of Moshe. Photo: Volodymyr Muzychenko.

෴ ෴ ෴

The Hasidic dynasty of tsadiks in Volodymyr-Volynsky was continued by Shelomoh of Karlin's son Moyshe Gotlieb (d. 1821), Moyshe's son Shloyme, and his grandson Nachum, who headed the city's Hasidic community. The last tsadik of Ludmir was Nachum's son Gdalyahu. One of Shelomoh's pupils and disciples was Uri Ben Pinchas of Strelsk, also known as ha-Saraf, the Burning Angel (b. 1757, d. 1826), who headed the Hasidic community of Lviv. Another of Shelomoh's pupils was Rabbi Asher from Stolin.

As Allan Nadler writes,[69] branches of Karlin-Stolin Hasidism—the Ludmir and Hasidic dynasties headed by Shelomoh's descendants, beginning with his sons Moyshe of Ludmir (d. 1829) and Dov Ber Tulchyn (d. 1833)—exist to this day in the Bronx (New York City), Buenos Aires (Argentina), and Israel.

Today Shlomo Wilhelm, a descendant of Shelomoh Karliner, heads the Orthodox community in the city of Zhytomyr, Ukraine, and is the Chief Rabbi of Central and Western Ukraine.

At the beginning of the nineteenth century, Volodymyr-Volynsky was home to Rabbi Noach, the pupil of Rabbi Ya'akov Yitshaak, the Seer of Lublin.

KHANE-ROKHL WERBERMACHER

Volodymyr-Volynsky is the birthplace of the female tsadik Khane-Rokhl Werbermacher, one of the most colorful figures of Hasidism and a charismatic leader of the city's Hasidic community.

The date of her birth differs from source to source. Most biographies indicate 1815. Citing official documents from this period, which were found in Palestine, the American scholar Nathaniel Deutsch gives 1806 as her date of birth.[70] She died in Jerusalem in 1892. Khane-Rokhl was renowned for her ability to heal the sick and was popularly known as "The Maid of Ludmir" (Yiddish, Di Ludmirer Moid). Strange as it may be, this prominent figure is practically unknown to Ukrainian regional specialists and historians.

The life of this unique woman—the first female rabbi in the history of Hasidism—has received much attention from scholars based abroad. She is now the focus of research by specialists in Hasidic history, the role of women in the Jewish community, and the development of feminism as a general social phenomenon. The first scholar to write about her life as a Jewish woman who fought for equality with men in

---

[69] http://yivoencyclopedia.org/search.aspx?query=ludmir.
[70] Nathaniel Deutsch, *The Maiden of Ludmir: A Jewish Holy Woman and Her World* (Berkeley: University of California Press, 2003), 75.

emotional and religious life was the Russian historian Shmuel Abba Horodecky (1871–1957), in his four-volume *Jewish History of Hasidism*.[71] The story of her life from a folkloristic perspective is the subject of an article by Hayah Bar-Itzhak.[72] Other scholars who have studied the life of this extraordinary woman include Nathaniel Deutsch, professor of religious history at the University of Chicago and author of *The Maiden of Ludmir: A Jewish Holy Woman and Her World*, and Hanna Krall, who wrote a short story called "The Great-Grandson."[73] A key section in the present volume is devoted to memoirs written by Khane-Rokhl's no less extraordinary great-grandson Janusz Bardach, who will be discussed later. Khane-Rokhl's story was transmitted from generation to generation within his family and in Jewish communities throughout the world, and at times it is difficult to distinguish between the truth and the stuff of legends.

Khane-Rokhl Werbermacher (meaning "weaver") was born into a wealthy Hasidic family who lived in the center of the city in a red-brick building located on Farna Street. Her well-to-do father Monesh gave her a good education, which included a comprehensive study of the Torah. There is conflicting information about her mother's name. According to Deutsch, her name is unknown, although her role in Khane-Rokhl's upbringing was undeniable. In her book, Tirzah Firestone calls her Leah.[74]

There are two versions of the story of Khane-Rokhl's birth, but both refer to the important role played by a well-known rabbi. According to one account, Khane-Rokhl was her parents' late and only child, born only after her mother received a blessing from Tsadik Mordekhai of Chornobyl. She sought his blessing in the desperate hope of bearing a child in order to save her marriage, because her husband Monesh was

---

71   S. A. Gorodetskii, *Evreiskaia starina 1909 g.*, vol. 2, http://lechaim.ru/ARHIV/172/deva.htm.
72   Haya Bar-Itzhak, "The Legend of the Jewish Holy Virgin of Ludmir: A Folkloristic Perspective," *Journal of Folklore Research* 46, no. 3 (September/December 2009): 269–92.
73   Kh. Kral', "Pravnuk," http://www.judaica.kiev.ua/eg9/eg913.htm.
74   Tirzah Firestone, *The Receiving: Reclaiming Jewish Women's Wisdom* (San Francisco: Harper San Francisco, 2003), 10.

threatening to divorce her. Hasidic laws permit divorce if a marriage has been barren for more than ten years. Although she invited her husband to go with her to obtain a blessing, he refused categorically, declaring that no blame accrued to him, and if anyone should seek the help of a tsadik, it was she.

Upon meeting the childless woman, Tsadik Mordekhai said that the situation was not her fault, and her husband should be the one who should pray to God for a child and seek a blessing. Mordekhai's heart was stirred with pity for the woman. He told her to go home, and said that with God's permission she would have a daughter. A year later she gave birth to Khane-Rokhl.

After her mother died, young Khane-Rokhl spent long hours sitting next to her grave. One day when she was leaving the cemetery at twilight, she tripped over a gravestone and fell. She was discovered only the following morning and remained unconscious for several weeks. This time her father went to Chornobyl. "Return home," the tsadik said. "Your Khane-Rokhl is well. She will bring you much joy and much grief."

Upon his return, her father saw that his daughter had regained consciousness; she was in a good mood and felt much better. Her strength was returning with every passing day. When she finally rose from her sickbed, she knew the entire Torah by heart. She told her father that she had visited Heaven and received a new soul. The great Tsadik Mordekhai confirmed her words: "We do not know whose religious soul lives in this girl." With this recognition, she acquired a new, special status.

Scholars are convinced that Khane-Rokhl's visit to a Uniate (Ukrainian Greek-Catholic) convent that existed in Volodymyr-Volynsky at that time also had an impact on her world perception.

Khane-Rokhl lived apart from everyone: her female peers made fun of her. She avoided conversations and spent all her time studying and praying. When she prayed, she would don a *tallis*,* like a man. She began commenting on the Writings of the Tanakh, and everyone was amazed at the originality of her ideas. Soon a group of believers gathered around her. She answered questions, offered advice and, according to various accounts, expelled demons. One of her visitors asked her to restore his hearing. At first she hesitated, then timidly she touched the ears of the sick man, who suddenly shouted: "I can hear!" After this, sick people from the entire region of Volhynia, Lublin, and Lviv began flocking to her. She became known as the "Maiden of Ludmir," and thanks to her good works she attained renown as a holy woman and miracle-worker.

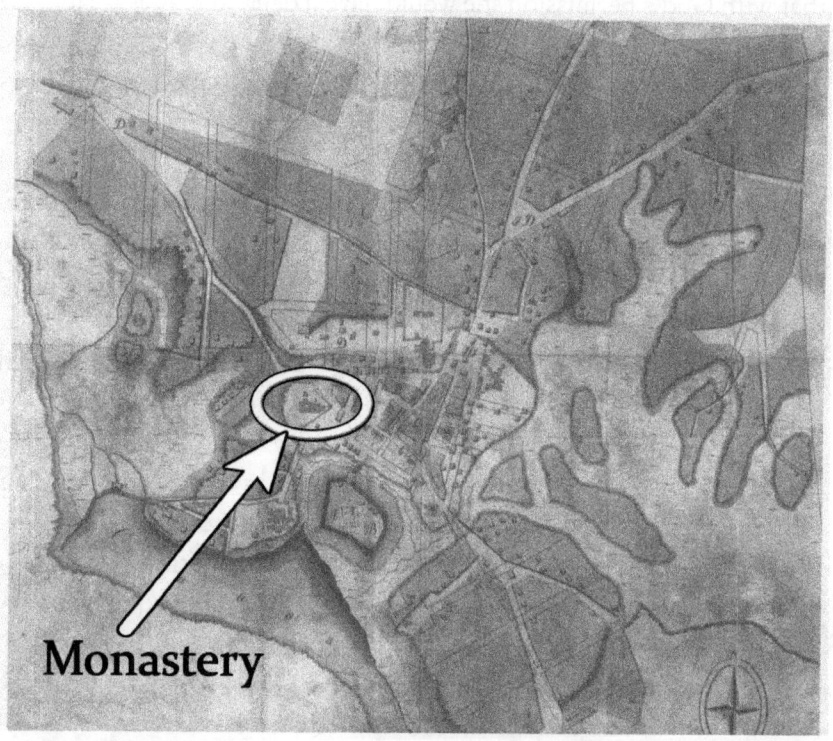

Ludmir/Volodymyr-Volynsky. This Russian government map (1807) shows the Uniate women's monastery that the Maiden of Ludmir may have visited. The original is held at the Russian State Historical Archive (RGIA) in St. Petersburg.[75]

---

75 Deutsch, *Maiden of Ludmir*, 102.

Khane-Rokhl refused to marry. She began to carry out all the religious commandments, even those that were not compulsory for women, and she continued her Torah studies. Her behavior was a challenge to traditional Jewish perceptions of the law and gender differences, which caused strife in Jewish society. She faced strong opposition from the hopelessly traditional Hasidic community, in which women's roles were restricted to bearing children and taking care of their households, but under no circumstances could they take on the role of spiritual leader. People said that she was possessed by a man's *dybbuk* (demon).

Gradually, she became the nucleus of a group of disciples, who were called the "Hasidim of the Maiden of Ludmir." When the house on Farna Street became too cramped to accommodate everyone, her father built her a prayer house (Hebrew, *bet ha-midrash** [study house]) nearby, on Sokalska Street. The building contained a special room where Khane-Rokhl received her disciples. In his 1909 book, Horodecky notes that this building was also called a *grünshtibl* (Yiddish, literally a little green Hasidic house of prayer) and was used as a prayer house by the members of the Rotmistrivka (Yiddish, Rakhmistrivke) Hasidic dynasty.[76] It was most likely demolished in the postwar period.

The fame of the Maiden of Ludmir spread to all the surrounding small towns and villages, and many people, both men and women, visited her, paying obeisance to her as a holy woman; even educated men and rabbis came to see her. But she refused to allow anyone to approach her: she customarily sat inside her room, the doors to which were kept open, and the people gathered in the next room listened to her through the open doors. There are eyewitness reports about her low voice, which resembled a man's.

---

76 Gorodetskii, *Evreiskaia starina 1909 g.*

The grünshtibl, the Bet ha-Midrash of the Maiden of Ludmir, early twentieth century.[77]

At this time the chief rabbi of Volodymyr-Volynsky was Moshe of Ludmir, who was supported by the city's prosperous Jews. But the poorer members of the community preferred the sermons of the Maiden of Ludmir and flocked to hear her speak. Extant Jewish stories contain a number of references to her sermons and teachings. She told her disciples: "Those who are accompanied by holy thoughts on their life journey are not alone and unfortunate because their noble thoughts protect them from loneliness."

Khane-Rokhl spent much time as a traveling preacher, a magid. Well-known tsadikim of the time expressed amazement—and irritation—at the emergence of their new female colleague. Other people came simply to see this phenomenon for themselves. It is said that she called every visitor by name, even those whom she did not know. Tsadik Mordekhai of Chornobyl also visited the prayer house of the Maiden of Ludmir; this was the man who had given a blessing to her

---

77 *Wladimir Wolynsk*, 231.

mother and restored Khane-Rokhl back to health. He was considered the most esteemed among the tsadikim of that period; according to Hasidic tales, he was the deputy of the thirty-six righteous men scattered throughout the world, on whom the world rests.

At a certain point, when Khane-Rokhl was being increasingly pressured, her father, wishing to avoid further conflict, asked his daughter to consult with his rebbe, the Magid (Tsadik Mordekhai) of Chornobyl, about her activities. The magid tried to convince her to change her unusual behavior, to marry, and to live her life as a traditional Hasidic woman.

After visiting the rabbi, Khane-Rokhl temporarily suspended her activities as a Hasidic leader and teacher. She even married, although the marriage was never consummated, and she and her husband divorced after one week. She eventually remarried, but that marriage was short-lived as well.

Later, Khane-Rokhl immigrated to Palestine, where she settled in Jerusalem. Together with an elderly kabbalist*, she devoted herself to activities which, according to the two of them, were supposed to usher in the coming of the Messiah.

According to a census of the members of the Hasidic community in Ukraine's Volyn region who were living in Palestine in 1866, Rabbanit* Khane-Rokhl, born in Ludmir, arrived there in 1863 at the age of sixty. According to another census, the female rabbi and tsadik Khane-Rokhl came to Palestine in 1859 at the age of sixty-nine. She lived on Hebron Street in the Old City (Jerusalem). Yossl Akiba described her as a rather sympathetic woman of short stature, who wore an old-style Jerusalem hat called a *yamperke*, and the color white figured prominently in her clothing; white was worn by the majority of elderly women in Jerusalem at the time.

Every day, Khane-Rokhl prayed at the Western Wall* dressed in a tallit and tefillin*. Nathaniel Deutsch believes that she was financially independent and was thus able to continue her activities as a Hasidic leader. She gathered the Hasidic community around herself, managed its affairs, and founded a new Hasidic court. On the Sabbath her disciples visited her in order to hear her treatment of the words of the Torah and her commentaries. On Rosh Hodesh* she accompanied them to Rachel's tomb to pray there and seek her assistance.

Khane-Rokhl Werbermacher, the Maiden of Ludmir, died in Jerusalem on 17 July 1892 (the twenty-second day of Tamuz 5652). She was buried on the Mount of Olives, where the most respected Jews of the world and righteous people are buried. The Hasidim believe it is the place that will mark the arrival of Moshiach (Messiah), the son of David, and the first people to be resurrected will be the individuals buried there. She is the only person from Volodymyr-Volynsky to be accorded the great honor of being interred there.

For a lengthy period of time, the exact place of her burial was not known. Thanks to Deutsch's many years of research, archival holdings yielded old maps of the Jerusalem Burial Society, which helped identify the grave of the Maiden of Ludmir.

1) The location of the Maiden of Ludmir's gravesite

1. Mount of Olives
2. Way to the Citadel
3. The Temple Mount
4. The Jewish Quarter
5. Silwan
6. Intercontinental Hotel
7. Mount of Olives Cemetary
8. Jericho Street
9. Data: Natan Torah Burial Society
10. Scale: 300 meters

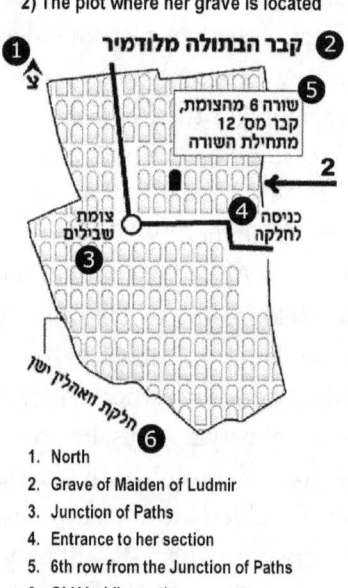

2) The plot where her grave is located

1. North
2. Grave of Maiden of Ludmir
3. Junction of Paths
4. Entrance to her section
5. 6th row from the Junction of Paths
6. Old Vachlin section

Diagram showing 1) the location of the Maiden of Ludmir's gravesite and 2) the plot where her grave is located.[78]

---

78 *Haaretz*, 4 July 2008, http://www.haaretz.co.il/hasite/spages/449208.html.

The grave of the Maiden of Ludmir.

A group of pilgrims visiting the grave of the Maiden of Ludmir on the Mount of Olives.

Like many graves in this cemetery, Khane-Rokhl's grave was unmarked for many years, as the original gravestone was destroyed during the Jordanian occupation. Rabbi Zalman Shachter-Shalomi established a fund for its restoration, collecting more than 3,500 dollars in donations for a new monument. Israeli native Ruth Gan Kagan, a recently ordained rabbi, resolved to do a *mitsvah** (good deed) by erecting a gravestone designed by the architect Abigail Zohar. On 11 June (23 Tamuz) 2004, a new gravestone was unveiled at the grave of Khane-Rokhl, which features a place for placing commemorative candles and *kvitl* (notes containing appeals and requests to God, similar to those that are traditionally left at the Western Wall and the graves of the Holy Righteous). After 116 years, her disciples now have another opportunity to read the *kaddish** at the grave of their spiritual leader.[79]

Today, pilgrims visit her grave to pray and ask God for intercession because, like the biblical matriarch Rachel, she is considered a saint. People believe that appeals addressed to God on this spot will be heard and fulfilled.

One hundred years later, the new owner of the house that once belonged to the Maiden of Ludmir is her granddaughter Chaya, who married a merchant named Motl. A former importer of sable fur from Russia, he prospered and bought several more substantial buildings on Farna Street. Like the majority of the Jews in the city, Chaya's sons and their wives and children perished in Piatydni at the hands of the Nazis.

In progressive Jewish synagogues, female rabbis are no longer a novelty; there are many of them today, including in the Jewish community in the Ukrainian city of Lutsk. But the first Jewish feminist and woman to head a Jewish religious community was Khane-Rokhl Werbermacher.

---

79 Debra Kolodny, "Celebrating the Life of the Maiden of Ludmir," http://www.aleph.org/pdf/MaidofLudmir.pdf.

Rabbi Ruth Gan Kagan at the grave of Khane-Rokhl Werbermacher.

The legendary image of the Jewish girl Khane-Rokhl from a small Ukrainian city has always sparked interest among not only historians and specialists of Hasidism, but also writers, composers, and poets. The famous Jewish writer Isaac Bashevis Singer (1904–1991) retells the story of the Maiden of Ludmir in his novel *Shosha*.

Many poems and prose works have been written about the first female rabbi in history. Khane-Rokhl figures in a work by the Polish writer Hanna Krall. In December 1997, the play *Ha-Betula mi-Ludmir* (The Maid of Ludomir), by Josepha Even-Shoshan, was staged at the Khan Theater (Te'atron ha-han ha-Yerushalmi) in Jerusalem by the director Ofira Henig.[80] In 1950, the short story "Ha-Betula mi-Ludmir" appeared in a collection of short stories about the life of Hasidim by the writer and journalist Yochanan Twersky (1900–1967).

Nathaniel Deutsch believes that the life story of the Maiden of Ludmir served as the model for *The Dybbuk*, the famous Yiddish-language play by the dramatist and ethnographer Semen An-ski (Shloyme Zaynvl [Solomon] Rapoport, 1863–1920). According to this American scholar, although the play does not recreate every detail of

---

80 http://www.eleven.co.il/article/14439.

Khane-Rokhl's life, it contains many analogous features, for example, a woman with a man's voice, the issue of forced marriage, a holy person who tries to expel evil spirits, etc. Proof of this is the fact that, prior to writing his play, An-ski visited Volodymyr-Volynsky on two occasions, querying city residents about the story of the "Maiden of Ludmir."[81] In his turn, Alex Tarn wrote a mystical musical drama entitled *The Dybbuk*, which was based on the motifs of An-ski's eponymous play.[82]

**Rachel Botchan playing the starring role in The Maiden of Ludmir.
Photo by Kathy Willens/Associated Press.**

In 1996, the Folksbiene (People's Stage) Yiddish Theater in Manhattan, New York, staged the musical *The Maiden of Ludmir*. In his review, Lawrence Van Gelder of *The New York Times* wrote: "She was a woman ahead of her time.... *The Maiden of Ludmir* draws on the true story of Khane Rukhl Verbermakher [sic], whose profound Talmudic scholarship, fervor and wisdom prompted her to adopt the religious

---

81 Deutsch, *Maiden of Ludmir*, 20–23.
82 http://lit.lib.ru/t/tarn__a/text__0230.shtml

practices of Jewish men in Ukraine in the 19th century."[83] The play, based on the book and lyrics by Miriam Hoffman, was directed by Robert Kalfin, with Rachel Botchan in the starring role. The music was written by John Clifton, and the production was staged in Yiddish, with English and Russian translations. As Kathy Willens of the Associated Press wrote, this play is "a feminist tragedy."[84] The full text of this musical was published in the almanac of the Jewish Branch of the Union of Jewish Writers and Journalists in Israel.[85]

THE SYNAGOGUE

The majority of the Jewish residents of Volodymyr-Volynsky, as in most other cities, were devoted to their faith and traditions. Thus, the synagogue (Greek, "gathering") played an immense role in the life of the community; first and foremost, Jews came there to take part in communal prayer.

In the summer of 2009, the foundation of an unknown brick structure dating to the fourteenth and fifteenth centuries was discovered during archaeological excavations taking place on Drahomanov Street. Some characteristic features offer grounds for assuming that this was a synagogue built during the period of the Galician-Volhynian Principality.

Oleksii Zlatohorsky, the head of the Volyn Antiquities Company, associated with the Institute of Archaeology of the National Academy of Sciences (NAN) of Ukraine, commented on the discovery: "There is no information about the existence of a monumental structure in this part of Volodymyr-Volynsky either in written sources or studies done in the nineteenth and twentieth centuries. That this is a structure from the fourteenth-fifteenth centuries is attested by the building materials, especially the bricks. The type of foundation wall indicates

---

[83] Lawrence Van Gelder, "Woman Ahead of Her Time As a 19th-Century Rabbi," *The New York Times*, 14 December 1996, http://www.nytimes.com/1996/12/14/theater/woman-ahead-of-her-time-as-a-19th-century-rabbi.html.

[84] Kathy Willens, "Yiddish Theater," *Gadsden Times*, 9 January 1997, http://news.google.com/newspapers?nid=1891&dat+19970108&id=9r0fAAAAIBAJ&sjid=QNgEAAAAIBAJ&pg=1826,835646.

[85] *Yerusholaymer almanakh*, vol. 28 (Jerusalem: Eygens 2008).

that this may be a synagogue."⁸⁶ The floor of the structure is significantly lower than ground level, a typical feature of synagogues, which could not be built higher than Christian temples. This restriction was also inspired by the prayer, "Out of the depths I call to you, O Lord" (Psalm 129:1).

The largest of the city's known synagogues was probably built in the late fifteenth century. It was situated in an area bounded in the north by T. Shevchenko Street, in the south by Danylo Halytsky Street, in the west by Kovelska Street, and in the east by Roksoliana Street. According to other sources, it was constructed in 1801. However, it is more than likely that this is the date of the construction of a synagogue that was built on the site of an earlier one.

In the seventeenth and eighteenth centuries there were at least two synagogues in the city: one was built of wood, and the other was a brick choral synagogue.⁸⁷ It occupied a dominant place in the area inhabited by the Jews, and was described by O. Tsynkalovsky.⁸⁸

This was a brick building of rectangular form with a roof covered with tiles, somewhat lower in height than the Dormition Cathedral, which is still standing today. It featured an original façade consisting of four arched vaults with cylindrical protuberances above them. The traditional six-pointed star known as the *Magen David* ("Shield of David") appeared both on the front side—on a spire above the roof and beneath the arched vault—and in the form of a relief on the rear wall beneath the roof arch. Inside the synagogue, arch-like covers rested on four brick columns.⁸⁹

---

86 "Sjurprizi Istorii Volins ki Arheologi Podivuvali Svoimi Znahidkami," http://vidido.ua/index.php/poglyad/comments/sjurprizi__istorii__ volins__ki__arheologi__ podivuvali__svoimi__znahidkami/.
87 Deutsch, *Maiden of Ludmir*, 77.
88 O. Tsynkalovs′kyi, "Materialy do arkheolohiï Volodymyrs′koho povitu," *Zapysky naukovoho tovarystva im. T. H. Shevchenka* 154 (1937): 183–240.
89 *Wladimir Wolynsk*.

The foundation of a brick structure, probably a synagogue dating to the fourteenth to fifteenth centuries.

Large choral synagogue built in 1801; photograph taken in 1901.[90]

---

90 Ibid., 225.

Large choral synagogue; postcard from the early twentieth century. From the private collection of R. Mazurok.

View of the synagogue. Postcard from the early twentieth century. From the private collection of R. Mazurok.

Early twentieth-century postcard depicting the synagogue in Volodymyr-Volynsky. Artist: Emil Weiss (14 August 1896–6 January 1965). From the private collection of R. Mazurok.

Large choral synagogue. Illustration by an unknown artist.[91]

---

91 Ibid.

The interior of the synagogue: the aron ha-kodesh* and the bima* (amud), the pulpit used by the khazan (cantor).[92]

The synagogue in Volodymyr-Volynsky; postcard from the early twentieth century.

---

92 Ibid., 89.

At left: the large choral synagogue; postcard from the early twentieth century. From the private collection of R. Mazurok.

The spot on which the choral synagogue once stood; today: Roksoliana Street. Photo: Volodymyr Muzychenko.

The large choral synagogue built in 1801 (view of the rear of the building facing today's Roksoliana Street). Archival photograph.

The synagogue (aerial photograph).

The synagogue was dismantled in the early 1950s, and its remnants were removed to the village of Zhovtneve, where they were used as building materials for the construction of a military helicopter airfield. There are many city residents still alive who witnessed its destruction. The synagogue walls were so thick that tank tractors were used to pull it down—and even then with great difficulty.

The destruction of the synagogue began during the Nazi occupation. A city resident, I. V. Vozniuk (b. 1923), recalls: "Next to our house was a wooden synagogue. During the occupation, when the Jews were being taken to the ghetto, people began dismantling the synagogue. When I walked past it, [I saw] Jewish books in leather covers scattered on the ground, trampled and torn."

Until the emergence of the Hasidic movement in the eighteenth century, there was only one synagogue in all the Eastern European communities, with the exception of the largest ones. Community leaders took great care to ensure that the community did not splinter into separate groups. Communal prayer was considered important for maintaining order in the community. It was only with the emergence of Hasidism in Volodymyr-Volynsky that small houses of prayer called *shtibls* appeared.

During this period, synagogues were mostly built of wood, and the fact that Volodymyr-Volynsky had such a large synagogue is proof that the community was comparatively wealthy, since its members managed to gather funds for its construction and had considerable influence and connections that allowed them to obtain permission to build it. The synagogue was not only a place where religious services and rites took place; it was also a spiritual and administrative center, where community leaders held their meetings and court hearings took place. In addition, religious schools traditionally operated in the synagogue.

In her book, author Ann Kazimirski describes the appearance of the synagogue:

> The large synagogue was an impressive structure, with high ceilings, long passageways, rows of rich oak benches and a mahogany pulpit. Stained-glass windows adorned the synagogue with

different biblical scenes: Adam and Eve in the Garden of Eden ... Moses striking the Ten Commandments on a rock, Noah building the great ark, and others. The aron ha-kodesh [the Torah ark in a synagogue] housed seven Torah scrolls adorned with silver crowns and covered in purple, velvet wrappings. Rich people belonged to this congregation and their contributions paid for the Rabbi's salary and the upkeep of the synagogue.[93]

To the left of the *bima* stood a cupboard used to store various ritual objects, such as *yad* (pointers in the shape of hands), a *shofar* (a ram's horn blown during feast days), and cloths for the *bima*.

Synagogue services featured singing by cantors. One of the most famous was David Kliger, who sang to the accompaniment of a choir under his direction. He was an erudite scholar whose prayers greatly appealed to his supporters. After Kliger, the functions of cantor were carried out by Baruch from Lutsk, who sang without choral accompaniment. He was a young man with a strong, pleasant voice.

Cantor Meir Diner was the next to be appointed to this post. His prayers were accompanied by a choir of sixteen singers directed by him. After several years, he was appointed cantor in the city of Rzeszów.

Shmuel from Lutsk was the next cantor to be appointed. He was considered one of the finest choral directors of his time, and the choir that he taught and directed was highly esteemed by the members of the synagogue. The last cantor of the Volodymyr-Volynsky choral synagogue, Cantor Shmuel, perished along with the entire community in 1943.

Among the members of his choir were the tenor Moshe, son of Feibl Broder, a Hasid from Włodawa (Ukrainian, Volodava); the bass Tuvia Leibishes, grandfather of Rodeski the grocer; and the alto Froika, son of Yaacov Ginsberg, the owner of a kiosk on Farna Street. The latter brought joy to his singers with his strong, beautiful voice.

---

93 Ann Kazimirski, *Witness to Horror*, 2nd ed. (Montreal: Devonshire Press, 1997), 2–3.

The Hasidim did not pray in this synagogue, but they came there on Rosh Hodesh, Passover, Shavuot, and Sukkot to listen to the singing of the cantor and his choir.

The Bet ha-Midrash stood a few dozen meters from the large choral synagogue. This was a large wooden building, where the Small Bet ha-Midrash was located on the right side of the corridor, and on the left, the Great Bet ha-Midrash. Upon entering, a visitor immediately saw a large *bima** surrounded by a wooden enclosure that stood in front of the aron ha-kodesh.

Every day, starting in the early morning, Jews who were utterly devoted to their faith and had dedicated themselves to God and the people of Israel came here to pray; among the faithful were merchants, bootmakers, tailors, and shoemakers. When one *minyan** finished its prayers, it was followed by another, and so on until noon. During the second half of the day, this building was visited by young men who had set aside some free time to study the Torah. Later, people traveling with their wares to markets and bazaars came there. Merchants, businessmen, and Hasidim were among those who attended the *Maariv* (evening prayer). Preachers spoke here, and many people came to hear them despite their fatigue from working all day.

Cantor Melech prayed there for many years before the outbreak of the Second World War. It is said, he had a powerful voice and knew how to please listeners with his songs when he came there for festive occasions that took place in the homes of various city residents. He did not distinguish between rich Jews or their poorer brethren, and his unparalleled performances of traditional Jewish songs were accessible to all.

The tiny *shtibl* synagogues were small, low-ceilinged buildings. Their walls were bare of paintings, and there were only a few benches. The aron ha-kodesh contained Torah scrolls covered with ordinary linen, and there were no decorative crowns or velvet. These prayer houses were attended by poor people, who paid their rabbi in kind—with food products.[94]

Since ancient times there had been a yeshiva in the city, which was divided into three grades. Most of the students were from the villages and small towns surrounding Volodymyr-Volynsky: Kryliv, Ustyluh, Kysylyn, Lokachi, and others. According to the recollections of Lipa Mendelson, who studied there before the war, the first grade was taught by rabbis Moshe and Yitshak. The head of the yeshiva, Menachem Mendl, who taught second grade, lived in the yeshiva building with his wife and children: three sons and a daughter. He was a great scholar and fervent disciple of the Karlin-Stolin dynasty founded by Aharon. Moshe Goldberg Mendel and Asher Chaim Bdanski also worked at the yeshiva. The students of the Volodymyr-Volynsky yeshiva, like those who attended yeshivas throughout Poland and Lithuania, were given meals according to the "day" system, that is, they were paired up with seven families, each of which fed a student one day a week. Such families did this out of the goodness of their hearts. If a student could not be fed on a designated day because of the family's absence, he was given enough money to feed himself for that day. Mendelson could not remember anyone ever refusing to feed a yeshiva student.[95]

The synagogue in the village of Porytsk.[96]

---

94 Ibid., 2–3.
95 *Wladimir Wolynsk*, 227–28.
96 http://www.badacz/org/izrael/zydzi__w__polsce/dzieje__nowe.htm.

During this period (1786–1860) there was a Jewish printing house not only in Volodymyr-Volynsky but also in the village of Porytsk*. This institution had an appreciable impact on the spiritual life of the community, inasmuch as books were a key feature of Jewish life. It is no accident that the Jews have always been known as the "People of the Book," a reference first and foremost to the Old Testament. Jewish printing houses of that time published religious literature.

Relations between the Jews and Christians of Volodymyr-Volynsky were varied. Judging from sixteenth- and seventeenth-century documents of the Volodymyr court of the first instance, one may conclude that in those years both communities coexisted peacefully and had good, neighborly relations.

Among the documents of the "current record book" of the Volodymyr court for 1566 are: a complaint lodged by Bishop Feodosii of Volodymyr against the Jews Nachim Shymanovych and Isaac Davydovych concerning the poor upkeep of the mills in Piatydni and Khrypalychi, which they had leased from him; a declaration of the Jew Itsko Shmoilovych about his debt to Stanislav Hraievsky and about the use of Shmoilovych's house as collateral and its lease to Hraievsky, which attests to the fact that Jews often became debtors of local lords and even had to lease their own residences as payment against their debts.[97] In turn, wealthier Jews loaned money to Ukrainian peasants; this is the subject of a declaration drawn up on 1 April 1567 by Shloyme Dluhach, a resident of Volodymyr-Volynsky, about the non-payment of money owed to him by some peasants owned by Prince Aleksander Czartoryski.[98] Lessors were under pressure, but Jews could appeal to the courts and defend their rights, as attested by a complaint dated 4 March 1567, which was lodged by a lessor of the Kyivan palatine Prince Kostiantyn Ostrozky, the Jew Zrail Abramovych, against the lord

---

97 *Volodymyrs´kyi Grods´kyi sud*, 20.
98 Ibid., 21.

Mykhailo Dubnytsky "concerning threats and insults made to him by the latter in the home of the Volodymyr reeve Maksym Ludovych."[99]

Another document found in the archives is a complaint lodged by some priests in Volodymyr-Volynsky, which was submitted to the municipal court in 1590. The complaint states that on Jewish Street (*vulytsia Zhydivska*) a group of Jewish youths—"brats" [*bakhuri*]—threw stones at a Procession of the Cross from the Dormition Cathedral to the Church of St. Nicholas.[100]

The authorities deliberately created conditions whereby the Jewish population was forced to act as an instrument of the authorities' and magnates' oppression of the impoverished segment of the population. Since legislation strictly restricted Jews' places of habitation as well as their economic activities, which included only those that were regarded as being unworthy of respectable citizens, Jews in fact were pushed into a particular social niche. Thus, in serving as intermediaries and engaging in trading and money-lending, leasing taverns, and collecting taxes and duties from ordinary people, they ended up in the role of a lightning-rod for the ruling, affluent segment of the population, thereby sparking dissatisfaction among the impoverished autochthonous population. This is what led to the merciless brutality that took place during the Khmelnytsky Uprising and the period known as *Koliivshchyna*, an anti-Polish peasant uprising, during which rebels destroyed entire Jewish communities, sparing neither women nor children. Ordinary Jews, most of whom were far from wealthy, were victims of these pogroms. This explains why, unfortunately, relations between Ukrainians and Jews were not always amicable. Eventually, the Jewish community of Volodymyr-Volynsky became the target of persecutions by the native population, and Jewish pogroms and killings took place periodically in the city.

---

99   Ibid., 35.
100 "Sudebnyi prigovor nad zhidami, kotorye brosali kamniami v episkopa Vladimir-skogo Meletiia Khrebtovicha i v sviashchennikov, sovershavshikh krestnyi khod v gorode Vladimire, 22 maia 1590 g.," *Arkhiv Iugo-Zapadnoi Rossii* [AIuZR] (1481–1596 gg.), no. 63, ed. N. D. Ivanishev (Kyiv: Universitetskaia tipografiia, 1859), 265–67.

One of the most tragic pages in the history of the Jews was that of the anti-Jewish pogroms that took place during the Khmelnytsky Uprising (1648–1649), which were marked by the brutal and barbarous destruction of defenseless civilians, including women and children, and the expulsion or forcible conversion to Orthodoxy. In 1649, when Khmelnytsky's troops captured Volodymyr-Volynsky, Jews fled the city. Those who did not manage to leave the city were killed by the rebels.

In his chronicle, Natan Hannover describes the inhumane cruelty of Khmelnytsky's Cossacks:

> Just like in Volhynia in the h[oly] Volodymyr community, in the h[oly] Lutsk community, in the h[oly] Kremianets community and in their sub-kahals, there was a great slaughter, and many thousands of Jews were killed. In the h[oly] Kremianets community, one malefactor took a Jewish butcher's knife and killed several hundred Jewish children with it. He asked his friend whether this was kosher* meat or *treyf**. When he said: "treyf," he was throwing a child's body to some dogs. Then he set about slaughtering another little boy, he was stabbing him, and his friend said: "kosher." They examined the meat (as is usually done with the meat of goats and sheep) and, spearing it on a stake, they carried it through the city streets shouting: "Who wants to buy some goat meat or mutton?" May God avenge their blood.[101]

These tragic events and the savage attitude to the Jews on the part of Khmelnytsky's Cossacks are described by chroniclers of that period: "They took Kaniv: they flayed the living skin from all Jews. That was their Cossack custom."[102]

The Jewish historian Simon Dubnow describes these events as follows: "The killings were accompanied by barbarous abuses—they

---

101 *Hlybokyi mul: Khronika Natana Hanovera* (Kyiv: Dukh i litera, 2010), 104–5.
102 Nikolai Kostomarov [Mykola Kostomarov], *Bogdan Khmel'nitskii*, vol. 1 (St. Petersburg, 1884), 321.

flayed the skin off living people, sawed them in half, beat them to death with staves, roasted them on coals, doused them in boiling water; there was no pity even for infants. The people demonstrated the greatest brutality toward the Jews: they were condemned to ultimate destruction, and all pity for them was considered treason."[103]

After the uprising was crushed, the Jews returned to the city. However, many of them lived in poverty because their properties had been looted. The leaders of the community were forced to obtain substantial loans in order to save their people from utter impoverishment. The economic situation improved only in the late seventeenth century.

In his research on the fatalities among the Jewish population on the eve of the Khmelnytsky Uprising and population losses during its course, Shaul Stampfer concluded that on the eve of the uprising there were nearly 170 Jewish homes in Volodymyr-Volynsky,[104] only thirty-nine of which remained standing.

According to other data, on the eve of the Khmelnytsky Uprising taxes in the city were levied from 159 Jewish houses, home to nearly a thousand people. In 1653, twenty-five homes were taxed, and in 1662, only 318 Jews.[105]

During this period a significant proportion of the city's Jews scattered to the surrounding villages in search of new sources of income. Some found employment in the sphere of agriculture.[106]

Khmelnytsky's attitude to the Jews may be judged by a text of the peace treaty that was concluded with the Rzeczpospolita in 1649, which proclaimed that Cossack lands were now free of the Jewish presence: "Jews in Kyiv and past the Dnipro River are not to reside in Kyiv, and they are not to travel for trade either to Kyiv or to any cities and places beyond the Dnipro. And whatever Jews appear beyond the Dnipro, even those Jews in the Zaporozhian Host are to be robbed and sent

---

103 S. M. Dubnov, *Kratkaia istoriia evreev* (Moscow: Svarog, 1996).
104 Shaul' Shtampfer, "Chto proizoshlo s evreiami Ukrainy v 1648 godu?," pt. 2, http://www.sem40.ru/ourpeople/history/18222.
105 Lukin, "Volodymyr Volyns'kyi."
106 *Wladimir Wolynsk*.

back beyond the Dnipro." The complete absence of Jews in the areas under rebel control is attested by sources from that period; for example, the travel notes written about Left-Bank Ukraine by the Orthodox priest Paul of Aleppo in 1654–1655: "Its [Left-Bank Ukraine's] immense significance lies in the fact that there are almost no people of other faiths, just faithful and pious Orthodox."[107]

The writer and Orthodox Church leader Ioanikii Galiatovsky wrote in his treatise *Mesiia pravdyvyi* (The True Messiah, 1669): "Christian tsars, princes, and all lords should take money from the Jewish treasury for the construction of churches and shelters for the weak and poor.... We, Christians, should ruin and burn down Jewish temples.... We should take your synagogues away from you and turn them into churches; we should expel you, as enemies of Christ and Christians, from your cities in all states, kill you with the sword, drown in rivers, and destroy you by all manners of death."[108]

Despite the declaration of war by the Orthodox faith, in fact this war had nothing in common with Christianity, which, like Judaism, forbids murder, let alone the Cossacks' horrifically sophisticated methods of killing. This did not foster peaceful coexistence between Christians and Jews. As a result of these events, in Jewish memory the image of Bohdan Khmelnytsky is associated with the terrible crimes that were perpetrated against them.

In this context, the following questions arise: how heroic was the struggle of Khmelnytsky's Cossacks against the peaceful Jewish inhabitants of Ukraine, including women and children? Can one build happiness on the blood of innocents, and if so, is it worth confusing heroism with banditry? Sadly, these aspects of history are ignored in school textbooks.

Many Jews perished in the pogroms of 1653, when the city was occupied by Lithuanian troops of the Rzeczpospolita, and in 1658, during the Russo-Polish war, when the city was utterly sacked, the sole Jewish survivors being the members of two families. Those who

---

[107] Bulos Ibn Az-Zaïm (Pavlo Khalebs′kyi), "Podorozh patriarkha Makariia (uryvky)," *Dzvin*, no. 9 (1990): 119–24.
[108] *Narysy*, 52.

gradually returned to the city were not able to pay their taxes and were thus forced to obtain loans (in 1650, 1666, and 1671). Other kahals in the county were faced with the necessity to obtain loans, and when, along with the Volodymyr-Volynsky kahal, they failed to pay 10 percent of the monies that they had borrowed for the army's maintenance, as established by the Volhynian Diet in 1671, the tax assessor of Volodymyr County lodged a protest against the main kahal and its subordinate synagogues.[109]

Fortunately, these tragic pages did not determine Ukrainian-Jewish relations inasmuch as, despite certain political and ideological influences, ordinary people of all nationalities, who always form a majority, existed side by side, found a common language with each other and lived in peace and mutual respect. In Volodymyr-Volynsky, Christian churches of various confessions stood next to Jewish synagogues.

As a result of the material losses caused by the Cossack and Swedish armies in the 1650s–1660s and the fire of 1683, the Jewish community became a debtor of the royal treasury and private creditors.

Trade continued to occupy an important place in Jewish economic activities. Considering Jewish religious laws and the circumstance that commerce was mostly in Jewish hands, in 1683 Wednesdays were designated as market and bazaar days in Volhynia, as an alternative to Saturday.[110]

During the 1765 census, Jews complained to inspectors "students are not allowing [us] to bury the dead in the cemetery, royal privileges for which had been granted to them." They were thus forced to carry out the burial ritual at night. According to this census, 1,327 Jews paid the poll tax.[111]

※ ※ ※

---

[109] *Evreiskaia Entsiklopediia Brokgauza-Efrona*.
[110] Scott Ury, "Sabbath Rest," http://www.yivoencyclopedia.org/article.aspx/Sabbath_Rest.
[111] Tsynkalovs′kyi, *Kniazhyi horod Volodymyr*, 74.

In the eighteenth century, the Jewish community of Volodymyr-Volynsky, while still important, no longer wielded the same influence that it had had prior to the wars of the mid-seventeenth century. The Lutsk kahal gained importance. The Polish government conducted the first census of the Jewish population in 1764. According to its results, 1,401 Jews lived in Volodymyr-Volynsky, the second most populous area in the Volyn region (after Lutsk).[112]

The census of 1765 contains data on 1,327 Jews (not including 74 children) who lived within the limits of various "jurisdictions" and owned a total of 159 buildings. The entire kahal district was home to 1,733 Jews, not including the Volodymyr kahal.[113] According to the census results, there were twenty-seven Jewish houses situated on starosta lands, compared to thirteen houses owned by Christians.[114]

The economic crisis in Poland in the eighteenth century also had a negative impact on the city's Jewish population. By 1784 there were only 340 Jews left in the city[115] and 592 in the entire kahal district. Gradually, however, the number of Jews residing in Volodymyr-Volynsky began to increase, and by 1790 the community had doubled in size to 630 people (926 in the entire kahal district).[116]

From the moment the city came under Russian imperial rule, following the Third Partition of Poland in 1795, the community began to fall into decline.

Describing this period in the history of the city, with specific reference to 1789, the Ukrainian historian O. Tsynkalovsky wrote: "The Jews are complaining that they have to pay into the starosta's treasury: shopkeepers—500 złoty, tavern-keepers—3,897 złoty and 27 groszy; in addition, shopkeepers must pay 7.5 groszy for each market, burghers are forcing the kahal to make each Jewish home pay 1 złoty and 20 groszy." This attests to the complex economic conditions that affected the Jewish community during this period.

---

112 *Wladimir Wolynsk.*
113 *Rossiiskaia Ievreiskaia Entsiklopediia*, vol. 4.
114 Tsynkalovs'kyi, *Kniazhyi horod Volodymyr*, 72.
115 *Elektronnaia Evreiskaia Entsiklopediia*, http://www.eleven.co.il/article/10945.
116 *Evreiskaia Entsiklopediia Brokgauza-Efrona.*

In taxation books, since its annexation to Russia, Volodymyr-Volynsky was mentioned as a county city for the first time in 1799. According to their data, the demographic situation looked like this:117

Table 1: The Population of Volodymyr-Volynsky in 1799–1805

	1799	1800	1801	1805
Jews	1,834	1,999	1,909	1,943
Christians	1.076	680	672	673
Jewish merchants	15	22	37	34

Thus, during this period the Jewish community once again experienced demographic and economic growth following the decline connected with the crisis in Poland and oppressions that the community had suffered at the hands of the Russian authorities. Polish, Ukrainian, and Jewish institutions existed side by side in the city, which boasted a pharmacy, a brickworks, a mill, a railway station, shops, street markets, and taverns (including one owned by a Pole named Kozlowski).

Municipal institutions included a school, a courthouse, a treasury, a hospital, and a prison. Jewish homes were scattered throughout the city, but were concentrated primarily in the vicinity of the central square. There were two Jewish cemeteries in the city, one old and one newer.

There are data on the Jewish horse trade, which supplied the Polish army in 1782 and the production by Jewish manufacturers of goods for this trade.[118]

⚜ ⚜ ⚜

During the economic crisis that swept Poland during the final years of its independence in the eighteenth century, Jewish obligations reached high proportions, in connection with which they lodged complaints to inspectors in 1789. At the time, Jewish stall owners were

---
117 Deutsch, *Maiden of Ludmir*.
118 *Wladimir Wolynsk*, 98–99.

obliged to pay 500 złoty to the starosta's treasury, and tavern-keepers had to pay nearly 3,860; for the right to have a rabbi, Jewish communities had to make a yearly payment of 1,300 złoty, as well as a number of smaller sums.[119] Beginning in 1794, for the right to engage in the merchant trades Jews had to pay two times more than Christians.

After the city became part of the Russian Empire, the tsarist authorities introduced a number of oppressive measures targeting the Jewish community. During the nineteenth century, a special system existed in Russia whereby Jews had to pay a higher tax, which was discriminatory in terms of nationality. As of 1844, the authorities began to levy a tax for the right to light candles before the Sabbath. In 1884 the Russian government introduced the so-called "box levy," which obliged Jews to pay a tax on meat consumption (levied on each animal or fowl slaughtered according to kosher law) and on the sale of every pound of kosher meat. Additional levies were collected in the form of a tax on inherited property and industries owned by Jews, as well as on income from leases of shops, granaries, and residential homes. Taxes were also levied on the use of Jewish clothing; every year Jews paid out 230,000 rubles to cover this one tax alone. From 1862 onward, Jews were allowed to print Jewish books, but there was a standard payment for each printed page.

In addition, there existed economic and religious bans concerning Jews' places of settlement and life.

In the Russian Empire, the kahals were abolished in 1844, although they continued their activities until 1918.

In the early 1880s, the tsarist authorities designated basic regions in Ukraine where Jews were permitted to reside. The city of Volodymyr-Volynsky ended up as part of the so-called "Pale of Settlement," which encompassed eight out of fifteen gubernias in the Russian Empire. Volyn Gubernia was one of the largest areas of Jewish settlement. The Jewish population was forced to reside in cities. The high concentration of Jews in urban areas stemmed from legislated measures restricting Jews from settling in rural areas. In addition, during the reign of Tsar

---

119 *Evreiskaia Entsiklopediia Brokgauza-Efrona.*

Alexander III, who was particularly intolerant toward the Jews, the so-called "Temporary Regulations" were enacted on 3 May 1882, according to which small towns were transformed into villages. As a result, Jews residing in these populated areas were compelled to move to larger towns that had retained their town/city status. This government measure led to the next influx of Jews to Volodymyr-Volynsky.

In 1883, Jews were forbidden to live in cities in which they were not born. They were permitted to live no closer than fifty versts (53.3 kilometers) from the Polish border.

Jewish habitation in cities also influenced the basic trends of their economic activities, among which commerce and various trades (shoemaking, tailoring, cabinet-making, carpentry, construction) and petty trade (mostly in agricultural and consumer products) remained predominant.

෴ ෴ ෴

In the early part of the nineteenth century, there were thirty-four Jewish merchants in the county of Volodymyr-Volynsky; meanwhile, there was not a single Christian merchant in this area.[120]

This situation remained unchanged until the late nineteenth century, with various types of trades and commerce being the most common occupations of Jews in the city and county. Nearly 600 women sold agricultural products and worked as servants in private service.[121]

According to the reports of the members of an ethnographic and statistical expedition in 1872, whose goal was to study the life of the Jewish population of Volyn Gubernia, "the greater proportion of Jews lives very poorly and in cramped quarters, in constant worry for their daily bread. The extraordinary poverty of the lower strata strikes one at every step. Only solidarity and mutual assistance, which are highly developed among Jews, rescue many from starvation."

---

120 M. Lutai, "Do istoriï ievreis′kykh poselen′ v Ukraïni i na Volyni," in *Mynule i suchasne Volyni*, 266–268.
121 *Evreiskaia Entsiklopediia Brokgauza-Efrona*.

The construction of a Jewish hospital commenced in 1888. This event was reported by Shlomo Goldman in an article that was published in issue no. 245 of the newspaper *Ha-Meilits*.[122] The beginning of construction work was solemnly marked and attended by all distinguished figures in the city. The construction was made possible by donations made by wealthy Jews.

The Jewish population of Volodymyr-Volynsky continued to expand during the nineteenth century. According to the 1861 census, there were 6,122 Jews living in the city[123] (out of a total population of 8,636).

The *Brockhaus and Efron Encyclopedic Dictionary* contains an entry dated 1892 about Volodymyr-Volynsky during this period. It notes the following information: "Altogether the city has … 1 synagogue and 7 Jewish houses of prayer … a total of 8,185 inhabitants. There are 1,083 Orthodox, 613 Roman-Catholics, [and] 6,389 people of the Jewish faith."[124] The phrase "houses of prayer" refers to the small Hasidic synagogues known as *shtibl*.

According to the First All-Russian Census of 1897, the population of Volodymyr-Volynsky numbered 9,883 people, of whom Jews comprised 59.3 percent (5,869 individuals).[125] The entire county was home to 28,934 Jews, or 10.4 percent of the total population. Within fifteen years (by 1912) the population of the city increased by 61 percent to 15,955. Among the city residents, 7,329 (74 percent) were mostly tradesmen, petty traders, servants, minor officials, and members of the intelligentsia (doctors, teachers, and religious figures).

Both the city and the county were multinational, with Jews forming the largest ethnic group.

---

122 *Wladimir Wolynsk*, 154.
123 Tsynkalovs'kyi, *Kniazhyi horod Volodymyr*, 79.
124 *Entsiklopedicheskii slovar' Brokgauza i Efrona*, vol. 12 (St. Petersburg, 1892), 642.
125 *Evreiskoe naselenie Rossii po dannym perepisi 1897 g. i po noveishim istochnikam* (Petrograd, 1917), 12–20.

Table 2: National Composition of the City and County of Volodymyr-Volynsky in 1897[126]

	Ukrainians	Russians	Poles	Jews	Czechs	Germans	Tatars
County	198,504	5,918	22,449	23,006	1,629	15,639	52
City	1,367	1,735	776	5,837	14	100	18

∽ ∽ ∽

Learning being one of the primary values of Judaism, obtaining an education was perceived as a commandment. Jewish communities placed special emphasis on education. Two thousand years ago, Jews were the first to introduce mandatory education for boys (until the late eighteenth century, Jewish girls were taught at home). Learning as a form of transmitting knowledge from generation to generation was one of the factors that allowed the Jews to survive as a people and to carry their faith, culture, and language down the millennia. Education, especially religious studies, was a continuous process and, in addition to special private schools, Learning took place in *heders** (Hebrew, "room") that were attached to synagogues and *shtibls*. Thus, there were practically no illiterate Jews. Clearly, this guaranteed the emergence of individuals capable of achieving success in all spheres throughout history.

An entire network of Jewish educational institutions arose in Ukraine, even before the emergence of Ukrainian confraternity schools (*bratsva*) in the sixteenth century.

Education was one of the trends that developed in the Jewish community of Volodymyr-Volynsky as well. A state school for Jews was established in the city in 1909. In the 1900s the city boasted a yeshiva, a religious institution of higher learning, where students studied the Torah under the tutelage of the finest teachers. By the late nineteenth century there was a *Talmud-Torah** school in Volodymyr-Volynsky.

---

126 V. Kuz´, "Zakhidna Volyn´ v tsyfrakh Vserosiis´koho perepysu naselennia 1897 r.," in *Munule i suchasne*, 262.

THE JEWISH CEMETERY

Jewish communities always paid great attention to honoring the memory of their deceased ancestors. The dead, including religious community leaders, were buried only in cemeteries, and these places were considered sacred. In Volodymyr-Volynsky, archaeologists uncovered Jewish *matsevahs** (gravestones) dating to the fourteenth century.[127] A Jewish cemetery once stood on Drahomanov Street (formerly Horodelska); today it is the site of Gagarin Park. This cemetery was one of the oldest on the European continent. Many distinguished people are buried here: authors of immortal manuscripts, founders of religious schools, community activists, and other eminent figures who made important contributions to the city's development. The cemetery stretched from Drahomanov Street, crossed Vulytsia Nezalezhnosti (Independence Street), and extended to the intersection of Sahaidachny and Kotliarevsky Streets. Standing on the site of the former cemetery today are School No. 2 and its sports field, as well as a sports school (the former Kosmos Cinema), where, every day, schoolchildren walk over graves. Nearby is an apartment building that was reconstructed from the remains of a semi-completed building slated for the district committee of the Communist Party.

Documents from the Volodymyr-Volynsky municipal department of public utilities contain information about the existence of another Jewish cemetery that was once located at 39 Dubnytska Street.[128]

A gravestone is considered a sacred object by Jews. It is thought to be connected with the eternal soul of the departed, and everything that concerns it is sanctified by ritual. Matsevahs are erected one year after the death of the deceased, and they are of considerable historical and cultural value.

---

127 Lukin, "Volodymyr Volynsʹkyi."
128 State Archive of Volyn Oblast (Derzhavnyi Arkhiv Volynsʹkoï Oblasti, DAVO), R-1049, list 1, file 1, fols. 37, 46.

During the Second World War, the Nazis used matsevahs as paving materials for local streets—barbaric desecration of the memory of the deceased, which was intended to debase the descendants of the Jewish dead. Up until a few years ago, on the sidewalk on Vasylivska Street (formerly Soviet Street), one could still see the faded inscriptions on the matsevahs. Only a spiritually blind person could fail to spot the symbolism behind this desecration. After the residents living on that street began insisting that all their troubles and illnesses stemmed from the fact that they were walking on Jewish gravestones, the matsevahs were removed to an unknown site.

The destruction of the Jewish cemetery, launched by the Nazis, was completed during the Soviet era. By that time, there was no one to tend to the graves of the departed: the bodies of practically the entire Jewish community were lying in ditches beneath Piatydni. For that reason, no one was buried there. The last interments took place during the war, although it cannot be omitted that some burials took place after the city was liberated.

"I remember the Jewish cemetery," I. Vozniuk recalls. "During the war, the Germans dumped thousands of gravestones from the Jewish burial ground into a bog behind the railway on the way to Lutsk."

According to one eyewitness, Serhii Dmytrovych Cholokhov, after the war, numerous matsevahs were removed from the cemetery and dumped into huge pits (possibly craters made by aerial bombs) in the vicinity of 51 Sahaidachny Street. Unfortunately, people who disagreed with the government's actions often ended up in the "resorts" (an ironic name for the forced labor camps of the GULAG) of Siberia; thus, no one dared to object. In my opinion it is not reasonable to reproach the city residents for this. The policies and ideology of the Soviet state militated against the burial of Jews in a separate cemetery, and the handful of people who survived the Holocaust and ended up abroad were unable to exert any influence on these events because foreigners were strictly forbidden to travel to the borderland zone, which included the city of Volodymyr-Volynsky.

The Jewish cemetery in Volodymyr-Volynsky in an illustration by the artist Emil Weiss. Postcard dating to the early twentieth century.

The Jewish cemetery. Archival photo.

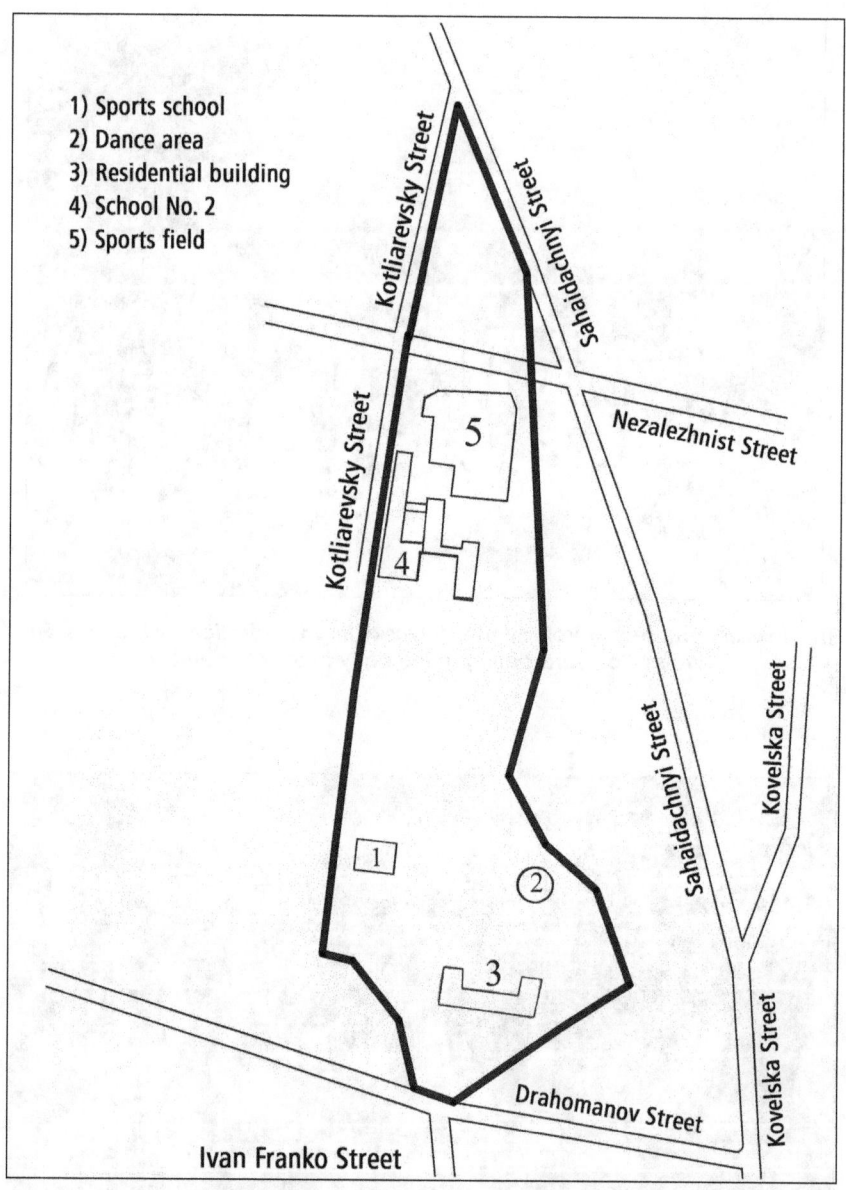

Layout of the cemetery. The bold line marks the limits of the cemetery.

The sidewalk on Vasylkivska Street. Photo: Nathaniel Deutsch.[129]

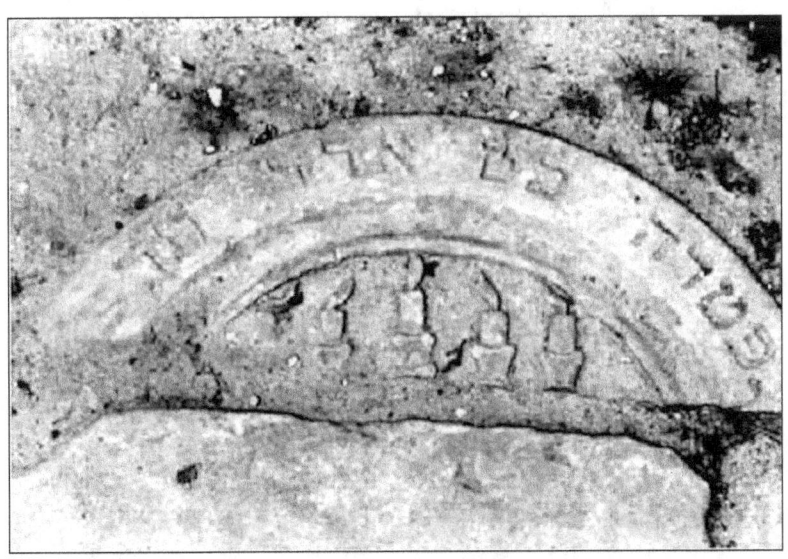

Matsevahs used for paving the sidewalk on Vasylkivska Street. Photo: Nathaniel Deutsch.[130]

---

129 Deutsch, *Maiden of Ludmir*.
130 Ibid.

Matsevahs discovered by the author in the yard of a private residence on Vasylkivska Street. Photo: Volodymyr Muzychenko.

A matsevah discovered by the author in a city courtyard. Photo: Volodymyr Muzychenko.

A grinding disk fashioned out of a matsevah. Photo: Volodymyr Muzychenko.

The Jewish cemetery.[131]

Some of the matsevahs were used to make other gravestones, but those were used for Christian cemeteries. From a resident of the city, Mr. B. M. Kniazevsky purchased a pierced grinding disk fashioned out of a matsevah (see photo) and presented it to the author.

---

131 *Wladimir Wolynsk*, 143.

THE LIFE OF THE COMMUNITY IN THE TWENTIETH CENTURY

On 5 May 1900, there was a great fire in the city. Spreading quickly, it destroyed 250 buildings, including six prayer houses and sixty-eight Torah scrolls; the central synagogue also suffered damage. Most of the burned buildings belonged to Jews, and approximately 2,000 people were left homeless and without an income. Many Jews prayed in the open air. The newspaper *Ha-Meilits*, which was published at the time, issued an appeal for donations to assist victims of the fire. Afterward, a fund and several relief organizations were established in the city to collect alms for them.[132]

The catastrophe spurred the community into founding the Mutual Aid Fund in 1901, which offered Jews no-interest loans. There was already a pharmacy in the city that offered discounts to the poor, where they could obtain medications at half the price.

Jews participated actively in political life. There were various political parties in Volodymyr-Volynsky, where a branch of the Hovevei Zion Party began functioning in the late nineteenth century. A branch of the Bund appeared in 1906, as well as the Zionist Socialist Party.

According to the newspaper *Ha-Meilits*, by 1903 the city had a hospital, pharmacy, and shops. Most Jews were engaged in the grain and horse trades.

The first railway was established in 1906, linking Volodymyr-Volynsky with the city of Kovel in the north.

According to the census of 1910–11, there were 7,060 Jews in Volodymyr-Volynsky, out of a total population of 15,622. At this time, there were nine prayer houses and a synagogue.[133] In the 1910s, besides a Talmud-Torah, a Jewish technical college was established in the city, where there was already a functioning yeshiva.[134]

With the outbreak of the First World War in August 1914, the urban population, including the Jewish community, shrank. One of the

---

132 *Wladimir Wolynsk*, 158.
133 Tsynkalovs'kyi, *Kniazhyi horod Volodymyr*, 80.
134 Lukin, "Volodymyr Volyns'kyi."

causes was an epidemic of cholera brought by refugees and soldiers in 1915. In the summer of that year, Cossack units of the Russian army and members of the local population of Volodymyr-Volynsky carried out an anti-Jewish pogrom,[135] and the central part of the city was burned down by Russian troops.[136]

In the summer of 1915, the playwright S. An-ski visited Volodymyr-Volynsky, where he witnessed firsthand the difficult conditions experienced by the local Jewish community. After lengthy discussions, he succeeded in convincing the municipal leaders of the need to create a special relief fund to aid the members of the Jewish community. He himself donated a thousand rubles for the purchase of crucial necessities. He advised that a delegation be sent to St. Petersburg with a request for state assistance to the community. A decision was passed to dispatch the rabbis of Volodymyr-Volynsky and Ustyluh, who left four days later.

Jewish shops in Volodymyr-Volynsky; Austrian postcard, 1918.

---

135 Rossiiskaia Evreiskaia Entsiklopediia, vol. 4.
136 Tsynkalovs'kyi, Kniazhyi horod Volodymyr, 83.

Volodymyr-Volynsky: a Jew wearing a tallit and holding a prayer book; photo dating to 1916–17.[137]

In 1915–18, the city was under Austrian occupation. The occupying government created a people's militia, whose members included approximately 200 Jews; thus, the city was protected from pogroms in 1918.

After the Austrian army departed, the Polish army entered Volodymyr-Volynsky, whose troops also carried out anti-Jewish pogroms.[138] Jewish residents suffered indiscriminately each time that the city passed from the control of one government to the other, as the arrival of each successive government was marked by a pogrom.

In 1920, the Soviet writer Isaac Babel visited the city. Laconic but eloquent entries in his diary,[139] which served as the basis of his

---

137 http://yivo1000towns.cjh.org.
138 *Rossiiskaia Ievreiskaia Entsiklopediia*, vol. 4, http://rujen.ru.
139 Isaak Babel', *Konarmeiskii dnevnik 1920 goda; Avt. Sb. "Konarmiia"* (Moscow: Pravda, 1990).

short-story collection *Konarmiia* (Red Cavalry), describe the dismal situation in the impoverished, war-maimed city.

After nearly two years of raging battles and successive occupations by Polish and Red Army troops, on 13 September 1920 Volodymyr-Volynsky reverted to Polish control.

The Jewish quarter of Volodymyr-Volynsky in the early twentieth century. Archival photo.

The Jewish quarter of the city. Postcard dating to the twentieth century. From the private collection of R. Mazurok.

A water-pump near the synagogue in Volodymyr-Volynsky, 16 August 1925. Photo: Alter Kacyzne.[140]

After the war, the community once again required assistance, and such help was provided by the American Jewish Joint Distribution Committee (known as the JDC, or "Joint"), which was dedicated to distributing humanitarian aid.

According to the census of 1921, the population of Volodymyr-Volynsky stood at 11,623, of whom 5,917 were Jews (51 percent). The results of the 1937 census reveal that the city had grown to 30,000 residents, of whom 12,000 were Jews.[141] Lukin cites the figure of 11,554 Jews, comprising 40 percent of the city's population.[142]

In the 1920s and 1930s there were approximately twenty synagogues in the city. In the 1920s and early 1930s, the rabbi of Volodymyr-Volynsky was Itskhok-Isaac Grossman; in the 1930s, it was

---

140 http://yivo1000towns.cjh.org.
141 *Wladimir Wolynsk*.
142 Benyamin Lukin, "Volodymyr Volyns'kyi."

Yaacov-Dovid Morgenshtern (b. ?–1941), who perished during the Nazi occupation.

Some of the synagogues that existed in the city during this period belonged to various Hasidic branches: Kotsk, Ruzhin, Turov, Lubavitch, and Shtibl-horn Zlatopol. Predominant among them was the Turov Hasidic sect.

∽ ∽ ∽

The development of Jewish education sped up at the beginning of the twentieth century. This is not surprising, as by this period the Jewish community already had a long tradition of education. Formed over many centuries, it was based on the Jewish people's devout spirituality.

Pupils of a Jewish school during the First World War, 1916–17.[143]

---

143 *Wladimir Wolynsk*, 179.

Teachers of the first Jewish school in Ludmir, period of the First World War. Seated (from right): Asher Heller, Solovobsky (first name unknown), Apenrikh (first name unknown), and Novak (first name unknown). Standing (from right): Yoshua Kleiner, Tsam (first name unknown), Mendel Lybsker, Binar (first name unknown), Abraham Bryk, Idamashek (first name unknown), and Shuster (first name unknown).[144]

Schoolteachers and their pupils are depicted in photographs dating to this period. One of these schools, known as the "First Jewish School of Ludmir," was located on Lietnicha Street (today: Shukhevych Street). Its founder and director was Dr. Novak.

The building of a Talmud-Torah elementary religious school for boys, which functioned until the beginning of the Second World War, has survived to the present day. Below, one can see a brick relief of the Star of David. Like many other photographs, a photograph of this school, depicting Jewish pupils and their teachers, was preserved thanks to the efforts of former residents of Volodymyr-Volynsky, who brought these pictures with them when they immigrated to Palestine and other lands. This school photograph depicts children who were soon murdered in Piatydni along with their parents and teachers. The same fate befell the many children who lived in the Jewish orphanage.

---

144 Ibid., 167.

In May 1917, a network of educational and cultural organizations called Tarbut (Hebrew, "Culture") was established in Poland, Romania, and Lithuania. According to the Treaty of Versailles, Poland was obliged to foster the development of education and culture of its national minorities. Beginning in 1922, the main Tarbut center became Poland, where, thanks to the Zionist movement, this organization played a significant role in Jewish cultural life between the two world wars. Despite financial difficulties and the Polish government's hostile attitude, activists succeeded in expanding Tarbut's cultural and educational activities. All disciplines, with the exception of the state language, were taught in Hebrew; a revival of the Yiddish language also took place. Dedicated Jewish activists and patriots put their hearts and souls into this cause. Religious texts were studied as part of the Jewish culture. The Tarbut network encompassed children's kindergartens, elementary schools, gymnasiums, evening schools, teachers' courses, and agricultural schools, as well as libraries and publishing houses, which issued journals, textbooks, and various teaching materials. *Eretz-Yisrael** and the question of the national revival of the Jewish people in its historic Fatherland were the building blocks of the Tarbut's curriculum. The schools embraced by the Tarbut system envisaged both elementary and professional education.

The building of the Talmud-Torah school on 2 Zelena Street.
Photo: Volodymyr Muzychenko.

The pupils of the Talmud-Torah school and their teachers.[145]

The building housing the Talmud-Torah school, 2 Zelena Street.

---

145 Ibid., 155.

There were also Tarbut schools in Volodymyr-Volynsky. The first one was opened in 1925. The following individuals were members of the organizing committee: head, Mikhael Brekner; vice-head, Yaacov Elin; M. Sheinebaum, Chaim Kaufman, Chaim Klinmints, Avraam Ingber, Pinchas Sheinkestel, Yehoshua Klainer, Chaim Peril, and Zev Apeldman. At the time, the school had only thirty-three pupils, who were divided into three classes. In those days there was a pre-school with Hebrew as the language of instruction. Yaacov Elin writes in his memoirs: "In 1934 nearly 500 pupils studied in institutions of the Tarbut network."[146]

For some time after Volyn came under Polish control, in the territories adjacent to Poland's eastern border the Polish authorities encouraged educational instruction in the Yiddish, Hebrew, and Ukrainian languages in an effort to help the population forget the Russian language as soon as possible. However, once the Polish government consolidated its rule in these territories, it began introducing Polish as a language of instruction by administrative means, disregarding the legal principles that were established by the Versailles peace conference and enshrined in the agreement signed between Poland and the League of Nations. The state was supposed to provide assistance to the educational and religious institutions of its national minorities. In reality, the situation of schools with Hebrew as the language of instruction worsened, especially after "Joint" stopped sending aid. In order to cover the shortfall of funds and to obtain donations, various events were organized. The school obtained assistance from the city only in the last year of its existence.

---

146 Ibid., 182.

The administration of the Tarbut school and its pupils. Seated (from right, middle row): Chaim Kofman, Pinchas Sheinkestel, Shalit (first name unknown); Zeitsik (first name unknown), the school principal; Rozenhak (first name unknown), head of Poland's network of Tarbut schools; Yaacov Elin, Chaim Kleinmints, and Tsytrynel (first name unknown). Standing (from right): Avraam Ingber, unidentified individual, unidentified individual, unidentified individual, B. Goldberg, Mrs. Podlis-Shalit (first name unknown), Leibl Hrushka, Mordekhai Apter, Moshe Boikes, Tsam (first name unknown), and Moshe Sheinbaum.

Teaching subjects in the Hebrew language was no easy task, considering that it was not used in everyday life. However, thanks to the arrival in Ludmir of graduates of the Tarbut seminary in Vilno (Vilnius) and of such experienced educators as Zeitsik and Podlis, under the guidance of Yosef Okon (who later became a leading figure in Israel's education ministry), their enthusiasm and dedication began to bear fruit. The work experience of the Ludmir Tarbut became a model for similar institutions throughout Poland. Adhering to the Zionist ideology, students were taught how to work productively. The trend of expanding Tarbut institutions was noted everywhere, but few of them achieved the same results as in Volodymyr-Volynsky.

According to Yosef Okon, more than 400 boys and girls were educated in Tarbut institutions.[147]

---

147 Ibid., 181–82.

In 1935, another Tarbut school was founded in the city. This two-year agricultural school was a unique and highly successful project. The activists who founded the school committee were Yosef Okon, Bubis (first name unknown), D. Bokser, Dr. Birman (first name unknown), Dr. Babchuk (first name unknown), A. Heller, Libres (first name unknown), Kuproser (first name unknown), and Pinchas Sheinkestel. Agricultural institutions in Poland had to meet the state's high requirements, and a license to operate the school was obtained with great difficulty. The curriculum was confirmed by the Polish Council of Governors, which meant that the pupils of the Tarbut agricultural school enjoyed the same rights as those attending state schools. This was the only Jewish school of its kind in the entire history of Poland. Its director was Yosef Okon, and the teaching faculty included Nachum Sinicki (agriculture, cattle-breeding); Yanka Semitsky (beekeeping); Kohan and Kopits (first names unknown; agriculture); Huberman and Lendsberg (first names unknown; general subjects); and Rachel Liberman and Yosef Segen (horticulture, decorative plants).

The school offered theoretical and practical training for young people who were heading to Palestine to work the land. The professional training curriculum included courses on horticulture, planting of trees and shrubs, cattle-breeding, and beekeeping. General education subjects included arithmetic, chemistry, physics, history, geography, and Polish language. Jewish subjects included Hebrew language, Bible studies, and Jewish culture. All subjects were taught in Hebrew. The school operated a dormitory, and the only pupils who went home at the end of the school day were those who lived in Ludmir. The school had access to 250 *dunams* (1 dunam=1,000 square miles) of fertile land located in the Polish colony of Hanusyn, some four or five kilometers from the city, in the direction of the village of Bilyn. Practical training in agricultural work took place here. One hundred and ninety dunams were given over to fields, approximately fifty became orchards and gardens, and on the remaining ten dunams stood a complex consisting of a dormitory, classrooms, a kitchen, dining room, teachers' accommodations, and various farm buildings: a barn, a stable, a chicken coop, a barn for storing straw, a cellar for conserves, etc. The land belonged to a Polish police officer named Kosowski, who leased it to the school. It was primarily chernozem-type soil, which produced excellent harvests. Applying the principle of crop rotation, the school grew barley, wheat, potatoes, turnips, clover, vetch, and rye. Decorative plants were also grown. Some plots were designated as experimental. Combining studies with practice, the curriculum enabled the school to maintain a balanced budget. Next to the school was a farm that raised silkworms and Angora rabbits (not for their meat, which was not considered kosher, but for their fur). Students were also taught how to card wool and knit.

The student body consisted mostly of the children of merchants and tradesmen who had no prior farming experience, an economic activity that eventually became their lifelong occupation. Pupils from poor families were given tuition reductions or a free education, even though tuition fees were the school's only source of income.

Nine classes—a total of 360 students from all over Poland—graduated from this school. Only a small number of its graduates managed to immigrate to Palestine, and even fewer survived the Holocaust. The school ceased to exist immediately after Volodymyr-Volynsky became part of the Soviet Union in 1939.[148] In the last years of the school's existence, the director was Semitsky, an engineer by training.

During this same period, there were several other schools with Hebrew as the language of instruction: Beit-Yaacov, (The House of Yaacov), school for orthodox girls, and Yavne; a private Jewish gymnasium (with Polish as the language of instruction); and a yeshiva, whose graduates became rabbis in synagogues.

Bringing up young people was immensely important to the Jewish community. Branches of youth-scouting organizations operated in Volodymyr-Volynsky, such as the socialist Zionist organization *Ha-Shomer ha-Tsa'ir* (The Young Guard), branches of which existed in various cities throughout the region, including Lokachi, Ustyluh, and Porytsk. The youth organizations *Ha-Tsofim* (scouts), *Ha-Shomer ha-Leumi* (National Guard), and *Ha-No'ar ha-Tsiyoni* (Young Zionists) were also active in the city.[149]

---

148 Ibid., 181–86.
149 Ibid., 206–14.

The teachers and pupils of the Tarbut agricultural school.[150]

The building housing the Tarbut school, located at 24 Haidamatska Street. Photo: Volodymyr Muzychenko.

---

150 Ibid., 185.

Jews are traditionally guided by a sense of responsibility vis-à-vis each other. In every family, children were taught from a young age to give charity—*tsedakah*—to the poor. Jewish hospitals functioned as institutions aimed at helping elderly people and individuals with physical handicaps and, later, orphans; refuges for such people came into existence as early as the beginning of the seventeenth century, and existed in the largest cities of the time. Eventually such institutions became an indispensable part of Jewish communities everywhere. Since charitable works are an important component of the Jewish system of values, Jewish communities always provide care for those unable to support themselves. Thus, various committees functioned in Volodymyr-Volynsky, providing care to orphans, elderly people, and the poor. One such association was the TOZ* society, which offered a variety of social services. In 1916, the "People's Kitchen" provided food to those in need.

The Jewish scouting organization Ha-Shomer ha-Tsa'ir.[151]

Medical care was provided by doctors, who enjoyed great authority among the members of the community. As of 1934, there were seventeen doctors in Volodymyr-Volynsky (two of them were Ukrainians).[152] Most of the doctors in the city were Jews, and they treated anyone who turned to them for help, regardless of their national origins. Among

---

151 Ibid., 213.
152 Tsynkalovs'kyi, *Kniazhyi horod Volodymyr*, 99.

them were the physicians Katz (first name unknown), Israel Oderman, Babchuk (first name unknown), and Dr. Shekhter (first name unkown), whose building is still used by residents of the city. The most well-known dentists were Bardakh, Kaminsky, Novak, Kipnis (first names unknown), and Henry Kazimirski. On the eve of the Second World War, the city was home to an otolaryngologist, Dr. Bubis (who studied in Belgium with H. Kazimirski), a gynecologist named Dr. Oitser, and the surgeon Dr. Podlipski (first names unknown).

The "People's Kitchen": members of its committee and the people whom it supported—mostly children, 1916.[153]

The members of the TOZ committee responsible for the care of orphans and their charges.[154]

---

153 Ibid., 133.
154 Ibid., 312.

The directors of the home for the elderly and its residents.[155]

Committee in aid of the poor and orphans, 1929. Pictured are Dr. Muzykansky (first name unknown), who lived for some time in Ustyluh, and orphans at a summer camp. The administration of the TOZ branch.[156]

The TOZ organization.[157]

---

155 Ibid., 251.
156 Ibid., 311.
157 Ibid., 601.

Summer camp for children, 1930. The woman in the center is their counselor Rakhel Weingarten.[158]

Children and their camp counselors Pesl Barenkholts and Aizenhart (first name unknown) at a summer camp for orphans, 1937.[159]

---

158 Ibid., 345.
159 http://yivo1000towns.cjh.org.

The directors of the summer camp for orphans, 1922.[160]

The new orphanage premises. Pictured on the photo are the individuals who donated funds for its construction.[161]

---

160 Ibid.
161 *Wladimir Wolynsk*, 597.

A committee called "Culture," whose members represented various religious and political organizations in the city, was established before the First World War. It provided assistance to the poor and oversaw the affairs of the hospital, the Sholem Aleichem Library of Jewish Literature, and the theater.

A drama group associated with the library was founded at the beginning of the twentieth century. Eventually it developed into a full-fledged theater, staging productions based on the works of Jewish playwrights and writers. Prominent among them was the famous Jewish writer Sholem Aleichem. The productions attracted not only local residents but also out-of-town visitors, who came especially to attend the plays. The theater existed until 1941.[162]

Committee of Jewish civic, religious, and political organizations, which supervised hospitals, the library and theater, and provided relief for the poor. First row, seated, from right: Beni Karp, Pesia Boim, Kakhat Kliger, Yaacov Kornfeld, Shoshana Ingebar, and Zosia Zhyntop. Standing, right to left: Yosef Skolar, Yaacov Budenshtein, Bina Kohen, Bluma Kohen, Chana Finkelshtein, Bergman (first name unknown), unidentified individual, Moshe Babioda, and Shmuel Shats.[163]

On photographs dating to this period, Jews resemble ordinary Europeans, which attests to the integration of the Jewish community

---
162 Ibid., 235.
163 Ibid., 193.

into the surrounding community. Thus, alongside the age-old traditions of life lived in a closed space, in isolation from the outside world, arose a new generation that was focused on new and progressive ideas. The community was comprised of both devout Orthodox believers and those with a completely secular world perception—people with materialist views and convictions.

The community played an active role in civic and political life. In May 1923, the Jewish residents of Volodymyr-Volynsky organized self-defense detachments aimed at protecting Jews from pogroms, and in the 1930s they protested decisively against an anti-Semitic boycott resulting from Poland's loss of Russian markets, the economic crisis, and the demarcation of new state borders in Eastern Europe.[164] In Volodymyr-Volynsky operated branches of various Jewish political parties, including the Poalei-Zion Party. The ideology and activities of Zionist organizations were aimed at encouraging Jews to move to Palestine with the ultimate goal of founding the state of Israel. Among the first émigrés were the Jews of Volodymyr-Volynsky.

Members of the branch of the Poalei-Zion Party: Seated from right: Aron-Moshe Libers, Abram Zafram, Itskhak Shmukler, Israel Shraier, Leib Lerer, Abraham Weinboim, and Eliezer Weisgarten. Standing: Aron Khofen, Choren Khigsh, Nisan Aizen, Shtern (first name unknown), Moshe Babioda, and Zakhariia Flot.[165]

---

164 *Encyclopaedia Judaica*.
165 Ibid., 173.

Souvenir photograph taken before the departure to Palestine of Dr. Israelis's family. Center: Dr. Israelis and his wife.[166]

The first group of émigrés from Volodymyr-Volynsky before their departure to Palestine, 1925.[167]

---

166 Ibid., 305.
167 *Wladimir Wolynsk*, 197.

The Volodymyr-Volynsky committee of the Zionist Party.[168]

Zionist organizations helped young, unmarried men and women to emigrate and settle in Eretz Yisrael. They were the first Jews to leave—pioneers in the historic Fatherland—who worked mostly in agriculture and the trades. Young people were trained for this type of work by the international youth organization *Ha Halutz**, which operated a branch in Volodymyr-Volynsky. The first Ha Halutz groups appeared in the early part of the twentieth century, although the idea behind its creation emerged as early as 1881, after a wave of pogroms swept through the Russian Empire. This organization was part of the Zionist workers' movement. Judging by an extant photograph, the membership of the Volodymyr-Volynsky branch was considerable. Ha Halutz's educational program included both theoretical preparation (theory of Zionism, social studies, history, and geography of Eretz Yisrael, and

---

168 Ibid., 196.

Hebrew language courses) and professional training (mostly agricultural practices; in addition to preparing farmers, these courses also trained personnel for various technical specialties; for example, the Tarbut in Volodymyr-Volynsky was a technical school).

The Ha Halutz youth organization.[169]

In 1926, eighty-four percent of the businesses in the city were owned by Jews. A local resident named Yaroslav Kyba reported that on the premises of a former mill owned by a Jew named Shulman he found prewar labels for the semolina that was produced there. The labels depicted three medals that the mill won at trade fairs in Leipzig, attesting to the superior quality of Shulman's product. During the interwar period, trading was mostly done with the city of Lviv. A large part of the community engaged in petty manufacturing and the provision of services. Jews continued to occupy an important place in the cattle, grain, and retail trades.

During the municipal elections of 1929, Jews won half of the seats on the city council: twelve out of twenty-four.

---

169 Ibid., 597.

Members of the city council.[170]

According to data gathered by the Main Statistical Division for the year 1931, the population of Volodymyr-Volynsky stood at 23,500, of whom 11,985 were Jews, comprising fifty-one percent of the total number of residents. At this time, Ukrainians formed twenty-two percent of the population.[171]

By the end of 1934, the city's demographic face changed. In general, despite the incorporation of surrounding villages into Volodymyr-Volynsky, the number of residents did not increase appreciably. According to the municipal magistracy, the city had 27,117 residents, of whom 10,406 were Jews.[172] In comparison with previous years, the Jewish population had shrunk somewhat; nevertheless, their numbers were still considerable. During this period, most of the shops in the city were owned by Jews, who resided in the central part of the city. Tsynkalovsky notes the existence of a private Jewish gymnasium in this period.[173]

In 1935 the building housing the hospital located on Lietnicha Street (Shukhevych Street) was transferred to the community, which then established a Jewish school on its premises.

---

170 Ibid., 311.
171 Tsynkalovs'kyi, *Kniazhyi horod Volodymyr*, 98.
172 Ibid., 99–100.
173 Ibid., 100.

The Hebrew-language newspaper Ha-Khaver (Comrade), 1932.[174]

The Yiddish-language weekly newspaper Unzer lebn (Our Life), 1930.[175]

---

174 *Wladimir Wolynsk*, 593.
175 Ibid., 591.

During this period, the Jewish community published several Yiddish-language periodicals, such as the non-party, democratic newspaper *Unzer lebn* (Our Life) and *Ha-Khaver* (Comrade), the latter published by the student union of the Tarbut school.

While the Jewish educational system was being totally dismantled in the Soviet Union, in Volodymyr-Volynsky, which was still part of Poland, it continued to function until Soviet troops invaded on 17 September 1939 as a result of the terms of the Molotov-Ribbentrop Pact.

On the eve of the Second World War, Jewish culture was highly developed in Volodymyr-Volynsky. Various political parties were active, and there were various Jewish schools in the city, including a Talmud-Torah and the Beit-Yaacov a heder*, which was an elementary school for younger children, where they studied the Holy Writings in the Hebrew language. The local yeshiva had 138 students.[176] There were also a library, a hospital, a people's bank, a Jewish orphanage, a residence for the elderly, and two movie theaters.

At the ORT* trade (technical) school, students were trained to become tailors and seamstresses. The school's founder was Mikhael Brekner; its director was Natan Shtern, whose home was located in the vicinity of today's pedagogical college.

---

176 *The Encyclopedia of Jewish Life Before and During the Holocaust*, ed. Shmuel Spector, 3 vols. (Jerusalem: Yad Vashem; New York: New York University Press, 2001), 3:1454–55.

The ORT trade (technical) school, 1932. Seated from right to left: Natan Shtern, Israel Shraier, Itskhak Bubis, Mikhael Brekner, Kilburd (first name unknown), Sandelshtein (first name unknown), and Finkelshtein (first name unknown). Second row, standing at right: Itskhak Shtern and Shpigel (first name unknown).[177]

The members of the Betar organization.[178]

---

177 *Wladimir Wolynsk*, 191.
178 Ibid., 215.

The members of the Betar organization.[179]

During the first half of the twentieth century, a branch of the *Betar** youth organization was active in Volodymyr-Volynsky. It was founded in 1923 by the leader of the Zionist movement, Vladimir Jabotinsky, in order to train soldiers for Jewish detachments in Eretz Yisrael, as well as to provide protection from pogromists for Jewish communities in the diaspora, including in Poland. In the various branches of this organization, young people were trained to defend the Jewish people and their future state. This legal organization preceded the formation of the future Israeli army. Members of the organization wore brown uniforms, whose color symbolized the soil of Israel; the organization's hymn was "Shir Betar" (written by Jabotinsky), and its slogan was, "In blood and fire Judea fell, in blood and fire Judea will rise again!" The Betar movement exists to the present day.

On the eve of the Second World War, a Jewish sports club called the "Amateurs" was active in the city, as noted by Hanna Krall[180] and Janusz Bardach,[181] as well as the club *Ha-No'ar ha-Tzionis* (Young Socialist).

∽∽∽

---

179 Ibid., 217.
180 Kral', "Pravnuk."
181 Ia. M. Bardakh and Ketlin Glison [Kathleen Gleeson], *Chelovek cheloveku volk: Vyzhevshii v GULAGe* (Moscow: Tekst, Zhurn. "Druzhba narodov," 2002).

After Soviet troops captured Volodymyr-Volynsky, the teaching of religion was banned, but the heads of the Tarbut schools managed to obtain the city council's permission to continue instruction in the Hebrew language on condition that the teaching of Judaism was suspended. However, this agreement lasted for only two months, and in November 1939, after the regional organs of Soviet power from the city of Rivne intervened in this matter, Yiddish became the language of instruction in all Jewish schools, thus putting an end to Hebrew-language instruction. Eventually, Jewish schools were closed. The activities of all Jewish (Zionist) parties were suspended, and in 1940 their leaders were deported to Siberia. Most Jews' hopes for a better life quickly evaporated, even among those who espoused leftist views. The new Soviet government began confiscating—looting, to be more precise—property from more prosperous Jews. Even those Jews who had a positive view of Communist ideology quickly realized what the new Soviet government had brought.

Young people were called up into the Soviet army and sent eastward. Among the draftees were Jews, including Moisei Khalemsky, who survived the war and returned to Volodymyr-Volynsky.

Building owned by Dr. Shekhter. Photo: Volodymyr Muzychenko.

Postcard from 1910 depicting Jewish shops located on the corner of Shevchenko and Kovelska streets, opposite the Roman Catholic church. A sweet shop owned by Yankel Roiter stood right on the corner. From the private collection of R. Mazurok.

The last Passover seder* celebrated at the orphanage, 1939.[182]

---

182 *Wladimir Wolynsk*, 599.

Rabbis Yaacov-David Morgenshtern (left) and L. Goldshtern showing the city sights to a visiting rabbi.[183]

Leib Filarent, the sofer (Torah copyist), and his family.

---

183 Ibid., 202.

The private businesses of petty entrepreneurs ground to a halt, and people tried to endure as well as they could after losing their means of survival: they kept cows and grew vegetables on small private plots.

In his autobiography, Janusz Bardach recalls the following incident: "One day Dr. Bubis paid us a visit. This stout, jovial fellow was an otolaryngologist and a great friend of my parents. He had come to ask for my father's help. The Soviet military command had given him twenty-four hours to give up three of his buildings, having promised to leave him his house and medical office located in one of his buildings, and not bother it ever again. If he objected, he was threatened with confiscation of all his property, his medical license, and even with deportation."

The deportation took place nonetheless. "On 5 December, toward evening, Yurii Savchenko rushed over to our house with the news that that night there would be mass arrests and a deportation. He predicted that my father's name was on the lists."[184]

There are data on the deportation that took place in the summer of 1940, when the new Soviet government brutally deported many active Zionists and wealthy Jews, including well-to-do refugees from western Poland, who were loaded onto cattle trains and sent to the eastern regions of the USSR.[185] This was "internationalism in action": the deportees were classified only by class categories. Subject to the deportation were all those who did "not fit into" the framework of worker-peasant origins and status, and people who were classed as "landowners" and "exploiters." Those who refused to obtain a Soviet passport—in the hope that the city would soon revert to Polish control—were also deported.

During the deportation operation, when people were being rounded up and driven on trucks to the railway station, NKVD (abbreviation for the People's Commissariat for Internal Affairs) troops destroyed the building owned by Dr. Shekhter, smashing everything that they could not steal: expensive furniture, paintings, and a piano. Bardach describes these events: "Even now I cannot recall without horror and indignation

---

184 Bardakh and Glison, *Chelovek cheloveku volk*, 40.
185 *Rossiiskaia Evreiskaia Entsiklopediia*, vol. 4.

[the scene] where three drunken NKVD soldiers who, upon failing to find the owners of the house, shot the night caretaker and the gardener, and then, one after another, raped the gardener's wife and killed her."[186]

Although the first victims in Volodymyr-Volynsky had already been killed in early September 1939, during the Germans' air and artillery bombardment of the city, even greater horror awaited the Jews with the Nazi invasion.

Large choral synagogue photographed between 1921-1924.

---
186 Ibid.

The Tragedy of the Jews of Volodymyr-Volynsky

> *I am freeing mankind from the restraining source of reason ... from filthy and rotten humiliations that the individual experiences as a result of the chimera that bears the name of conscience and morality. With enthralling clarity I oppose Christian doctrine on the unending importance of the individual human soul and personal responsibility to the salvational doctrine on the worthlessness and unimportance of the individual human being.*
> **Adolf Hitler**[1]

> *The result of the war will be ... the destruction of the Jewish race in Europe.*
> **Adolf Hitler**[2]

> *The Germans took away all the Jews-Christians, and in the Catholic Church there remained a single, last Jew, the One on the cross. Then He came down from the cross and said to His Mother: "Mame, kim...," which, translated from the Yiddish, means "Mother, let's go."*
> **A parable that circulated in the ghetto**

---

1   *Niurnbergskii protsess: Sbornik materialov*, 2 vols. (Moscow, 1954), 1:519.
2   Adolf Hitler, *Reden und Proklamationen, 1932–1945*, commentaries by Max Domarus, vol. 2 (Würzburg, 1962–), 1056–58.

The impact of Nazi ideology on the lands of prewar Poland was felt even before the outbreak of the Second World War. Janusz Bardach describes this period in his book:

> In 1936, because of the hostility of my Polish classmates, I had to switch from the state school to a private Jewish gymnasium. As a result of the ubiquitous boycott of Jews in my native city of Volodymyr-Volynsky, many Jewish shops and stalls were closed. In 1937 my father had to prove the compatibility with Polish requirements of the dentistry diploma and license that he had obtained; in 1921, when he began to work in Poland, there had been no need for this. At the present time, the Polish authorities were constantly questioning documents from the Kharkiv [Ukrainian SSR] Dentistry Technical College, even though it was closed after the October Revolution.³

On the eve of the war, a patriotic mood engulfed young Jews, who were encouraged by the Zionist movement, which had a great influence on the youth. First and foremost, their efforts were aimed at the establishment of their own state in Palestine. This is attested by the entries recorded in a notebook by an unknown girl which was found by a city resident named B. M. Kniazevsky (1926–2012) in 1942, after the destruction of the ghetto. During this period it was fashionable to keep notebooks (Polish, *pamiętniki*), in which friends recorded their thoughts and wishes for each other. Here is a couplet from a Polish-language poem:

> "Thunder strikes, the earth groans,
> The Arab torments Israeli children."

When the war broke out, Bardach and a friend went to the draft board office to sign up for the army so that they could defend their people. There they were told: "You are all Jews. Why are you raring to defend Poland? Why don't you go and fight in Palestine?" Bardach writes:

---

3 Bardakh and Glison, *Chelovek cheloveku volk*, 17.

The refusal to register us as volunteers for the Polish army was another sick reminder that Jews were aliens in Poland.

We had to sit around twiddling our thumbs, yet at this time the Nazis were bombing our cities.... Rumors began circulating that the Nazis were advancing on the city from the west and the south. On 10–11 September the local police and civil authorities fled: they feared not only the Nazis but also revenge from the people whom they had persecuted earlier....

...The sudden flight of officials plunged the city into anarchy. Ukrainian nationalists with pro-Nazi inclinations did not waste any time: they directed the local militia to smash Jewish stores and houses. In response to this, my friends and I, together with the members of the "Amateurs," the Jewish sports club, organized a defense group. The fear of being attacked and looted—because one could be beaten and even killed—was so strong that no one felt safe for a second. Contradictory reports about the location of the German army intensified the chaos....

On 12 September 1939, the members of the "fifth column"—ethnic Germans who had Polish citizenship and were secretly collaborating with the Nazis—appeared on Farna Street dressed in German military uniforms. Among them I recognized my former classmates Bubi and Rudy, the Schoen brothers, who were the sons of the local pastor. They did not see me, and I hurried back home.... When we had last spoken two years ago, Bubi said that my family and I had to leave Poland because something bad might happen to the Jews.[4]

The Jews of Volodymyr-Volynsky, along with other refugees, tried to save themselves by crossing over into the territory of the USSR, but they were stopped on the Soviet border, near the city of Ostrih.

---

4   Ibid.

On 19 September 1939, Volodymyr-Volynsky was occupied by Red Army units, in accordance with the terms of the Molotov-Ribbentrop Pact. After the city was annexed to the USSR, the Polish population began to shrink and the Jewish population began to increase. During this period, the population increased to 37,000, of whom 17,000 were Jews.[5] According to other data, during this period the Jewish population of the city rose to 25,000.[6] Nearly 15,000 Jewish refugees,[7] who had been forced to leave Polish territory, arrived in the city. Eyewitnesses recounted that these people were starving and so exhausted that they would faint and fall on the ground. Aware of the Nazis' policy toward the Jewish people and the fate that awaited the Jews of Germany and other Nazi-occupied countries, they tried to escape death: "In October–November Volodymyr-Volynsky was bursting with Jewish refugees, some of whom had returned from the former Soviet border, which was never opened to them; others had snuck in illegally from German-occupied territories after crossing the Buh River.... The refugees could go to synagogues and prayer houses, and local Jews offered them food and shelter. We accepted as many refugees as our house could fit."[8] They hoped to save themselves from Nazi persecution, after having abandoned German-controlled territories, but they ended up in a trap.

৵ ৵ ৵

The Nazis occupied Volodymyr-Volynsky on 23 June 1941. Whereas the residents of cities farther away from the border had time to get their bearings, and the municipal authorities managed to collect themselves and organize the evacuation of at least part of the population, there were no such opportunities for the Jews of Volodymyr-Volynsky: they were trapped.

---

5   *Wladimir Wolynsk.*
6   *Elektronnaia Evreiskaia Entsiklopediia,* http://www.eleven.co.il/article/10945.
7   *Rossiiskaia Evreiskaia Entsiklopediia,* vol. 4.
8   Bardakh and Glison, *Chelovek cheloveku volk,* 37.

After the Nazis occupied Volodymyr-Volynsky, the city became part of the administrative-territorial order of the *Generalkommissariat Wolhynia and Podolia* (Volyn and Podillia), which was part of the *Reichskommissariat Ukraine*. The city was designated as the center of the *Gebietskommissariat*, one of six in the Volyn region. A military command was installed there, and by September the city was under civilian administration. It became the administrative center of Volodymyr-Volynsky District (*Gebiet*), which included the districts of Ustyluh, Verba, and Porytsk. The administrative body of this district was the Gebietskommissariat, and Wilhelm Westerheide was appointed district commissioner.[9] According to M. Bass, a former prisoner of the ghetto, the Gebietskommissariat was located in a building that today houses the Ukrainian Greek-Catholic monastery on 47 Kovelska Street.

With the arrival of Nazi troops, a new order—terrible and brutal—was established in the city. Any violation was punishable by death. For 1,124 long days and nights, a terrible darkness fell upon the city, bringing death and destruction. During its thousand-year history, Volodymyr-Volynsky had never seen such bloody orgies as those that were organized by the Nazis in the twentieth century.[10]

Before the German troops arrived, the central part of the city was heavily bombarded—the very section that was densely inhabited by Jewish families. As a result, approximately 500 people died.[11] The Nazis were advancing rapidly through the USSR, and soon the city ended up in the Germans' deep rear.

After the city was occupied, a police force was formed out of local Poles and Ukrainians. Jews were not accepted into its ranks because they were now the main target of the force's activities. The Jewish population now began to be persecuted.

In the fall of 1941, a German gendarmerie post staffed by several German gendarmes was established in the city, to which several dozen Ukrainian policemen were attached.

---

9   *Kholokost na territorii SSSR: Entsiklopediia*, ed. I. A. Al'tman (Moscow: Nauchno-prosvetitel'skii tsentr "Kholokost," ROSSPEN, 2009).
10 Isaievych and Martyniuk, *Volodymyr-Volyns'kyi*.
11 *Wladimir Wolynsk*.

There were only about a dozen Gestapo in Włodzimierz, but these were sufficient to control twenty thousand Jews, for they had recruited about a hundred Ukrainian policemen, who enthusiastically did most of the Gestapo's dirty work for them. These Ukrainians had had nothing before the war; now they had plenty of food, carried weapons, which they used freely, and were encouraged to beat and torture Jews whenever they felt like it.[12]

Ivan Vozniuk (b. 1923), a resident of Volodymyr-Volynsky, recorded the following in his memoirs:

I had lost money at cards and didn't know how to earn some more. There were some people at the shop where I was supposed to buy eggs with the money I had lost, and among them was a neighbor whom I knew, Anatolii Matusevych. He was in the criminal police, so he urged me to join the police. I don't even remember how he dragged me into it. I had an immature mind....

We were called the *Schutzmannschaft* and they gave us a green uniform to wear and fed us.

Soon I was posted to the prison for a few days. When a German was taking me out, there was a boy standing there with his hands tied with barbed wire, and he asked me to take him away. What could I do?... The thick walls [of the prison] did not get warm even in the summer. There was starvation. After returning home, I fainted and then came to after water was poured over me.

One day our *Hauptwachtmeister* [Chief Constable] came and verified us according to a list. It turned out that half were missing—they had fled to the Ukrainian partisans [i.e., insurgents, who fought against the Germans and the Soviets—M.D.O.]. This was because the evening before he had forced

---

12 Henry Orenstein, *I Shall Live: Surviving against All Odds, 1939–1945* (New York: Beaufort Books, 1987), 72.

them to crouch up and down as punishment for not listening attentively when he was speaking.

They sent us wherever they wanted. We did guard duty at the prison, guarded posts—both ours and the German one. They sent us to Stenzharychi; there was a post there, but no Germans with us. We went there for parties. With me were some older fellows around 30 or 40 years old; they had families. They did not pay us anything in the police. They only fed and clothed us.

While we were in Stenzharychi, the Germans shot the Jews in the ghetto. After we came back from Stenzharychi, I was walking through the ghetto and behind a trunk inside a house I found a sheepskin coat. I put it on and came home wearing it. And I also found a piece of fabric, from which my sister sewed something later, but the material, which had been lying in the damp, fell apart….

Some 20 or 30 of us men were enlisted and dressed in the German SS uniform, and we groomed horses.

One day we were escorting Jews who were being transported to Piatydni. We had them disembark before the bridge, and I don't remember anything else…. The Jews were loaded onto a small vehicle at the prison; I remember that an old granny couldn't climb up, so a German was pushing her in and then he closed the truck….

In the winter I was sent as part of another detachment to Pinsk in Belarus. There, people did not want to transport logs to the match factory; they were not submitting. So we were supposed to force them to submit to the Germans. Some local people were assigned to us, because there was one [fellow] from Kobryn, one from Pinsk. There was no German with us. There were two older authorized representatives; one of them was Ohorodnichuk, a nationalist; he read poems….

But toward morning we were captured by partisans, Ohorodnichuk was killed…. One partisan took my boots and gave me his bast shoes. We dashed to another village a few kilometers away, where some commander spoke to us—he reprimanded us severely.... Then we were called out one by one, and each one was questioned thoroughly: where we were born, who our parents were.... But they let us go, threatening that the next time they would speak to us differently. So we went back to the police again—where else could we go? We went on to Pinsk. There we were brought to a house and given the clothing of Jews who had been shot. The clothing was lying in piles. I took some footwear.

Immediately after the occupation, the fascists launched the destruction of the Jewish population. By 5 July 1941, with the help of anti-Semitic representatives of the local Ukrainian population, 150 Jews[13] had already been captured and killed in the courtyard of the prison located behind the wall. This was probably carried out by the "South" subunit of the police regiment, which was based in the city at the time.[14]

By 31 July, approximately 200 Jews had disappeared. SS men and SA troops were grabbing them on the street, taking them from their homes as though to work, but they never came back. By 29–30 August, between 300 and 400 Jews had disappeared, according to various data. The deadly bacchanal was gaining force, and during the next roundup approximately 800 people disappeared.[15] Above all, young people and healthy individuals were disappearing. The technology of destruction in all the ghettos was identical throughout: the first to be destroyed were young people, who might put up effective resistance, and intellectuals, who could gather them together, plan, and lead organized resistance. On 29 September, 250 people disappeared during a roundup; in October, two groups of 500 and 600 working people and

---

13 *Elektronnaia Evreiskaia Entsiklopediia*, http://www.eleven.co.il/article/10945.
14 *Kholokost na territorii SSSR*.
15 Ia. Tsaruk, "Holhofa nad Luhoiu," *Slovo pravdy*, 10, 12, 18, 20, 24, 26, 27, and 31 July 1991.

a group of 120 educated individuals, members of the intelligentsia, disappeared.[16]

A mass killing of Jews in the city took place on 1 October 1941, which that year coincided with Yom Kippur*, and in late October, 890 Jewish residents of Ustyluh were killed. The shootings were carried out by the Second Company of a police battalion whose headquarters were located in the city of Lutsk since September 1941 (company commander: Police *Hauptmann* Hans Wimer).[17] This battalion was part of the Russia-South Army Group commanded by Friedrich Jeckeln, the "highest-ranking SS and Police leader of Russia-South," and later an SS army general. A postwar investigation determined that Jeckeln's victims numbered approximately 275,000 Soviet civilians. In January 1946, Jeckeln was sentenced to death. He was hanged in Riga on 3 February 1946.[18]

Nearly 1,200 people were killed between 5 July and 29 September 1941. Most of them were killed with axes, iron pikes, and rifle butts, while some people were buried alive. Dozens of people were killed at their workplaces.[19] Moshe Margalit learned about this in his uncle's house, from the conversations of policemen who were attached to the Judenrat, a Jewish self-governing administration established by the Nazis on occupied territories.

Data gathered from various sources differ. This is understandable, as at the time no one was making accurate estimates; it was virtually impossible to do this. But even the lowest possible figures indicate that already at this stage the destruction of the Jews had a mass character.

It is impossible to understand and excuse those Ukrainians and Poles who, in collaborating with the Nazis, helped commit these insane acts, and also those who served in the Jewish police in the ghetto and the members of the Judenrat, who consciously set out on the path of

---

16 *Encyclopedia of Jewish Life before and during the Holocaust*, vol. 3.
17 A. Kruglov, "Schiesst ihn Tot: rol' shtaba Ekel'na i podchinennykh emu podrazdelenii v istreblenii evreev Ukrainy letom i osen'iu 1941 g.," in *Problemy istoriï Holokostu*, vyp. 3 (Dnipropetrovsk: Porohy, 2006), 54.
18 Ibid.
19 *Wladimir Wolynsk.*

collaboration. Looking back on history and being aware of it, or at least in possession of information that is accessible today, one may say that those people ended up in circumstances in which even their insignificant egoism, not to mention overt baseness, led to fatal tragedies for hundreds and thousands of people. Nazi ideology and the Communist regime, the latter of which revealed its true face within a mere two years after the city was occupied, devalued human life to the lowest level and sparked enmity in people, which produced deadly fruits in the form of mutually merciless and savage killings. If Ukrainian-Polish relations were difficult, a fact that was exploited by the Nazis, who egged these two nations against each other, then in relation to the Jews, the Nazis created an atmosphere of hatred among everyone else, and they did everything possible to encourage people to kill. As Reichskommissar of Ukraine Erich Koch declared:

> I need a Pole, upon encountering a Ukrainian, to kill the Ukrainian and the reverse, so that a Ukrainian will kill a Pole. If, meanwhile, they shoot a Jew, this is exactly what I need....
>
> Some people have an extraordinarily naïve idea of Germanization. They think we need the Ukrainians and Poles, whom we have forced to speak German. But we don't need either the Russians or the Ukrainians or the Poles. We need fertile lands.[20]

The Germans' policy lay in the mutual destruction of the nations on Nazi-occupied territories, but the Jews were first on their list.

It is more than likely that the pretext for Ukrainian participation was an announcement that the Nazi occupiers plastered throughout the city, calling on residents to come and see what the "NKVD personnel, the Jews" had done to prison inmates. When it was retreating from the city, the NKVD did not manage to deport the prisoners, and they were killed right in their prison cells. The Nazis very ably exploited this crime that the Soviet government had perpetrated against those whom

---

20 D. N. Medvedev, *Sil'nye dukhom* (Moscow: Izdatel'stvo "Pravda," 1989).

it wanted to destroy—first and foremost in order to sow hatred toward the Jews in the city and enmity among those who, until recently, had lived in peace with one another. This probably explains such incidents as people denouncing their Jewish neighbors: for example, Rabbi Yehuda-Arie Goldenberg and his three sons, who concealed themselves in a hideout near their house, were shot after being denounced by their neighbors.[21]

*The former prison, which was converted to a TB hospital after the war.
Photo: Volodymyr Muzychenko.*

In 2010, archaeological excavations were launched on the premises of the prison, in the course of which were discovered numerous mass graves. The skeletons of hundreds of victims, lying face down in rows, included women, children, and elderly people. There is every reason to suppose that some of them were still alive when they were buried. According to one theory, these were citizens of Soviet-ruled Poland, who were shot by the NKVD; according to another version, bolstered by eyewitness testimonies, they were Jews who had been killed by the

---

21 http://www.sztetl.org.pl/.

Nazis.[22] Only the Nazis laid out corpses in such a pedantic fashion—row by row, group by group, head to head, and all lying face down. Nearly all the corpses were naked. No crucifixes, traditionally worn by Christians, were found in the mass grave; therefore, the victims who had been shot were not Christians.

But no matter who these victims were, their killers were criminals. At the present time the victims' identities have not been definitively established (if this is even possible) because the exhumation process has not been completed.

The exhumed remains were reburied in the local cemetery; funeral liturgies were held according to the Ukrainian Orthodox, Ukrainian Catholic, and Jewish rites. Other mass graves were uncovered during the archaeological excavations. The bodies of these murdered people are still lying in graves on the premises of the former prison, behind the wall. To this day no one has conducted any investigation in these mass graves, nor has any memorial plaque been installed there. One can only hope that this matter will be concluded once all the victims are buried with the proper honors and once we learn the truth of what happened there in 1939–1944, no matter what it takes to do so.

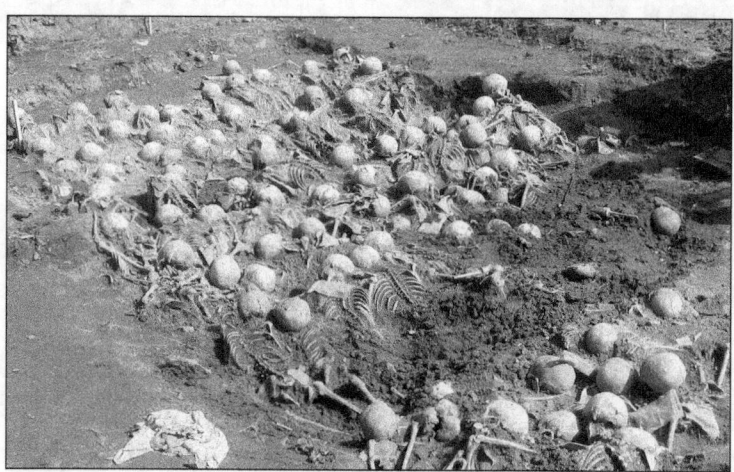

Mass grave uncovered by archaeologists in 2011 on the territory of the former prison. Photo: Volodymyr Muzychenko.

---

22   V. Muzychenko, "To koho zh rozstrilialy na horodyshchi u Volodymyri?" *Volyn'*, 6 October 2011.

On 7 July 1941, the Nazis ordered the creation of a twelve-man Judenrat, which was located in a two-story building on the corner of Kovelska and Lutska streets (opposite today's bus station). At the time, no one was aware of the Germans' plans. Those who were appointed to the Judenrat worked there in order to help their community survive. The first Judenrat was headed by Rabbi Ya. D. Morgenshtern, who died the following month, in late August. He was buried in the cemetery, where Gagarin Park stands today.

The next head of the Judenrat was a lawyer named Veiler or Venger (first name unknown), who was arrested along with the other members of the Judenrat.[23]

In September 1941, Veiler was shot. The next head of the Judenrat was a lawyer named Pass (first name unknown).[24]

On 1 September 1942, Yakob Kohen, a member of the Judenrat, committed suicide together with his wife and thirteen-year-old son after the German occupiers demanded that he assemble 7,000 Jews for transport. Unable to decide who should live and who should die, he refused to accept the responsibility of delivering people to certain death.[25]

Nearly all the members of the Judenrat were shot in September 1942. A new Judenrat was then formed, headed by the only surviving member of the preceding one, a former hairdresser named Leib Kudysh, who, thanks to his organizational skills, arranged small workshops where the residents of the Jewish ghetto worked. He collaborated constantly with the Nazi occupiers and profited from the sufferings of the ghetto prisoners: he speculated in labor certificates and helped confiscate valuables from Jews by taking hostages and demanding large ransoms in gold and silver from their families. Nevertheless, this did not help him avoid the fate of other Jews. During the last "action" (as the Germans called mass executions) he was shot right in the middle of the street. By that time his services were no longer required because

---

23 *Encyclopaedia Judaica*, s.v. vol. 20, 564–565.
24 *Kholokost na territorii SSSR*.
25 Isaiah Trunk, *Judenrat: The Jewish Councils in Eastern Europe under Nazi Occupation* (New York: Macmillan, 1972), 445.

there was no one left. The other members of the Judenrat were Korolevsky (first name unknown), Simcha Bergman, and Sheinkestel (first name unknown), who before the war was a mathematics and physics teacher and a prosperous and respected individual.[26]

From time to time announcements were displayed throughout the city, informing the residents about various demands that were required of them, above all of Jews. One such leaflet, which was circulated in Lutsk, is held at the State Archive of Volyn Oblast.

ОГОЛОШЕННЯ

Виходити ЖИДАМ на вулиці поза дільницю, яка замешкана жидами, найсуворіше заборонено.

ВИНЯТКИ:

Жидам з посвідками, на обороті яких маєтъся відповідна помітка, вільно проходити бічними вулицями в часі від

    6,30 год. — 8,30 год.
    12,00 год. — 14,00 год.
    17,00 год. — 18,30 год.

Проходити головними вулицями (Ковельською, Головною, Північною, Київською) вільно тільки до найближче положеної бічної вулиці.

Провадженим жидівським робітничим колонам вільно проходити вулицями в указаний вище спосіб протягом цілого дня поза годинами загально забороненими. Зупинятися заборонено.

Жиди, які порушать це розпорядження, **БУДУТЬ ПОКАРАНІ СМЕРТЮ.**

Луцьк, дня 13.XII.1941 р.

                              Комісар Округи
                                  ЛІНДНЕР.

Copy of the leaflet courtesy of the Lutsk Congregation for Progressive Judaism.

---

26 Kazimirski, *Witness to Horror*, 65.

TEXT OF LEAFLET:

JEWS are forbidden to be on the street past the district populated by Jews; this is strictly forbidden.

EXCEPTIONS:

Jews with certificates, on the reverse side of which is a relevant notation, may pass freely through side streets in the hours between

6:30–8:30
12:00–14:00
17:00–18:30

Traversing the main streets (Kovelska, Holovna, Pivnichna, Kyivska) is allowed only up to the nearest situated side street.

Escorted Jewish workers' columns are permitted to traverse streets in the above-mentioned manner throughout the entire day; after hours it is strictly forbidden.

It is forbidden to stop.

Jews who violate this order WILL BE PUNISHED BY DEATH.

Lutsk, 13 December 1941   DISTRICT COMMISSAR
                               LINDNER

Municipal Printing House in Lutsk, order no. 759
(Seal)

German occupiers abusing Rabbi Moshe Hagerman, Olkusz, Poland.[27]

---

27 *Wladimir Wolynsk*, 320.

The members of the Judenrat went from Jewish house to Jewish house, handing out all the directives of the occupying government. According to one directive, Jews were ordered to wear a white band with a blue, six-pointed star on their arms.

According to Orenstein's memoirs, "The Judenrat, executing the orders of the Germans, supervised the distribution of food, registered Jewish workers, and delivered them to the places to which they had been assigned. Most members of the Judenrat had no choice but to do the Germans' work for them; either they had served in the Jewish town administration before the war, or they were prominent citizens and appointed by the Germans specifically to this post. Refusing such an appointment would have meant certain death."[28]

The Judenrat also appointed 120 men to the Jewish police. In order to improve their families' situations, some Jewish policemen curried favor by helping the Germans enforce the regulations against their Jewish brothers. In some cases, they beat and abused their fellow Jews entirely on their own initiative.[29] Nevertheless, the same fate awaited them as that which befell their coreligionists. Vladimir Jabotinsky was correct in saying, "Every nation has the right to its own scoundrels." During the mass shootings, some Jewish policemen from the Judenrat placed the corpses into pits and the clothing of those who had been killed. They did not kill anyone because the Germans did not supply Jews with weapons.

All contact between Jews and the Polish and Ukrainian populations was forbidden. In early August 1941, a new order was promulgated: beginning on 15 August, all Jews fourteen years and older were obliged to wear yellow patches. The patches were nine centimeters in diameter; one was worn on the right side of the chest, and the other on the middle of the back.[30]

---

28 Orenstein, *I Shall Live*, 72.
29 Ibid.
30 *Wladimir Wolynsk*.

The residents of Volodymyr-Volynsky recalled how the Germans forced Jews to pave sidewalks with gravestones from the Jewish cemetery.

The German Wehrmacht was in charge of dispatching cargo to the front, and the lading work was carried out by teams of Jewish workers from the city. When they were taken on these jobs by the Wehrmacht, all of them came back home, but if Jewish laborers ended up working for the SA, they might return or disappear without a trace.[31]

In mid-August 1941, food ration cards were introduced for the Jewish population, with the fixed ration of one kilo of bread a week per person; soon this quantity was reduced to 700 grams.

It was difficult to conceal the fact that Jews were being killed, and people began to organize hiding places in the hope of saving their children and themselves. This is how Henry Orenstein describes one roundup in his autobiographical book *I Shall Live*:

> The moment we saw the trucks arrive with the Germans and Ukrainians we got into our *skrytka* [hideout] ... there were sixteen or seventeen people in it: the four of us, the landlord's family, including his daughter and son-in-law, and another tenant and his family. There was barely enough room for us all to squeeze in.... Even standing up, our bodies were pressed tight together. It was pitch-dark.
>
> Soon we heard the sounds of a search party in the house. We could hear them walking about, laughing and cursing, knocking on the walls listening for secret openings, alert for the cry of a baby. They went down to the cellar, up to the attic. They were in the house for only three or four minutes, but it seemed an eternity. My heart was pounding so hard I was sure they could hear it. One sneeze from any of us, and it was all over. Finally we heard the German in charge say, "There's nobody here, let's not waste any more time."

---

31 Tsaruk, "Holhofa nad Luhoiu."

As soon as they left the house, the landlord's son-in-law let out a whoop of joy. He was instantly hushed. We knew that the Germans often left one of their party behind after the rest had gone, hoping to catch Jews as they came out of hiding. This son-in-law was a dangerous fellow; even before the war he had never been quite right in the head, and the anxieties of the occupation had unhinged him still further. He now started complaining that everybody was pushing him, but in fact no one was; it was just too crowded in there. He was standing near one wall, so he put his hands on it and started pushing the others back, to make more room for himself. He was strong, and the rest of us were being squeezed unmercifully. A few people started complaining and apparently he found this amusing, because he suddenly started to laugh very loudly, terrifying us all. His father-in-law kept apologizing for him and pleading with him to be quiet. The ventilation was very poor, and after two or three hours the air became so heavy that some of us were close to fainting. Finally we took a chance and opened the door a crack.

We stood in the skrytka all day, until dark....

Later in the day we learned from the Judenrat that about two thousand Jews had been seized by the Germans ... and taken away to their deaths....

We had had too many eyewitness reports of the mass killings, both from Jews who had not been mortally wounded and who had managed to escape from the execution pits after the Germans had left, and from Gentiles who had watched the killings from a distance.[32]

Today it is difficult to recreate these events in detail. On the one hand, few of their direct participants remain alive; for obvious reasons, those who were the hunters in this "hunt" did not write memoirs.

---

32 Orenstein, *I Shall Live*, 73–75.

On the other hand, once the 1938 pact between the NKVD and the Gestapo was revealed,[33] it became clear why the study of questions pertaining to the Holocaust was neglected in the USSR after the victory over Nazism, and why inscriptions on monuments erected at the sites of mass shootings called Jews "Soviet civilians." The events in Babyn Yar and other places of horror were passed over in silence for decades. Instead, the Soviet government fabricated the so-called "Doctor's Plot" (in which a group of prominent Moscow doctors [predominantly Jews] was accused of conspiring to assassinate Soviet leaders), waged a war against cosmopolitanism [a term applied mostly to Jews—M.D.O.] and readied train cars for deporting Jews to the Soviet Far East.

There is one well-known case of German soldiers refusing to send Jewish workers to be killed. When Jews worked for the Wehrmacht, at the end of the day the SA and the SS would come to take away these unfortunates. Some German soldiers, considering themselves honest warriors, found out about this and refused to hand over the Jews to be killed. Then the representatives of the SA and the SS went to the Gebietskommissar and brought back written confirmation from him, stating that he was permitting them to take back these Jews for their own needs. But the soldiers knew what was meant by the word "needs," and so they hid them in the barracks, where they fed them for several days and then sent them home.[34]

In January 1942, on the order of Gebietskommissar Westerheide, Jews began fencing in large areas in the city's downtown for the creation of a special Jewish neighborhood—a ghetto. It covered a significant area of the central part of Volodymyr-Volynsky (see the "Area plan of the first ghetto" on page 133).

Various sources state that on 27 February 1942 (according to other data, 24 February[35]) 250 Jews were deported as forced laborers to Kyiv oblast, where they perished.[36] In his memoirs, Moshe Margalit recounts

---

33 http://www.nazireich.net/forum/viewtopic.php?t=4139&sid=15d85fff3edfb223bcea255fa625c48b.
34 Tsaruk, "Holhofa nad Luhoiu."
35 *Encyclopaedia Judaica*, s.v. vol. 20, 564, 565.
36 *Mistsia skorboty: Volyns'ka oblast'*, comp. I. Kabanchyk and O. Bohun (Lviv, 2005).

the failed attempt to send the ghetto Jews to Kyiv. Two members of the Jewish police force brought a directive ordering his brother Chaim to appear for the transport to Kyiv. The order threatened that if he did not respond to the summons, one member of his family would be shot. Those on the transport were released on 2 March, after being kept in frigid train cars for two days without food or water. After returning home, Chaim said that they would have died if they had not been released. The cancellation of the departure was explained by problems on the railways in connection with partisan activities. It cannot be excluded that this was not the only such case.

On 13 April 1942, all Jews were forced to move to the ghetto, which was locked from the outside on 1 May. The ghetto was fenced in by barbed wire rising to a height of three meters, but in such a way that the main streets were left open for truck transport, and it was guarded by policemen.[37] Jews from surrounding villages were also rounded up and brought to the ghetto. All the Jewish refugees from Poland, who had hoped to find a haven for their families on Soviet territory but had instead landed in a fatal trap, were also imprisoned in the ghetto. Surrounded on all sides by barbed wire and guards, the ghetto housed approximately 22,000 Jews.[38]

The ghetto, whose basic purpose was to ease the process of the "final solution of the Jewish question," became a place where Jews were concentrated, a transit point prior to their annihilation. In addition, the prisoners in the ghetto were a source of practically unpaid labor for Nazi Germany. Kept in inhumane conditions, their life in the ghetto was horrible: a high concentration of people, crowded conditions, hunger, and cold.

During the Middle Ages, the Jews of Eastern Europe lived in separate areas known as ghettos, which were determined by their culture and religious affinity. These areas were home to synagogues, ritual bathhouses (*mikveh*), schools, and other civic institutions. As a rule, a cemetery, considered a holy place, was located nearby. It was only after the horrors of the Second World War that the word "ghetto" began to

---

37 Tsaruk, "Holhofa nad Luhoiu."
38 *Elektronnaia Evreiskaia Entsiklopediia*, http://www.eleven.co.il/article/10945.

be associated with life in conditions not compatible with perceptions of human dignity; suffering and death. The word "Jew" also began to elicit such associations, and it had become a term of abuse back in the eighteenth century. It was no longer an indication of nationality but became a humiliating death sentence.

In May, the ghetto was divided into two sections. In one part were housed those whose specialist skills were required and who had obtained the proper attestation from the Judenrat. The rest of the ghetto residents were housed in the other section. The Nazis were thus preparing the superfluous population, including children, elderly people, the sick, and the weak, for liquidation.

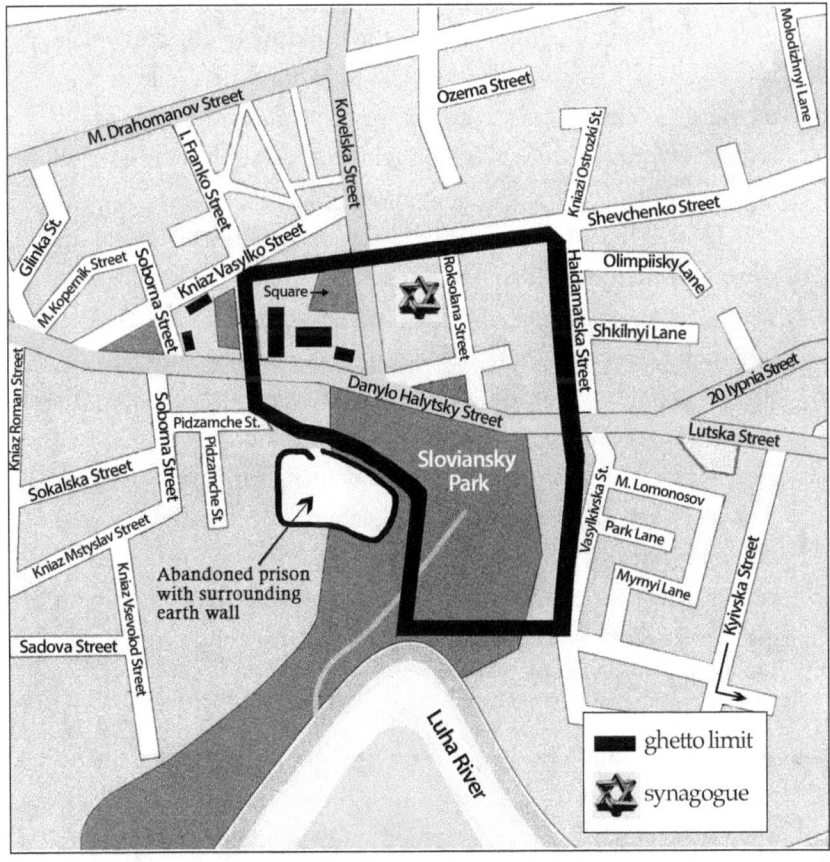

Area plan of the first ghetto drawn by Volodymyr Muzychenko according to the recollections of eyewitnesses. On map: 1=hillfort wall; bold line=boundary of the ghetto; Star of David=synagogue.

Jews were forbidden to leave the ghetto on pain of death. People suffered from the lack of essentials, such as food and medicine. The lack of elementary hygiene and the prevalence of lice and scabies were endemic. Jews were forced to do the heaviest work. According to the memoirs of M. Bass, at the railway station Jews unloaded cases of various types of ammunition, including aerial bombs. Those who could not endure this physical labor were killed by the Germans on the spot. The ghetto Jews performed the arduous work of laying the Berky-Vinnytsia communications cable for the German army.

> In order to lay this zinc, multi-core cable with a thickness of up to ten cm the Jews dug a trench all the way from Ustyluh past Volodymyr-Volynsky. From the building of the geological survey expedition, which was on Ustyluzka Street, all the way to the little chapel on the corner of Soborna and D. Halytsky streets, approximately 300 men laid that cable, having carried it in their arms in the rain and snow.
>
> In the late autumn and during snowfalls the prisoners were forced to stand in the Luh River up to their waists in water, using their feet to clear out the bottom of the trench, in which the cable was to be laid. Those who saw those unfortunate people, wet, cold, and hungry, could not recount this calmly: "An SS officer is walking around in boots polished to a gleam with a whip in his hands, just waiting for someone to try and creep out of the cold water! If anyone so much as slowed down his pace of work, the whip danced wherever it landed; if you crawled out of the trench, it was death on the spot. If you lost consciousness, they would drag you out of the trench, and the bullet was immediate."[39]

The only people who could leave the ghetto were those who had obtained a work card (work certificate). Small groups of laborers were led to work. The work plan was issued by the Judenrat. After the Jews

---

39 Tsaruk, "Holhofa nad Luhoiu."

were locked inside the ghetto, the Germans suspended the supply of already meager bread rations. There was widespread starvation in the ghetto, and only workers were able to obtain food by exchanging items for food when they returned to the ghetto after their workday. Approximately 5,000 Jews from the Volodymyr-Volynsky area were also housed in synagogues and schools.

The situation worsened from day to day. People were becoming exhausted by hunger, depressed by their dire straits and the inhumane treatment that was being meted out to them. They were demoralized and terrified, and their sole desire was to survive or at least to save their children. However, the Nazis' plans did not include allowing a single Jew a chance to survive. As a result of the unsanitary conditions in the densely populated district, people fell sick and died. The dead were buried in the part of the city where the high school (former School No. 4) stands today, and also next to the Tarbut school building; the latter place is mentioned by Moshe Margalit as the place where his uncle was buried.

Not all the city residents could look upon the sufferings of these people with indifference. Some Ukrainians helped the Jews however they could. "People brought whatever they had from the villages. Some gave for nothing, others—for money, gold, valuables, fabric. For example, Semén Prokopovych Borys, from the village of Lobachyn, gave a sack of peas to the ghetto that was on Chekhov Street just like that, saying 'one day we'll settle up.'"[40]

The destruction of the Jews continued between August and December of that year. The Nazis dumped the corpses of their victims in mass graves that were dug in the prison yard.[41]

In his report, *Sonderführer* (Specialist Leader) E. Kumming wrote that during the opening of the new officers' club in Volodymyr-Volynsky on 9 December 1941, "District Commissioner Westerheide criticized the bad organization of the execution [of Jews in the city of Rivne—V.M.]. The layer of soil on top of the executed was only one meter deep, which is why dogs dug out the bodies the following day.

---

40 Ibid.
41 *Elektronnaia Evreiskaia Entsiklopediia*, http://www.eleven.co.il/article/10945.

He also noted that the Jews of Volodymyr-Volynsky (approximately 17,000) would already have been liquidated if not for the difficulties arising from local soil conditions. 'You have no idea of the masses of earth that must be moved from the site.'"[42]

> Abschrift
>
> Sonderführer (B) 9. 12. 41
> E. K u m m i n g
>
> An
> Abt.Frd.Heere Ost (II c)
>
> Während der durch O.K.H. - Gen. St. d. H.O.Qu. IV Abt. Frd. Heere Ost - Chef Nr. 1870/41 g.Kdos. v. 28.10.41 Ziffer 5 befohlenen Reise konnte folgendes festgestellt werden :
>
> 1. Nach Aussagen der zum Oflag XI a in Wladsimieros gehörenden Offiziere und Wehrmachtsbeamten (Oberlt. D u v a l und Oberlt. L ü s s e n h o p - beide Abwehr -, Zahlmeister S c h w a r t i n g , die K.V.I. J a h n s , T e l t h ö r s t e r , B i t t i n s , S i e b e n und B ö t t e l) wird zur Zeit die ganze jüdische Bevölkerung der Ukraine liquidiert. Aus Kiew sollen 42000 - 48000 (die Angaben schwanken) in die Umgebung unter dem Vorwand einer Umsiedelung herausgeführt und nach Abnahme der Kleidungsstücke in einer grossen Mulde erschossen worden sein.
>
> 2. Eine ähnliche Exekution stieg am 29.10. in Rowno. Die Soldaten hatten ab 19.00 Uhr Ausgehverbot. Etwa 17000 Juden (einschl. Frauen, Kindern und Kleinkindern) wurden in der Umgebung erschossen. Vorher mussten sich alle ausziehen, die Frauen durften ihre Schlüpfer anbehalten. Nach Erzählung im Kasino des Oflag XI a werden die für die Exekution bestimmten Leute sternenförmig zu dritt mit dem Gesicht zum Boden übereinander gelegt und mit Maschinenpistolen erledigt. Nach der Exekution werden die Muldenränder gesprengt, sodass die Mulde durch die aufliegenden Erdmassen zugedeckt wird. Der Gebietskommissar von Wladsimieros, W e s t e r h e i d e , bestätigte diese Exekution während einer Unterhaltung (am 9.12., Einweisung des neuen Offzw.-Kasinos in Wlad.) zwischen ihm und Hptm. M e s s m a n n (Gen.d.Art. b.Ob.d.H.), wobei der Unterzeichnete an demselben Tischende sass und dem Gespräch folgen konnte. Gebietskommissar W e s t e r h e i d e kritisierte die Exekution wegen ihrer schlechten Durchführung, da die Erdmassen über den Exekutierten nur 1 m hoch waren und die Hunde am nächsten Tage die Exekutierten herausholten. Er sprach auch davon, dass die Juden von Wlad. (rund 17000) bereits liquidiert worden wären.

Text of E. Kumming's report.[43]

---

42 Raport zonderfiurera E. Kumminga o ego sluzhebnoi poezdke vo Vladimir-Volynskii v 1941 g. po zadaniiu OKKh (otdel Frd. HeereOst II s), http://labas.livejournal.com/tag/ns.

43 Ibid.

Gebietskommissar of Volodymyr-Volynsky Wilhelm Westerheide made frequent visits to the ghetto with his mistress Johanna Eleonore Zelle, née Altvater, for her amusement: she would roam the ghetto killing women and children by shooting them in the mouth. She would call out to children, bring them around the corner of a building, tell them to open their mouths, and close their eyes.[44]

This is mentioned by M. Bass, a former prisoner of the ghetto: "Johanna Zelle, the assistant of the Gebietskommissar, was noted for her singular cruelty and sadism. While roaming the city on horseback with the district commissioner, she amused herself by killing Jewish children right on the street with a pistol." Whenever she appeared at the ghetto with the district commissioner, everyone hid in the buildings, and the streets became totally silent.

Aron Nukhimovych Babukh, who endured the horrors of the ghetto in Volodymyr-Volynsky, attests to the Nazis' brutality: "Gebietskommissar Westerheide always walked around with a whip. I often saw him using it to beat someone for not lining up quickly enough. A few days before the mass shooting Westerheide shot Simcha Bergman, a member of the Judenrat, with his pistol."[45] He also saw Johanna Zelle ripping a baby from its mother's arms and, holding it by the legs, smash its head against the wall of a building.[46] A similar incident was recounted by M. Bass.

In August 1942 the Germans mobilized workers from the ghetto to dig three pits near the village of Piatydni, located six kilometers from Volodymyr-Volynsky, in the direction of the large village of Ustyluh. For the purpose of spreading disinformation in order to preclude mass resistance and to calm down the Jewish population, the Germans explained that the pits were for an underground fuel storehouse that would be located next to the site of a projected aerodrome. People from the village of Mykulychi were also pressed into service.

---

44 V. K. Molchanov, *Vozmezdie dolzhno svershitsia* (Moscow, 1984), 118.
45 Iu. Shul'meister, *Gitlerizm v istorii evreev* (Kyiv: Izd-vo politicheskoi literatury, 1990), 244.
46 *Luts'k: Memorial'na knyha* (New York, 1961), 454–55.

Hanna Bohush, a resident of Piatydni, recounted: "They assembled a whole truckload of people—both old and young—to dig the pits. They didn't say where they were taking them. It was frightening. When we were brought there, all the places where the digging was supposed to take place were already marked out. The people dug, not knowing whether it was for others or perhaps for themselves.... And I dug as well."

Many people suspected the real purpose of these pits, because rumors were already circulating among the Jews that the Germans were killing them en masse. Yet, could a normal person even imagine what had been planned and prepared with German pedantry by the Nazi ideologists, who propounded the rule of the Aryan race over what they termed "sub-human" nations? The mind refused to believe in the reality of what was happening. Everyone should realize that what happened in Volodymyr-Volynsky was not a local crime. This was a global, diabolical plan which, thanks to the indifference and inaction of bystanders, and often their active collaboration, was implemented in most of the countries on the European continent.

In his memoirs, Henry Orenstein writes:

> News of "actions" against Jews were now arriving thick and fast from neighboring towns and cities: Łuck [Ukr., Lutsk], Równo [Rivne], Pińsk. As yet there had been no total exterminations in this area, but thousands of people who had been captured by the Gestapo had been taken to the outskirts of town and killed. An action was clearly imminent in Włodzimierz.
>
> This meant a new and urgent need for hiding places, which had to be very cunningly disguised. Many families were constructing these *skrytkas* (hideouts) in their houses, and people who didn't have one tried desperately to secure a hiding place elsewhere. Our landlord built a double wall with a door that was perfectly matched with the paneling of the wood, and in front of the door he placed a cabinet. In order to get into the skrytka between the two walls, one had to open the door

of the cabinet, swing out a shelf, crawl inside the cabinet, push through its back wall, and open the hidden door leading to the skrytka. Then you closed the cabinet door, got into the skrytka, swung the cabinet shelf into position, and closed the door in the wall....

In some houses, skrytkas were built in a crawl space between the ceiling and the roof, with a cleverly disguised entrance. It was a game of hide-and-seek in which the prize was one's life, and a cleverly constructed skrytka meant the difference between life and death.[47]

The Jewish dentist Henri Kazimirski, who worked in a German clinic where he was passing himself off as a Pole, transmitted information to the ghetto about the anticipated shootings of Jews, but most people did not believe that this was possible, and they accused him of panic mongering.[48]

During the night between 31 August and 1 September 1942, the ghetto was surrounded by policemen, and at dawn the Germans and their accomplices entered the ghetto and began rounding up Jews and herding them onto trucks that were dispatched to the pits in the vicinity of the village of Piatydni. This was the beginning of what the Germans called an "action," during which the Nazis, with the help of the local police, carried out the "final solution of the Jewish question"—the complete destruction of the Jewish population. This action would have been followed by the resolution of other "questions": Ukrainian, Polish, and Roma.

From her hiding place, Ann Kazimirski observed the entire process, which she later described in her book *Witness to Horror*. At first, she heard a terrible lamentation, but after some time the Jews became more passive; they were unarmed and thus unable to do anything. She and her husband Henry saw Gebietskommissar Westerheide walking around the ghetto, making sure that everything was going smoothly.

---

47 Orenstein, *I Shall Live*, 73.
48 Kazimirski, *Witness to Horror*.

A playful smile was on his face, as though he was very amused at what was happening.[49]

One after the other the trucks filled up and departed to Piatydni. The killings lasted fourteen days. Day and night, policemen tore up floors and smashed walls in their search for Jews who had concealed themselves.

In his book *Reminiscences of the Years Spent in Volyn*, E. Rosa writes: "Jews who had hidden themselves in the ghetto buildings were found by the policemen and killed." The author witnessed a policeman shooting a Jew who was hiding on the second floor of a building. As the man, who was still alive, was falling, his trousers caught on the ledge of the building, and he yelled. Then the policeman took out his knife and cold-bloodedly cut off the piece of material that had caught on the ledge, condemning the wounded man to certain death. Nearby, Rosa saw the corpse of a pregnant woman whose face was being gnawed by starving cats.[50]

An SD (*Sicherheitsdienst*, Security Service) team from Rivne, a group of gendarmes from Lutsk headed by Buh, the *Hauptmannschaftsführer* (Lieutenant) of the gendarmerie, the local gendarmerie, Ukrainian police force, and the 103rd Ukrainian Police Battalion based in Matseiv (Matsiiv/Lukiv), Turii district, took part in the action.

After the war, the former policemen N. Zaichuk, I. Leskovsky, S. Maksymuk, and T. Sokhatsky were arrested and tried in March 1948. During the investigation, they testified that several police subunits were merged into the 103rd Punitive Battalion of Matsiiv (Lukiv). As of June 1942, this battalion was used mostly for destroying Jewish ghettos in populated areas of the oblast. Zaichuk recounted that "he walked around Matsiiv, captured Jews who were hiding from the shootings in buildings, cellars, and hiding places, and delivered them to assembly points—to the ghetto." Sokhatsky recalled that, in addition to taking part in the shootings of Jews in the Matsiiv ghetto, "in July–August 1942 he departed for the shootings in the cities of Volodymyr-Volynsky, Horokhiv, Berestechko, Lokachi, [and] Turiisk."

---

49 Ibid., 51.
50 E. Rosa, *Vospominaniia let, prozhitykh na Volyni* (Toronto, 1996), 164–65.

Five Germans and ninety-seven policemen took part in liquidating Jews in the village of Melnytsia, Kovel district, on 3 September 1942.[51]

During the period of the mass executions of Jews (July 1942–August 1943), the chief of gendarmes in the district of Volodymyr-Volynsky was Lieutenant Grigov, who attained the rank of *Gebietsführer* of the gendarmerie by the end of the war. He died in 1978 without ever having been prosecuted; he was only questioned as a witness in the Westerheide case. His superior, Buh, was killed in 1943. Krause, who had led a liquidation action in late 1943, was investigated for some time after the war, but owing to health problems he was never prosecuted.[52]

On the first day of the action, Jews were transported on trucks under police convoy[53] straight to the pits, where they were forced to undress and then shot. Jews were also brought to the prison, where they were forced to undress and then transported naked to Piatydni or killed right there in the prison.

According to various data, between 13,500[54] and 18,000[55] Jews were killed in the period from 1 to 14 September 1942. Isaievych and Martyniuk's book gives the figure of 15,000. During this period the Jewish residents of Ustyluh and other neighboring towns were also liquidated.[56]

Yaroslav Tsaruk, who has studied the Holocaust in the Volodymyr-Volynsky area, spent much time gathering statements from eyewitnesses of those terrible events, which he eventually published in a series of articles entitled "Golgotha on the Luha River." The following excerpt requires no commentary:

> I would like to quote the words of one of many eyewitnesses, which correspond to other statements and describe those terrible times in the greatest detail. Lev Mykolaiovych Savych,

---

51 *Zhivymi ostalis' tol'ko my: Svidetel'stva i dokumenty*, ed. and comp. Boris Zabarko (Kyiv, 1999), 359.
52 *Kholokost na territorii SSSR*.
53 Rosa, *Vospominaniia let, prozhitykh na Volyni*.
54 *Rossiiskaia Evreiskaia Entsiklopediia*.
55 *Wladimir Wolynsk*.
56 Isaievych and Martyniuk, *Volodymyr-Volyns'kyi*.

a resident of our city, a retired miner born in 1926, began by saying that he was personally acquainted with a Jew named Yos, whose family lived on Ustyluzka Street. This was a very intelligent family that was raising two daughters. I walked to school with the younger one. It was on the way. She attended the Jewish school, where the inter-school educational-industrial plant is now located on Telman Street [today: Drahomanov Street—V.M.], and I attended the Ukrainian school. But I don't remember her name.... They sold grain.

I also knew the family of a Jew named Poiva. He had sons and a daughter; I was friends with the sons. One of Poiva's sons sang the Ukrainian song "I will pick flowers/I will toil in my beloved Ukraine." He had a nice voice. This family grew cucumbers, tomatoes, onions, garlic, and all sorts of things, and they also dried pears, apples, plums, and other [fruits], and engaged in trade. Another family with whom I was acquainted lived in the place where the third ten-year school is today [10 Kovelska Street—V.M.], and they sold confectionary goods. Nearly everyone in the city and throughout the villages knew a fourth family, the Golshteins. They lived in the same building where the municipal executive committee is located today [3 Soborna Street—V.M.].

The building owned by the Golshtein family on 3 Soborna Street. Photo: Volodymyr Muzychenko.

The family lived on the third floor, and the store was on the first two. The owner sold plows and harrows, and became so wealthy that you could buy practically all manufactured goods in his store. His younger daughter worked as an interpreter for the Gestapo, which was located in this same building because the store had been liquidated in 1939–1941. The Golshtein family lived in their house until the very end.

On 1 September 1942 the elders of the villages of Lobachyn (Stakh Vorobchuk), Mykulychi Druhi (Oleksandr Boiko), Zarichchia (Matvii Stepasiuk), and Fedorivka and Piatydni (Hnat Melnychuk) received the following order: at every house a digger with a shovel was to be designated and sent to the police. Villages were rotated, as it became known later—for what purpose, no one knew. We were assembled near the gymnasium (the teachers' college today) and a policeman was assigned as the leader—a Ukrainian with a Russian 7.62-mm. rifle.

We went in the direction of Ustyluh. The policeman was in front and we were behind him. The Gestapo representative had warned us in advance through an interpreter: if any of us escaped or failed to carry out our assigned work, the village from where he hailed would be burned down and its residents destroyed.

As we were approaching Piatydni we heard shooting. We guessed that executions were taking place there. One of us ran up to the policeman and asked what this meant. He replied that he knew as much as we did and that if they began shooting at us, he would give an order and we should scatter in all directions, and he had fifteen bullets and would shoot back. But in the meantime, we should behave calmly.

We saw three huge pits. We were led to the last one and placed behind the mound of earth. We sat there almost until evening. It was very hot. Someone brought water and we drank; no one felt like eating. The pits were very large and deep, approximately fifty meters long and fifteen meters wide, with a depth of between three and five meters. On one side of the pit there was a gentle slope. Here on both sides of the edge of the pit were raised areas, where on special small tables cobbled together with ordinary boards stood two fastened German hand machine guns. Next to each of them were a soft chair, a case of Champagne, chocolate, and cases of ammunition. Next to the machine guns were two Germans. One of the Germans who were shooting was called Hans—he was skinny and dark-complexioned—and the other one was Köhle—red-haired, stout, and taller than average. They wore boots with short boot-tops. They were naked to the waist, with only an ammunition belt across their shoulders, pistols, and helmets. Two cars with their tops down stood near the pits.

A truck filled with seated Jews was driving up. In the cabin was a policeman, and two were in the back of the truck. The word *Gewalt!* was written in chalk on the truck that had come from the city. At that moment two men in civilian clothing with armbands ran up with clubs. With the clubs they forced the unfortunates to the ground and ordered them to strip naked quickly; often entire families of Jews were arriving. Everyone got undressed. Footwear was placed in one pile, clothing on another pile, and money on another. Money was dumped in several piles: [German] marks, dollars, [Ukrainian] *karbovantsi*. All the gold was piled separately. Rings, wedding bands, and earrings were removed. Gold teeth were removed from whoever had them. Women and children unbraided their hair. At the end of the day these piles were very large….

On the first and second day I did not see any of my acquaintances, but we were sitting far away and were not allowed to look. On the third day, when the pit was nearly half-filled, Yos's family was brought. When they were going into the pit, the girl with whom I had walked to school fell down.…She tried to get up, but fell again, screaming. A guard had struck her with a whip. She screamed but could not get up. Then her father Yos went back, picked her up, and carried her into the pit. Shots rang out and I began to sob. The policeman struck me in the face and shouted: "Be quiet or else you'll end up there." I was the youngest one there. The older ones began to calm down the policeman and me.

After some time they delivered the Golshtein family, whom nearly everyone knew, as I have said. When the younger daughter, the one who was the interpreter, was entering the pit, the red-haired German grabbed her by the arm and seated her at the table next to him. He said something. The other one was shooting and she was screaming, striking her naked breasts, tearing her hair, wresting herself from the German. He forced her onto his lap and poured Champagne into her mouth. Then, holding her delicate hand in his big one, he led her to the pile of clothing, spread open a kerchief and on it placed women's underwear, some kind of footwear, and clothing, tied it up into a bundle, took a handful of marks, dollars, and valuables, dumped them into the bundle, and escorting the unfortunate woman about a hundred meters, released her with the words *musur, musur* (meaning, "Run away to the village of Mosur, to the woods,"). She began to move, but after walking about a hundred meters, she ran back shouting something. The German grabbed the girl by the arm, bent her over his knee, took off his belt, releasing it from the pistol, and spanked her six times. Then he stood her up and repeated: *musur, musur*. She left. All of us were sitting and looking at her and the German. The Jewish woman walked for about a kilometer, then stopped. Then the German grabbed the policeman's carbine and shot three times in her direction. The explosive bullets flew over her. She ran off. [Rushing ahead, I must note that today this girl lives in the US, and God willing, if she reads these lines, she will write about this event in greater detail—Ya.Ts.]

On the third day a Ukrainian girl, who was working for some Jews and wanted to remain with them forever, was killed.

The SS men took all the money and valuables with them, and the clothing and footwear were taken away on the trucks.

The Jews were being driven into the pit, and they lay down on top of the row of people who had been shot earlier; evenly, head to head; small, medium, tall—all even; face-down on the corpses, with their napes facing the German, who shot each one once, and only in the head. If a shot was bad, there were two people in the pit: one finished off the wounded people with a pistol, and the other straightened out the bodies. The German likes order. They shot one row, the next one after that, and so on. Both of the Germans had binoculars and sometimes they would look around, perhaps for relaxation. Besides the one near us, there were no policemen.

After the Germans departed, we stood on both sides of the pit and, without looking inside, we dumped earth into it. Some [of us] were vomiting, felled by nausea. We dumped [earth] for one hour, two, three; silently, without a word, without a sound."

The following account was related by Petro Semenovych Yakymiuk (b. 1915), from the village of Piatydni:

Jews were transported on vehicles from Ustyluh and Volodymyr-Volynsky. The main massacres took place in three pits. Beforehand, the unfortunates were stripped naked and arrayed in rows in a crouched position. Evenly, head to head, they were killed with one shot. Entire families entered [the pit]. One time, we, pit fillers from the surrounding villages, were lining up above the pit, and a German said through an interpreter that right now he would show us how to kill Jews. And we stood looking while he, the German, fired. I saw this with my own eyes. Then we were ordered to fill up [the pit with earth]. All of a sudden I see that one is alive and is brushing the earth off himself. I stopped and asked my neighbor: "Do I cover someone alive with earth?" The German saw this and, drawing close, fired several times at the person that was moving, and with all his might he slashed me across the shoulders with his whip. I fell. He walked over to the machine gun and called me over. From a pitcher he poured out a shot of liquid, drank it, and through the interpreter he forced me to drink. I drank four shots. Then the German walked up to the pile of clothing, selected some trousers, gave them to me, and sent me home. I did not want to take the trousers of a Jew who had been killed, but the interpreter told me: take them and then you can throw them away. That's what I did.

There were three pits, each three meters deep. After we filled up the first pit, the interpreter said that there were 15,000 Jews here. [Incidentally, this is confirmed by L. M. Savych—Ya. Ts.] There were fewer in the other two pits. The murdered people were laid out in several layers.

There is another witness, Mykola Vasyliovych Moskaliuk (b. 1924), who lived in the village of Mykulychi Druhi (Piatydni): "This happened around the fall. The shootings lasted a week, or perhaps longer. The village elder forced eight of us to plow the field at the manor. This was around one and a half kilometers from the site of the executions. At noon we watered and fed the horses. Not a single horse touched the feed. And the shots went bang, bang."[57]

Tsaruk continues:

There were also Jews fleeing en route to Piatydni. Danylo Antonovych Holiuk, a resident of the village, born in 1913, states that he personally saw Jews rioting on a truck; they threw off the policemen and ran into the Piatydni woods. Jews also escaped from the ghetto alone or with their entire families; it was becoming increasingly difficult to capture them, even though before the shootings they had not been given anything to eat for a month.

---

57 Tsaruk, "Holhofa nad Luhoiu."

Krause, Westerheide's assistant, personally liberated two beautiful girls, about sixteen or seventeen years old. One of them was Henia Hausman, and the other was Sarah, surname unknown. Today both of them live in the US.[58]

After the first round of liquidations in Volodymyr-Volynsky, approximately 4,000 Jews were left—all that was left of the immense Jewish community in the city and the districts of Ustyluh and Verba. Impoverished, oppressed, and starving, they were made to sort out the belongings of their murdered family members and friends in a building at the market: clothing, linens, footwear (according to other data, the belongings of those who had been shot were stored on the premises of the incompletely constructed Jewish gymnasium, which is now School No. 1 on 8 Stepan Bandera Street). They were also ordered to clean up the large ghetto, and were assigned other tasks.

Those who had been in hiding and believed the Germans' promises that they would no longer be bothered also returned to the ghetto, although in fact they had nowhere else to go; they had no other choice. All bans on rendering aid to Jews remained in force; therefore, besides the ghetto, there was no other place for the Jews in the city. Gangs were operating in the forests; whether Ukrainian or Polish, they destroyed the unarmed, persecuted, and defenseless Jews. Many of them were ready to die rather than endure such abasement.

Thus, this group of "illegal Jews," those who did not have permission to work, managed to survive for some time. This was not part of the plans of Germany's Nazi leadership, and two months later another horrific pogrom took place.

On 13 November 1942, during the second "action," which also lasted two weeks, nearly 2,500 Jews were shot. They were assembled in the prison courtyard, where they were herded by men prodding them with their rifle butts, and from there they were driven on trucks to the pits in Piatydni and killed. According to M. Margalit's reminiscences, the hunt for those who were in hiding lasted until the end of the year.

---

58 Ibid.

Captured Jews were brought to Kudysh, the head of the Judenrat, who was supposed to decide whether he needed a person for work, that is, whether to let him or her live. At the time Jews told Ukrainians: "They are going to liquefy us, and you will be doing the mixing."

The second "action" was marked by refined sadism: the executioners would grab infants from their mothers, smash them against trees, and toss the bodies into the pits, and the dead along with the living were covered with earth.[59]

According to the testimony of A. N. Babukh, during the second "action" he hid in some bushes on top of the prison wall and heard screaming and shots coming from there. Jews were being shot by those young fellows from the SA and the SS.[60] During the occupation a resident of the city, Volodymyr Stemkovsky, heard constant gunfire behind the wall. At this time Shloime, the last rabbi of Volodymyr-Volynsky, was shot along with others.[61]

Eliezer (Lazar) Reisfeld of Jerusalem, Israel, recalls:

> I was born in Zamość [Ukrainian: Zamostia] and was a refugee in Volodymyr from 1939. During the Second World War, in the period of Ukraine's occupation by the German fascist invaders, I was a prisoner of the Jewish ghetto in the city of Volodymyr-Volynsky.

Eliezer Reisfeld. Photo courtesy of E. Reisfeld.

---

59 Isaievych and Martyniuk, *Volodymyr-Volyns′kyi*.
60 Tsaruk, "Holhofa nad Luhoiu."
61 Orenstein, *I Shall Live*.

When the second pogrom was taking place in the large Jewish ghetto of Volodymyr-Volynsky, I was in the small Jewish ghetto. Some Ukrainians [policemen—V.M.] took me and my two friends from there and forced us to work, removing the bodies of Jews who had been killed in the second pogrom from the large ghetto and moving them to the prison. We were given stretchers for moving the bodies. A huge pit was dug on the prison premises; it was located approximately a hundred meters from the entrance to the prison. The policemen gave the order to throw into this pit the killed Jews whom my friends and I were bringing on stretchers from the large ghetto. When we first approached this pit, we saw that there were already many dead people there.

As we were approaching the prison, we saw policemen forcibly dragging a little Jewish boy of about seven years old in the direction of the prison. The boy was sobbing. A few minutes later we entered the prison and saw that he was already lying dead near the entrance; he had been killed. This was the very same little boy who had been dragged to the prison and who had been alive and crying just a few minutes earlier. We were ordered to take him and throw him into the large pit along with the other killed people. All those killed people whom we moved to the pit were Jews who were killed during the pogrom in the large ghetto. After this, the two friends with whom I was working were killed in the pogroms.

Horror reigned in the ghetto. Some people fell into despair at their inability to save their children. In an effort to survive at any cost, ghetto prisoners hid wherever they could: in cellars, burrows, niches, underground locations, and attics. After the war, when the building that had stood in the ghetto opposite today's bus station was dismantled, the remains of a young Jew were found in the flue (documents were found on him). There were many cases of mothers accidentally killing their own children: while hiding from the Nazis during the roundups in the ghetto, they would close their child's mouth or cover it with a pillow so as not to draw attention to their whereabouts. One such case occurred in the Volodymyr-Volynsky ghetto and is described by Ya. Tsaruk.[62]

According to various estimates, after the second liquidation the Germans left between 1,500 and 2,000 Jews alive: they were specialists from various professions that were useful to the Nazis, and their families (there were many different, high-caliber Jewish specialists). They were held in a third ghetto that was located in the southwestern part of the city, near the Luh River. The German administration used them as slave labor. This ghetto was smaller and covered an area stretching from Poshtova Street, along Chekhov Street, all the way to the river. This territory did not include the building at 10 S. Bandera Street, which housed the German hospital, or the neighboring building, number 8, mentioned earlier. Eleven Jews were appointed to maintain control over the Jews in the ghetto. Yankel Zavydovych, who was appointed chief, survived. He died in the US after the war.

In the early spring of 1943, the mass graves in Piatydni were dug up by local marauders, although the Germans said that dogs and wolves had done this. Corpses that had been dragged out by dogs were scattered all around the area. The ghetto Jews were ordered a second time to gather the bodies of their family members and cover them with earth. This scene is recorded in a photograph taken by an unidentified German soldier.

Mass graves unearthed in Piatydni, spring 1943.[63]

---

62 Tsaruk, "Holhofa nad Luhoiu."
63 *Wladimir Wolynsk*, 537.

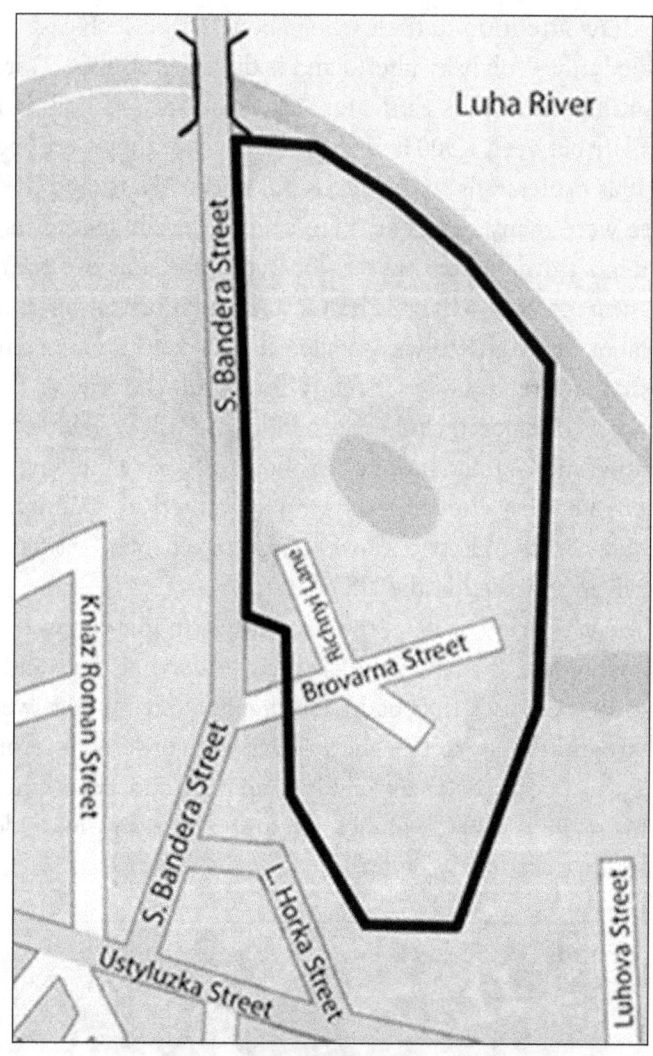

Diagram of the third ghetto sketched by the author according to the reminiscences of M. Bass and B. Kniazevsky. The bold line indicates the boundary of the ghetto.

This was not the end of the bacchanal of death. "In the second half of the summer of 1943 the Germans took 200 Jews to work and shot them all. Some people said that they had been killed in the prison; others, that they had met their end near Piatydni. The remaining Jewish specialists, approximately 500 men, were taken to the SD. These were troops headed by German commanders; all the soldiers were

Vlasovites.[64] They disappeared without a trace, but one thing is clear: none of them survived.[65]

A small number of Jews concealed themselves in hideouts both inside the ghetto and on the "Aryan side." However, few were lucky enough to survive the roundups organized by the Germans and members of the local police force. The latter were particularly successful at this hellish hunt for people because they were very familiar with the area and the people in the city and with outlying neighborhoods well. The unfortunate people who were trying to save themselves and their children were found in their hiding places and transported to Piatydni, where they were shot.

Those times are described by witnesses in an account dated 1991:

There were about twenty of them. Several families hid in the cellar of a building. They spent two days without food and water in the stuffy underground room. The elderly people are suffering and the children do not understand: they need heat, the sun, clean underwear, milk and cereal. They do not grasp fear or death. You cannot persuade them, calm them down. A Jewish woman named Begenmolts made the decision. She stood up in the center of the cellar, bowed to everyone, and said: "Forgive me, but I am going upstairs. I will go with my child. If I perish, then perhaps at least I will save you, but if I keep on sitting here, then they will hear the child's crying out there and that will be death for all of us. I will cover the crawlspace from outside so that they don't find you."

And she left. As soon as the child saw the sun it stopped crying. Just then a policeman came up and hit her, and she is asking him not to hit her and her little daughter, not to kill them. She was shot, as well as her little daughter. One of the

---

64 Soldiers from the Russian Liberation Army (ROA; also known as the Vlasov army), which was subordinated to the Nazi high command during the Second World War. The ROA was organized by former Red Army general Andrei Vlasov, who sought to unite Russians opposed to the Soviet Communist regime—M.D.O.
65 Tsaruk, "Holhofa nad Luhoiu."

people sitting in that cellar at the time survived. Recounting this incident forty-eight years later, he cried without any embarrassment in front of his listeners. We cried too.

The Ohtel couple did not have children for ten years. Then a daughter was born before the beginning of the war, before 1939. In the opinion of the mother and father, grandmother and grandfather, and all the other relatives she was the most beautiful and intelligent little girl in all of Volodymyr-Volynsky and the entire district. In early September 1942 their family was pushed from a truck onto the ground in Piatydni: everyone got undressed, the mother unbraided her long, long hair that reached down to her waist, and unbraided her little daughter's hair. They went into the pit hugging each other: all the Ohtels—the grandfather, father, mother, grandmother, and the little daughter, who was four years old. She doesn't understand anything: why is everyone naked, why is everyone crying, and why are people looking at her? Daddy's on one side and mummy's on the other. They hugged her and are leading her in. And why did they take her dolly away from her? They all lay down in a row on top of the corpses. The child became frightened and tried to get away, but her mother and father next to her squeezed her with their hands and looked at her. They remained lying there...

Leiba Hapin had two daughters. Each of them knew six languages: Yiddish, Ukrainian, Polish, German, French, and English. He lived in a building on (today's) Sholem Aleichem Street. His house was inside the ghetto boundary. When they began hunting down the Jews, loading them on trucks, and driving them away to be shot, Leiba and his family hid underneath his building. But it was damp there and poorly ventilated, and Leiba, who had a lung disease, was forced to crawl out to the surface. The family heard him being questioned about whether he had any gold, where his family was, and whether he knew where there was buried treasure. Then he was led out of the house. His family never saw him again.

There were cases of people who were still alive in the pit. In one case, a man named Yankel, who had survived, crawled out of the pit during the night and made his way naked to someone's house. The owner washed him, clothed him, and fed him. He lived in his cattle shed until the cold weather arrived.

Then one dark, cold night he made his way to the village of Ponychiv to his acquaintance Ivan Pylypovych Semeniuk, who warmed him up and gave him food. But Yankel the Jew was a cultured, modest individual, and he told the owner of the house that he would go to the ghetto because he did not want Mr. Semeniuk's family to perish because of him. He put some bread, butter, fatback, and onions in a bag and left….

Earlier, at the beginning of the summer, several Jewish families secretly built quite a large hideout in the forest near Shystiv. They organized a secret passageway from the ghetto. When the ghetto was surrounded and Jews were being caught and transported for execution, these families hid themselves in the secret passageway. Nearly forty people hid there. Nearby were people in two other hideouts, but they were discovered, taken away, and shot.

At night they left the boundaries of the ghetto and reached the Shystiv hideout, where they had hidden a supply of food, enough for several days. They stayed there from 13 to 25 December 1943. It was very cold, the earth was damp, and the air was heavy.

After ten days the food and water ran out, even though they had doled it out crumb by crumb, drop by drop. There was no room to lie down, and a tall person could not stand fully upright. And when the unfortunates had no more energy and some were fainting from the hunger, cold, and lack of water, they uncovered the crawlspace that was sealed up on the inside with earth one meter thick and tamped down, and slowly began crawling up to the surface. They breathed in fresh air and rubbed their legs, backs, and hands. The fate of the remaining people is not known, but toward morning those sixteen people reached a bunker at Dovha Loza. Several local residents, including Vasyl Mykhailovych Vozniuk, helped dig a bunker, in which plank beds were constructed and a supply of food was stored. They brought a lantern, built a brick structure resembling a stove, and obtained firewood.

People spent entire days in the hideout, and they went outside at night, and only when there was a snowstorm. They massaged their bodies, removed their clothing, and shook out the lice that were literally eating them up. Younger and more able-bodied individuals would walk to the village of Shystiv, but only at night and only when a snowstorm was raging, so as not to leave any footsteps. At night a resident of the village of Shystiv, Teklia Ustymivna Vozniuk, who moved to the village of Zarichchia after the war, would place a pan of cooked groats, a loaf of bread, a piece of fatback, onions, garlic, a pail of potatoes, and a jug of milk into a bush of mountain ash, covering everything with a cloth. Early in the morning she would remove the empty crockery from the bush. If everything was still there, she knew that something had prevented the Jews from coming.

January 1944 passed and then half of February. Soon, in a month, it would be spring: it would be warm, sorrel would start growing, and things would become easier. The important thing was to survive until then. But not everyone was destined to see this blessed time. On 20 February 1944 the bunker was attacked by a gang that shot eleven of the people, three of whom were children aged eight, nine, and fourteen; two were men, the rest were women. Five people survived only because at the time they were gathering brushwood some distance from the bunker. Today David and Rachel Goldfarb live in the city of Hartford (USA). Wolf Karduner, who died in this city recently, was profiled in articles published in the American press as a long-living individual. There is no information on the subsequent fate of Mikhel Boiarsky. Aron Nukhimovych Babukh lived in the Ukrainian city of Novovolynsk.

After their relatives were murdered and the bunker was destroyed, Mikhel Boiarsky and Aron Babukh went to Volodymyr-Volynsky. Aron's sister and husband were hiding in the city, and the two men hoped to locate them and save themselves together with them.

Half-naked, starving, and frightened to death, at first they went to their friends, the Vozniuks, whose house stood near the woods. They spent the night there and put on some clothing, and the housewife, Teklia Ustymivna, gave each of them a piece of bread, two boiled eggs each, and a bottle of milk, and told them: "I bless you in the name of Christ, even though you are not Christians, but may He protect the unfortunate and persecuted." Then she made the sign of the cross over them. Ahead lay the village of Shystiv. In the distance they saw a group of people and so as not to attract attention to themselves, they entered a house on the outermost edge. As it happened, when they opened the door, they saw two Banderites[66] sitting at the table eating. Spotting the Jews, one of them grabbed his carbine, but the other said calmly, "Leave them alone, they're friends of mine!"

They invited the two men to sit down, offered them food, and even gave them advice about how to enter the city to avoid mishap.

There was another acquaintance in the village named Vasyl Pasalsky. Hardly had the Jews entered the yard when his son, who was outside at the time, shouted: "Run, there are Banderites in the house!"

Thus, going from house to house, they passed through Shystiv and Zarichchia, and then entered the city. They went to see some Czechs, who were living in a building situated between the prison and the Dormition Cathedral. They kept them there until nearly evening and gave each of them a shovel, and with the shovels on their shoulders, they went to

---

66 Members of the underground Ukrainian national liberation movement led by Stepan Bandera, which fought against both the Nazis and the Soviets.

today's Telman Street and entered a red-brick house, where Aron's sister lived with some Poles, the Sawickis. They spent several days there, washed, caught up on their sleep in the warm surroundings, but the Sawickis themselves were risking death because they were sheltering Jews, which fact had already become to known to their closest neighbors, and so they told them how to get to Bilyn, where the Armia Krajowa (AK)[67] was stationed, and where they would be safe. That is what they did.

They reached Bilyn, where soldiers dressed in Polish uniforms with epaulettes were stationed with their subunits of the 27th Division of the AK. Also based in Bilyn were non-military Polish units for maintaining public order, which were launching attacks on the nearest Ukrainian villages.

At this time several dozen Jews had assembled in Bilyn. Some of them were related to each other, while others were lone individuals, but all of them were people left alive after the executions and had nowhere to go. This was the final refuge for these persecuted and beaten people, the last chance for their survival.

They quickly found their relatives, but they soon noticed that some Jewish families or individual members were disappearing.

Yankel Reiter, the owner of a house near today's Druzhba [Friendship] Restaurant, who once sold every variety of ice cream (which could be purchased at any time of the day or night, all year round), lived with his family. The Poles threw his daughter, along with his ten-year-old granddaughter, into a well, and his son-in-law, who escaped barefoot through the snow, survived and died in Australia in 1988. The Poles beat Yoina Goldberg, Motel Fuchs, and another Jew from Zamość, as well as Hirsche Babukh for disarming the retreating Polish army in 1939, even though

---

[67] The Armia Krajowa, or Home Army, was the dominant Polish resistance movement in German-occupied Poland—M.D.O..

they were only fifteen or sixteen years old at the time and, of course, could not have taken part in such actions. The Jews Aronvigel and Rombigel were also beaten.

There were some good people among the Poles, who quietly advised the Jews to flee because there was an order to kill them all surreptitiously.

One night the Jewish survivors left Bilyn and headed for the woods. Spring was coming and the forest being what it was, one could always find some sustenance there, and they were also fed secretly by Ukrainian peasants.[68]

Tsaruk continues:

Punitive actions were carried out by Polish gendarmes who were in Bilyn. One of them was Jurek Malinowski (who is buried in the Polish cemetery in Volodymyr-Volynsky). These killers, who were destroying the villages of Pysareva Volia, Zoria, Zabolottia, Stenzharychi, Turivka, Okhnivka, and others, were commanded by Lieutenant "Lech" (real name: Jerzy Krasowski), who lived in Warsaw until 1990. It was under his command that villages were burned down, and hundreds—perhaps thousands—of innocent Ukrainian citizens were beaten, cut to pieces, slashed, and burned; women and old people, infants, and even the unborn. Jews who had miraculously survived demanded that he be prosecuted. Our law enforcement agencies should join this cause because the killing of civilians is considered a crime everywhere.[69]

Volodymyr Antonovych Stemkovsky (b. 1933) witnessed a tragic incident in Volodymyr-Volynsky, which he recounted in his memoirs:

I want to recount the most horrible thing that I saw as a ten-year-old boy in the village of Zarichchia in the district of

---
68 Tsaruk, "Holhofa nad Luhoiu."
69 Ibid.

Volodymyr-Volynsky in 1943. From the village I walked to the school that operated at the Dormition Cathedral at the beginning of the war. I saw the ghetto on today's S. Bandera Street and Jews who were behind barbed wire. The ghetto was guarded by the Polish police. One day I was walking from school along this street, and ahead of me was an old Jew, who was carrying something. When he reached the outskirts of the village, he encountered two men, former Ukrainian policemen, whom people called "Stepan's boys." These two knocked the old man down and began slashing at him with an ax. We children were chased away.... I heard someone shouting: "Why are you tormenting him? Shoot him!" To which those [two men] replied, "It's a shame to waste a bullet!" Later, some Germans drove up and forced someone to bury the body of that old man.... I am thinking: why was this street named in honor of S. Bandera?[70]

While Ukrainians and Poles risked their families' lives by offering assistance to their Jewish friends and to refugees, some city residents betrayed Jews in order to gain possession of the property of those who had been shot, and simply to profit from the sufferings and deaths of Jews. Such incidents were described by Henry Orenstein in his autobiographical book *I Shall Live*, in which he describes his experiences in Ustyluh:

Toward the end of August it became clear that the Uściług "action" would come any day now....
Sam knew a Polish engineer who worked for a company that did construction work for the Germans on both sides of the river Bug [Ukr., Buh]. He made arrangements with the engineer to smuggle us into Hrubieszów [Ukr. Hrubeshiv; i.e., to Polish territory—V.M.]...it was now Monday, August 31.

---

70 V. A. Stemkovs´kyi, "Istoriia i trahediia sela Zarichchia," *Volodymyrs´kyi ekspres*, 28 April 2011.

The Tragedy of the Jews of Volodymyr-Volynsky

That very day, the Germans ordered that all Jews were to gather in the town the next morning, Tuesday, September 1, at nine. Sam gave the Pole half of all the money that we had left, promising him the other half after he had taken us to Hrubieszów. Our lives were in his hands.... He was to meet us at three in the morning. We were to wait for him in a World War I ditch not far from the Bug bridge....

At one o'clock we left the house.... In a few minutes we had reached the ditch.... Now we had only to wait.... Three o'clock passed, and he hadn't come.... At four-thirty a woman and a little girl came into the ditch, and a few minutes later a middle-aged man and his wife joined us. So did a young man, a locksmith. A few more Jews came, all desperate people with nowhere else to go. By five-thirty there were thirteen of us in the ditch.

It was going to be a glorious day.... It was September 1, the day of the action, and we were trapped....

We began to hope. At six o'clock we began a whispered discussion about the best route to take to the river.

It six-thirty when suddenly we a harsh German voice bark: "*Juden—raus!*" [Jews—out!].... They had us....

We were now approaching a narrow street that led to the tile shop where Felek and I had worked. Sam suggested that we shove our money and our watches into the hands of the Ukrainian policeman and run for it.

In a few feverish seconds we took off our watches, wrapped them and the paper money in a handkerchief, pushed it into his hand, and started running....

In about thirty seconds we had reached the back of the tile shop....

At about eight o'clock we heard a voice outside that we recognized. My heart was pounding hard. It was the voice of the Ukrainian supervisor of the shop, who was knocking at the storage room door. "I know you are there," he called out, "Don't worry, I'm your friend." In a quick, whispered consultation, we decided we had to take the risk and let him in. We unlocked the door. He came in and told us the Germans were shooting every Jew they could find. "You'd better stay right here," he said.

The only possession of any value that we had left was Felek's coat, a fine English brown herringbone tweed. "Give him the coat," I whispered. Maybe with such a gift he would not betray us. After hesitating a moment, Felek handed his coat to the Ukrainian, saying, "Here, take it. If we don't make it you'll have something to remember us by." The Ukrainian made a dismissive gesture, but he didn't need much persuasion. He took the coat, saying, "I will be back," and left.

New discussions ensued: "Is he going to betray us?" The Polish engineer had made us skeptical about trusting people, but we had no choice in the matter....

Late in the afternoon a Russian who was a friend of our Ukrainian supervisor came to the door. He was not a local man but a Soviet citizen who had come with the Russians [Soviet troops—M.D.O.] in 1939 and had been unwilling or unable to evacuate with the Russian army. He came into the storage room half drunk. His speech was slurred as he assured us that we had nothing to fear from him; he was a friend. On and on he kept assuring us of his friendly feeling. We couldn't figure out at first what he was getting at, until it occurred to us that he wanted something from us, money or a gift. But we had nothing left. Half of our money had gone to the Pole, the other half and our watches to the Ukrainian policeman. Felek now had no coat, and the coats of the rest of us were old and valueless. We didn't know what to do. Felek had a straight razor that we all used to shave with, but should we offer it to the Russian? Perhaps he would be offended by such an insignificant gift. We were reluctant, too, to give it up because we had talked about using it to cut our wrists. Better that than to be shot by the Germans. Giving the razor away would mean losing the chance to take our own lives.

The Russian kept gabbling away. Finally Felek said, 'We have nothing left but this razor.' He handed it to the Russian, who examined it, opened the blade, tested its sharpness, closed it, put it in his pocket, and staggered out of the room, as we tried to assure him of our sincerity. "Really we have nothing else left. Please believe us."

...Late in the afternoon the Russian returned, even drunker, and rambling still more incoherently. He became abusive, calling us "Nadoedlivye Ievrei" [pesky Jews—M.D.O.]. We knew it was just a matter of time before he betrayed us, and could only hope he was too drunk to do it before nightfall. When he left he was reeling, so drunk he couldn't walk without holding onto something. After he had gone, we counted the minutes....

On our second day there we heard a woman's voice humming a little tune as she approached the Lipińskis' house. We recognized the voice as that of an elderly woman known for her anti-Semitism even before the arrival of the Germans. She was always very solemn; Felek and Sam, who knew her well, had never before heard her laugh or sing. "Can you hear her now?" Sam said. "Happy as a lark. She's delighted to see Jews being killed...."[71]

Matilda Topolia, who survived thanks to Kateryna Lipińska, lived with her two sisters and her mother; they had a shop where they sold manufactured goods. They had many friends and acquaintances, but their best friends were the members of a certain Polish family. When the troubles came, these Jews asked their friends to hide them at least for a short time, probably for free. They agreed. This was right before the destruction of the Jews. When the "action" began, the Jews moved in with their rescuers. But these were different acquaintances, who declared outright that they had no desire to perish because of them, and so it would be better if they drowned themselves. They dragged the

---

71 Orenstein, *I Shall Live*, 89–95.

Jews to the Buh River, and after stripping them of their clothing, threw them off the high riverbank into the water. One of the sisters immediately sank to the bottom, while the other struggled in the waves until a log thrown from above struck her in the head and finished her off. As she was falling, Matilda, the third sister, grabbed onto an osier branch and hung suspended over the water. In the water below her mother was drowning, but she managed to utter a few words of a blessing to her last daughter, who survived.

After the killers left, Matilda reached the riverbank. Naked, she began making her way into a nearby forest, where she spotted a man grazing his cows. Embarrassed and trying to conceal her nakedness, she approached him and asked him to bring her some clothing. The peasant took off his jacket and walked quickly to the village. He returned soon with some clothing. Wearing this dress, the sixteen-year-old girl reached Ustyluh and by morning she had reached the Lipińskis' yard. That is how Matilda Topolia ended up living with Kateryna Petrivna's family. She did not leave the house in the daytime, only at night. No one knew about her. She survived until the arrival of the Soviet army on 20 July 1944. Afterwards she moved to Poland and eventually to the US. Today Matilda Topolia-Hertel lives in New York.[72]

Here is a quote from Janusz Bardach's book:

> I bumped into my classmate, a Pole named Eugeniusz Karkuszewski. Eugeniusz gave me the names and addresses of the city residents who had looted our building after my parents were shot.
>
> One of them was a Ukrainian family that I knew, and I went to see them. They invited me to come in, and for several intense moments my eyes went from my father's rocking chair to a small Roman statuette that my mother had loved, to the hutch with my mother's china, to the painting that had hung in the waiting room of my father's dentistry office. I could not utter a word and left in quiet despair.[73]

---

72 Tsaruk, "Holhofa nad Luhoiu."
73 Bardakh and Glison, *Chelovek cheloveku volk*, 264.

Many of those who tried to save themselves by fleeing to the woods were killed by anti-Semitic peasants and members of the Polish underground organization, Armia Krajowa. The Germans issued five kilograms of salt or a pair of boots for every captured Jew.[74]

At this time the Soviet partisan movement was just beginning to be active in northeastern Volyn. The entire district was controlled by armed groups of Ukrainians and Poles, all of whom had a hostile attitude to Jews who were trying to hide in the forests. Ukrainian nationalists, after the experience gleaned from Soviet rule in the prewar period and incited by Nazi propaganda, actively collaborated with the Nazis until it became clear that Ukraine's independence was not part of Hitler's plans.

Young Jews in the ghetto who had weapons tried unsuccessfully to establish contact with the Polish insurgents, but the Poles refused to accept them in their ranks. In April 1943, a group of young people armed only with pistols escaped from the ghetto, aiming to cross over into the Polissia region [of Ukraine], where Soviet partisans were operating. But on the outskirts they were attacked and killed by local bandits.[75] Nevertheless, Jews from Volodymyr-Volynsky joined partisan detachments and took part in the armed resistance. Among them were Moshe Krigser and his sister Eva, Roza Delburd, Karl-Yakutiel Goldenberg, and others. Not everyone who was armed was destined to survive. A partisan member named Dora Zilbert was killed in a battle near Volodymyr-Volynsky. She helped blow up four enemy trains at the railway station and took part in numerous clashes with German subunits and patrols.[76]

The Jews were hopelessly trapped, and once again they were forced to return to the ghetto from their hiding places. Even those who had taken the risk of leaving their families behind in the ghetto to survive without their assistance, those who had already lost loved ones, and those who had managed to escape to the woods, where they tried to

---

74 *Slovo invalida voiny*, nos. 11–12 (1995): 99.
75 *Wladimir Wolynsk*.
76 *Katastrofa i Opir ukraïns′kho ievreistva (1941–1944): Narysy z istoriï Holokostu i Oporu v Ukraïni* (Kyiv, 1999).

offer armed resistance, were frequently killed in clashes with Ukrainians and Poles. For example, in the fall of 1943, a Soviet Jewish partisan detachment led by Boris Bazykin was ambushed near Volodymyr-Volynsky by large formations of the OUN–UPA, and the majority of his fighters were killed in the ill-matched battle.[77] In addition to organized Ukrainian and Polish insurgents and freedom fighters, the forests were full of marauders and ordinary bandits during this period. Subsuming them all into one category does not make sense and is simply inaccurate, especially as applied to the activities of the Organization of Ukrainian Nationalists and the Ukrainian Insurgent Army, whose ranks included those who had fled the German-controlled police force.

The ghetto was finally liquidated on 13–14 December 1943. The Germans destroyed the approximately 1,500 Jews who remained in the labor camp. This time the Nazis brought them to a grove near the village of Falemychi (today, the site of the local sugar factory treatment plant) and shot them there.[78] In order to conceal the traces of these executions, the Germans stacked the bodies, poured gasoline over them, and burned them,[79] and the ashes were dispersed throughout the fields. The burning of the corpses was done by soldiers from General Vlasov's army, one unit of which was stationed in the city.[80] Moshe Margalit recalls a story recounted by some city residents, who were ordered by the Germans to dig out a truck that had become stuck in the snow after leaving the prison: underneath a tarpaulin at the back of the truck were naked people being driven away to be shot. The truck was headed in the direction of Falemychi.

The "action" was carried out by *Sonderkommando* 4B (commander: SS Sturmbannführer V. Krause), which had been stationed in the city since October 1943, as well as the German gendarmerie and the Ukrainian police.[81]

---

77 Ibid., 329.
78 *Wladimir Wolynsk*.
79 Isaievych and Martyniuk, *Volodymyr-Volyns'kyi*.
80 Kazimirski, *Witness to Horror*, 92.
81 *Kholokost na territorii SSSR*.

In an article entitled "A Black Column of Smoke" Yaroslav Tsaruk writes:

> It must be stated that Jews were shot not just near Piatydni (as is well known, there were two actions, each lasting up to fifteen days), but in other places as well. Not all the Jews were destroyed in one fell swoop: some (tailors, shoemakers, and other specialists) were kept alive to provide services for the German army, while others were used for introducing order in the abandoned, neglected ghetto. A certain number had scattered and [were] in hiding, but since they had nowhere to go, they returned to the small ghetto because the Germans had announced that they would no longer be killing anyone. By mid-January 1943 nearly 2,000 people had gathered there. On the orders of the city commandant, practically every day teams consisting of between twenty and thirty men were selected for various types of work, mostly to clear snow from the railway tracks and highways.
>
> These people rarely returned to the ghetto after their workday.
>
> During the war years, a small forest called Birok was located near the site of today's sugar factory treatment plant. That is where they shot Jews.
>
> In the daytime they clear snow from the railway, and toward evening they are led to some small woods that begin right behind the tracks, and destroy them. The bodies of those who were shot were stacked, doused with benzene or solar oil, and burned. Thick, black smoke wafted upwards in the cold January dusk, and with it the souls of the people flowed to their eternal rest....
>
> This scene was repeated in a day or two. At first, you can hear quiet, distant shots, and after some time a black, fatal column of fire rises once again from the earth, as though it is propping up the sky and not letting it fall onto this terrible, bloody soil. This lasted until late spring, when the ashes and

skulls that had not disintegrated were gathered into huge pits and covered with earth.

Today the small woods that witnessed the final moments of the lives of many people are gone; there is also no resting place for their young souls. May our memory forever resound in our souls and not allow those who were burned innocently there to be forgotten.[82]

The executions of the residents of the last remaining ghetto (called the "tradesmen's ghetto") was carried out by Sonderkommando 4B, under the command of Krause and his deputy Wilhelm Braune, together with the gendarmerie. On the orders of the commander of the security police and the SD of Lutsk District, Krause planned the "action" and, together with his deputy, were responsible for arresting Jews, conveying them to the place of execution, and supervising the killing process.[83]

"In the spring of 1943 I saw mass graves, barely covered with earth, in the vicinity of Volodymyr-Volynsky. The indictment speaks of 9,000 people who were shot. However, at the time we had information about 14,500 killed people, including quite a few children.... I will never forget this terrible grave until the end of my days." These words were uttered in Dortmund, during the war crimes trial of the former Gebietskommissar of Volodymyr-Volynsky, the 73-year-old Wilhelm Westerheide, and his mistress Johanna Zelle, who were accused of killing thousands of Soviet citizens.[84]

"This was their second trial, because during the first one—in 1978–1979 in Bielefeld—these SS executioners were exonerated by the 'guardians' of the law, in particular because the chief witness, 67-year-old Herbert B., a former junior officer of the Wehrmacht in 1942–1943, from the city of Hattingen, was unable to recall 'the color

---

82 Ya. Tsaruk, "Chornyi stovp dymu," *Slovo pravdy*, 23 April 1994.
83 Aleksandr Gogun and Aleksandr Vovk, "Evrei v bor'be za nezavisimuiu Ukrainu," http://lib.oun-upa.org.ua/gogun/pub07.html, 196.
84 Isaievych and Martyniuk, *Volodymyr-Volyns'kyi*, 41–42.

of Westerheide's uniform' during the mass liquidation that he carried out in the spring of 1943."[85]

Only a small number of people from the labor camp managed to hide and then escape. They were able to reach an area where Polish insurgents were based; they were operating north of Volodymyr-Volynsky, in the Polish colonies of Bilyn and Vorchyn. Some of the men who had escaped were accepted into their ranks. The others, along with their wives and children, remained in Vorchyn.

There was another attempt to mount armed resistance during the last "action." A group of armed but inexperienced young Jews occupied a fortified position in a bunker near the brickworks, but it was discovered by the Germans. An unequal battle ensued, in which thirteen people were killed.[86]

One often hears the question, "Why did the Jews allow themselves to be killed?" as well as various answers to this question. The truth is that the technology of destruction was planned to the very last detail by its perpetrators. The Nazis did everything to prevent resistance, especially organized forms.

This is attested by Otto Ohlendorf, the head of one of the *Einsatzgruppen SS*: "They were brought on trucks...as many as could be executed at once. Thus, all this was carried out as quickly as possible, that is, the interval of time between the actual execution and the realization that this would take place was very small."[87] When the unarmed people, surrounded by cutthroats, realized what was happening to them, they could not do anything. One can only imagine what they must have experienced in the final minutes of their lives, clutching their children in their arms as they stood next to their family members, whom they were powerless to protect. It is also worth noting that the Einsatzgruppen SS were specially trained operational groups of professional killers, who moved from place to place killing civilians, above all Jews, in a planned manner. Einsatzgruppe C, under the command of

---

85 *Elektronnaia Evreiskaia Entsiklopediia*, http://www.eleven.co.il/article/14439.
86 *Rossiiskaia Evreiskaia Entsiklopediia*, vol. 4, s.v. 266-267, http://rujen.ru.
87 *Niurnbergskii protsess*, 1: 674-76, 679.

Brigadeführer (Brigade Leader) Otto Rasch, operated on the territory of Ukraine, with the exception of its southern part.

Even physically weakened by cold, disease, and exhausting labor, the oppressed, unarmed, and uninformed people, who had been reduced to an animal-like existence, still tried to mount resistance as circumstances permitted.

∽ ∽ ∽

Volodymyr-Volynsky was liberated from the Nazis on 20 July 1944. To the credit of the courageous liberators, a 224-gun salute firing twenty times took place on that day in Moscow, the capital of the Soviet Union. Military formations that had distinguished themselves in the battles for the Ukrainian city were awarded the title "The Volodymyr-Volynsky Fighters," and many soldiers were awarded orders and medals.

The scale of Nazi crimes is attested by figures: whereas before the war, Volodymyr-Volynsky had a population of 37,000 people, only 7,000 were alive as of August 1944.[88] After leaving their hideouts or returning from the forests, those who had survived miraculously saw a city that was nearly deserted.

In his autobiographical novel *A Chronicle of One Life*, Roman Tsyvin, a resident of Volodymyr-Volynsky, describes what he saw after the city was liberated: "The Jewish cemetery. At first, I didn't even grasp what it was. Brown, stone stumps stood crookedly. Some had toppled over. Inscriptions in Old Hebrew. A terrible sight. I understand that no one will come here."[89]

Moshe Margalit, who lives in Israel today, recalls: "After the city was liberated in July 1944, when I left the hideout where I had spent many months, I saw a depopulated city. Most of the buildings were empty, since their inhabitants were buried in horrible ditches on the outskirts of Piatydni."

---

88   Isaievych and Martyniuk, *Volodymyr Volyns'kyi*, 41–42.
89   R. Tsivin, *Khronika odnoi zhizni*. The chapter "1946–1947 gg. Vladimir-Volynskii" is located online here: http://www.proza.ru/2006/06/29-237.

It is difficult to imagine what the people returning to the city after its liberation must have experienced when they learned the fate of their loved ones. Here is a fragment from Bardach's book:

> In May forty-four my unit and I ended up in Volodymyr-Volynsky. We entered on the third day after its liberation. I was told that during the occupation, doctors and their families were not taken to the ghetto, which is why our family remained for some time in our apartment. Later, when the Gestapo began to loot, rape, and kill, it became dangerous for our little girls Taubtzia, Rachel, and Fruma to remain in the house. They went to the ghetto voluntarily.
>
> I located Chaim Tsuker, my father's dentist, who told me that in July 1942 the Gestapo led all the members of our family into the courtyard. When he heard them coming, Chaim jumped out of the window and hid in an outbuilding. He saw my father suddenly fall to the ground. My father always carried potassium cyanide, declaring that the Nazis would never take him alive. Except for the little girls who were in the ghetto, everyone else was led into the woods and shot.[90]

With a single blow, the Nazi occupation destroyed the Jewish community of Volodymyr-Volynsky, which had lived in the city for 800 years.

---

90 Bardakh and Glison, *Chelovek cheloveku volk*, 263.

FROM THE KILLING FIELDS

The Reminiscences of Zippora (Feiga) Weinstock-Zaar (Tel Aviv, Israel)[91]

Zippora Weinstock-Zaar. Photo courtesy of Zippora Weinstock-Zaar.

There were six people in our family. My mother's name was Yocheved. My father, Yosyf Weinstock, owned a grocery store on Kovelska Street. As soon as the Germans entered our city, they looted all our property. Nevertheless, we managed to give some of it away to non-Jews, reckoning that afterwards they would return our property. But in a very short period of time all the Jews were forced to move to the ghetto. Among those who went to their death in the ghetto were my parents and my older brother Efraim. I was thirteen years old then. Only three members of our family managed to hide. And we continued to live, doing various jobs in order to feed ourselves, but without any hope whatsoever. Each of us knew what awaited us. The Nazis surrounded the whole ghetto with the German gendarmerie and helpers from among the local population. It is impossible to describe this picture. My sister Mania, younger brother Shlomo, and I managed to slip out of the ghetto and hide in a cave, but we were found there and brought to the

---

91 Yiddish-Russian translation by David Shkolnik (Rehovot, Israel). Russian-Ukrainian translation by the author.

prison. Our brother was also there. From there, small groups of Jews were transported to various jobs.

One time he left for some job, and we were driven by truck to Piatydni [a reference to the second "action"—V.M.], where a large pit had been prepared for us. During the journey we were forbidden to raise our heads, and it was impossible to escape. When we arrived at the place, we were told to undress, and they began to kill everyone who had been brought there with automatic weapons: they led them one by one up to the pit. My sister was also there. Our only consolation was that we knew that, in our family, our brother was alive.

As my turn came for the pit where I was supposed to be shot, I could no longer look at what was happening. Fortunately, I ended up among the very last people. When they shot me, I was wounded in three places and fell into the pit, which was full of dead people. The killers thought that I was dead. I lost consciousness and came to during the night when someone underneath the corpses uttered a few words. It was a woman's voice, but nothing more was heard. In the morning some Poles came to cover the pit. I did not want to be buried alive, and I lifted my head. They got a big scare when they saw me alive in the mass grave, and they told me to run away. I asked: "Where? I am naked and wounded!" But they were shouting, telling me to escape. I got out of the pit and went into a field, where I hid in a pile of straw.

When some Polish peasants came from the village to take away the straw and saw me, they brought me clothing and bread, and told me to leave that place. I spent several days in the village, and then I went to the city because there were still people in the ghetto who were working, including my brother. I wanted to enter the ghetto, but because of my wounds I couldn't.

I stopped by the home of a Polish woman named Wojciechowska, to whom we had given our house when we were moving to the ghetto. I had changed so much that she did not recognize me, and she took me for a beggar. When she finally recognized me, she nearly fainted from fear because she thought I was dead.

This woman began nursing me with whatever she could find. She bandaged my wounds and looked after me. I asked her to pass a message to my brother that I was alive. She went to the ghetto and told this to the Jews, but they refused to believe her. She described my features, and then my brother and his friends brought me into the ghetto. They hid me in such a way that the Germans could not find me, especially since I was wounded and needed medical assistance. It was very difficult. I had to be brought secretly to the hospital in the city (at the time it was located in a building that had previously housed the Polish bank PKO). There, a woman whose surname was Rokova gave me some medicines, for which I paid a large sum in gold that I still had left from home. I needed an operation, but no one there dared operate on me because doctors had to report such matters to the commandant's office. And this spelled death because it was forbidden to treat Jews.

From time to time the Germans carried out roundups in the ghetto and transported Jews to their death, especially those who did not have a work card. Sick people were not issued such cards. I hid from the Germans for nearly a year, for the entire time of the ghetto's existence.

In 1943 everything came to an end in one hour, when the Germans suddenly attacked us. I did not even manage to see my brother. I ran into a hiding place together with a family. We heard the cries of people who were being taken away.

It became clear that we could not remain for long in this hiding place. We left and tried to escape from the ghetto to some village. During our escape we were shot at, and several people were killed. A married couple and I were lucky enough to escape. We came to a place where we knew Jews were hiding. We spent several days there, but I did not want to stay longer. After I left, everyone who was hiding there was found and led away to be killed. I found out about this later.

After these unimaginable tribulations I returned to the city and went to the home of a Ukrainian, to whom we had given some of our possessions. I was hoping that perhaps my brother was there. At the very moment I found out that my brother had been killed I wanted to go some place where I could be shot too. My shattered heart ached: no one of my family was left. But such was my fate. The landlady of this home hid me so that the neighbors would not find out. There were other Jews hiding there, including the Shoiev family. I hid there until I was liberated by Russian [Soviet] troops.[92]

---

92 *Wladimir Wolynsk*, 527–28.

THE REMINISCENCES OF YAACOV HARARI (ENGINEER, BERKELEY, CALIFORNIA)

Yaacov Harari (Berger).

I was born in 1932 in the city of Volodymyr-Volynsky. I lived with my parents Itshak and Esther Berger and my younger brother Rafi on Lutska Street near the river Smoch. My parents had a fruit and vegetable store. In 1941, when the Nazis occupied the city, our family, along with other Jews in the city, was sent to the ghetto.

On the eve of the pogrom my parents sent me and my brother to the village of Zhytan, where we stayed for nearly two months. The Savchuk family, who had bought my parents' store, lived in this village. Their son Savko had joined the police. He was spreading rumors in the village that he had seen my parents loaded onto a truck and shot. We were hoping that he would not do anything bad to us because he knew us and, after all, we were only children.

But he caught us, my brother and me, in that village. He caught us and took us in order to send us to the city. His parents, who knew us very well, told him: "Savko, what are you doing?! These are our children, you know those children!" But he told his parents: "You're trying to save Jews? You yourselves will go to prison."

But he did not return to the city that day. He locked us up in his cellar and returned the next morning, brought us out of the cellar, and led us on foot to the city. We walked about ten kilometers.

He brought us to the German headquarters and left us there. After two or three hours another policeman came and, without saying anything, he brought us to the ghetto, behind barbed wire. We were lucky because this was the last day of the pogrom, and we escaped death this time, since we could have been sent directly to Piatydni along with everyone else.

Near the house where we lived in the ghetto my parents had made a hiding place in the cellar, where potatoes were stored in the winter. It was located underneath the floor, separated by boards, and from the outside it was invisible. There was room for no more than four people. I knew about this hiding place. We hid there during the roundups.

For a year and a half we lived in the hiding place located beneath the floor of the first-floor apartment of a three- or four-story building situated in a garden behind Shulman's mill on Lutska Street. The owner of the apartment was Lidia Prokopiuk, who in 1944 had a two-year-old daughter and a seven-year-old son [named] Volodia. This woman's face was deformed: she didn't have a nose. My parents gave her money from their savings, and all of us—we, she, and her children—lived off this money.[93]

---

93 http://www.hcnc.org/oralhistory/harari.html.

THE REMINISCENCES OF DEBORA INTERIEUR[94]

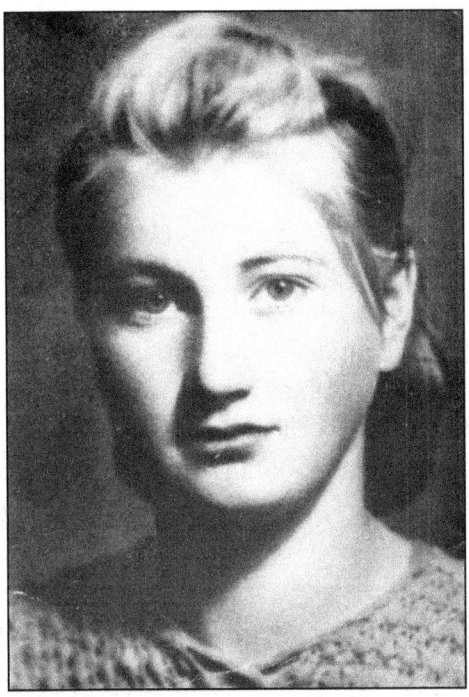

Debora Interieur (née Frimer).

Debora was born in 1930 in the city of Ludmir, Poland, to her parents Elke Frimer (born Laufman) and Moshe Frimer.

Debora's father Moshe was a blacksmith and her mother Elke sold embroidery items and tapestry in the villages around.

Elke was known as "Elke-cossack" because of her strength and diligence.

Elke and Moshe had six children: Israel, Pesach, Leah, Debora, Henya and another brother who disappeared at the beginning of the war whose name Debora cannot remember.

They spoke the Yiddish language at home, which was a very religious home.

---

94 An English résumé of an interview that took place in Israel as part of the Polish Roots in Israel Project.

At the beginning of the Thirties, 44% of Ludmir's population was Jewish. Although there were three schools in town where they gave lessons in Hebrew, Debora was sent to a state school. The reason for that might have been because when the Soviets entered the town in 1939, the Hebrew schools were closed.

The Germans entered Ludmir on June 25, 1941, and on July 6 the Gestapo people took control over the town's Jews. A Ghetto was established, wherein all the town's Jews were gathered.

Already before the ghetto was established, Debora, who was then eleven years old, sneaked out of the house without her parents knowing it, and she went to look for work in the nearby village. She found work with a family of peasants, taking care of their baby.

She remained in that village for several days, till one night she dreamt that the Germans were killing her father. She didn't stop crying until the peasant for whom she worked took her home to Ludmir, to see what was happening there. Upon their arrival in town, she witnessed her nightmare being realized in front of her eyes. She saw a German man shooting her father. Debora ran to her injured father shouting with all her strength, "Father, Father!" The SS man who shot her father hit her with his rifle and she fainted....

Later, when Debora came with the peasant man to her mother's house, she realized that her family was sitting Shiva (seven days mourning)...for her. Her family was sure that her disappearance from home was because she had been killed. No one in the family except her knew about the death of her father.

The Polish peasant asked her mother's permission to take Debora with him back to the village. Her mother agreed, after much pleading, that Debora could go for a few days only because they were building the ghetto and Debora would no longer be able to return to her family. The peasant took Debora with him to his house, where he gave her a large supply of food, and then took her back to her mother's house.

"That food helped us to exist for some time," says Debora. But eventually it was finished. Debora started sneaking out of the ghetto in order to bring food to her family. One time she arrived at a nice villa, and when looked through the window she saw a beautiful woman who was standing naked in the kitchen, and from the other room a man's voice was heard, demanding her to bring him coffee. Debora didn't understand that she had happened to arrive at a house where escort girls gave sexual services to German officers, but that woman saw her. She understood that she was a Jewish girl who sneaked out of the ghetto to look for food. She instructed Debora to lie down quietly outside and went to bring coffee to the man in the next room. Then she returned and gave Debora a basket full of goods and hurried to send her away.

When Debora arrived at the gate of the ghetto, she wondered how she could sneak in with the food basket she received, without being noticed. At the same time a group of Jews who were marched back to the ghetto arrived, after finishing their work. Debora sneaked in among them and asked one of the men to hide her under his black coat (a Kapota—a long coat worn by orthodox Jews). The man hid her, and that way she managed to enter the ghetto without being caught. As a token of gratitude she gave the Jewish worker a cake for his children.

On another occasion, while she was trying to sneak out of the ghetto, she was caught by a Judenrat officer. She was severely beaten by the Jewish policeman, and the man who saved her from his hands was, of all people, a Ukrainian policeman.

Debora returned home trying to hide the scars from her mother, but with no success. Her mother saw that she was beaten and begged her to stop sneaking out of the ghetto, but Debora continued. "I had no choice, I had to bring food home," she said.

Once, on her way back from the village, just before entering the ghetto, she saw a "selection" taking place. A truck was parked in the square and Jews were being loaded on it, among them her mother and her brothers and sisters. She never saw them again.

Debora ran to the fields and wandered around for day among the surrounding villages without any purpose. She had nowhere to go, and no one waited for her. She slept in fields under the open sky and ate raw potatoes. But the survival instinct of that brave girl was strong. She wanted to live.

One day, she arrived at a village where she met a peasant woman. She asked her for some food. The woman took her to her house, bathed her, and gave her cooked food and clean clothing.

She apologized for not being able to let her stay in her house, since the Germans were coming to search for escaping Jews and she could not put her children in danger. The peasant woman gave Debora a necklace with a cross to wear on her neck, and sent her away. On the way she encountered an S.S. man. When Debora saw him, she immediately made the sign of the cross, and when he asked her name, she gave him a false Polish name. Her self-confidence, the cross on her neck, and her Aryan looks saved her. The officer was sure that he was looking at a Polish Christian girl.

Debora kept walking till the evening hours when she found a place to sleep in a field among reaped straw sheaves. The following day she found a hiding place in a barn of a peasants' house, among the piles of grain crops.

The lady of the house suspected that someone was hiding in her barn, and in the evening she came and said loudly that if someone was hiding there, he should not be afraid, she would help him. And indeed Debora came out and she was taken to the house, where she received warm food and a bed for the night. The next day she was again sent away.

Debora went to the forest, where she wandered alone for three days. On the third day, she suddenly heard from afar voices of people talking. She cautiously advanced in the direction where the voices were coming from and saw a group of partisans. She approached them, and they felt sorry for her and took her to a peasants' farm near the forest. (It appeared later that the farm owner was the commander of the partisans' group.) At the farm she received food and a place to sleep in the cowshed. The next morning she woke up and started walking around the farm. Suddenly she saw from afar two Germans who were approaching in the direction of the farm and she immediately pretended that she was working in the field. When the Germans arrived, they took her by force to the cowshed attic that was made of straw, where they started questioning her about hiding partisans. Since she claimed that she knew nothing of what they were talking about, the frustrated Germans threw her from the attic and she fell down on the concrete floor of the cowshed.

After the Germans left empty handed, the lady of the house found her lying down injured and with high fever. She took the injured child and treated her until she recovered.

Debora joined the partisans' group and stayed with them till the end of the war. Her role was to watch and warn her friends in case of danger. She was also told to take off the rings and watches and jewelry from dead bodies of Germans who were killed in fights against the partisans.[95]

THE MEMOIRS OF ANN KAZIMIRSKI

Ann Kazimirski.

Ann Kazimirski was born and raised in the city of Volodymyr-Volynsky, in Poland, where Jews had lived for twelve centuries. At first, her father Joshua taught Russian, and her mother Matilda was one of his students. Later, her father could no longer earn a living from teaching, so her

---

95 http://www.sztetl.org.pl/?a=showCity&action=viewtable&cat__id=16&city__id=1314&id=12973&lang=en__GB.

parents became coal and lumber merchants. They were able to educate her brother Benny and her. Her education included attendance at a Jewish school and a private high school, as well as music lessons.

She was seventeen when the Germans invaded Poland. Her father and eighteen-year-old brother Benny were in the first group of Jews to be captured and then beaten in the city's prison. She saw her best friend Sarah being raped by German soldiers. Sarah died as a result of this savagery.

The Germans killed Ann's grandfather Aaron, who was a very pious Orthodox Jew. He was a role model for his children and grandchildren, who taught them to revere nature and hard work, and to honor the Sabbath. But her grandfather's Jewish world, which, as he believed, was a beautiful land created by God where people could live and be happy, was nearly completely destroyed by the Holocaust. It became a world of concentration camps, ghettos, and systematic mass killings.

Shortly after the start of the German occupation, the Jews of Volodymyr-Volynsky were rounded up and sent to the ghetto, which was surrounded by barbed wire. At this time the first of three "actions" took place. During the first "action" Ann, her husband Henry, and her mother hid in the attic of the military dentistry clinic. A German dental technician, who was a friend of Ann's husband, allowed them to hide there. This man, whose name was Hahn, risked his own life to save them.

Ann Kazimirski's identity card issued by the Judenrat of Volodymyr-Volynsky. Photo from her memoirs, Witness to Horror.

The clinic was to the right, on the kitty-corner from the ghetto. One morning they heard horrible screaming. Through the small attic window they saw that a pogrom had begun. People were being beaten with staves and shoved into trucks that were standing all around. With their hands raised in the air, they were crying: "Why have You abandoned us?!"

Mothers were screaming. Some clutched their infants, trying to hide them under their dresses. But the Nazis grabbed the babies and tossed them into the trucks. The ground and children's clothing were stained with blood. Ann shut her ears, unable to listen to the cries. To this day she can still hear this in her dreams.

During the second "action" they hid in a barn, and later in an attic in the home of a Polish woman named Maria Wierzbowska. They stayed there for a few weeks, until her husband discovered them. He was an estate steward and had a hostile attitude to Jews, and when he discovered their presence, he threatened to denounce them to the Gestapo. They were forced to go to the ghetto.

They stayed in the ghetto until 13 December 1943, when the third and final pogrom began. The goal of this third "action" was to make the city *Judenrein*, free of Jews. German soldiers swarmed into the ghetto and shot at Jews at random. Many were killed while attempting to escape by climbing up the barbed wire.

Miraculously, Henry and Ann found a cramped hiding place in the attic of a house, but they became separated from her mother. During the next few days, from their hiding place they observed the Germans and Ukrainian policemen scouring the ghetto, searching for the remaining Jews. To her horror, one morning she recognized her mother in a group of five people who were being dragged from their hiding place in a nearby building. The five of them were placed against the wall and shot. She never forgot how the red bloodstains looked on the white snow: helplessly, she saw her beloved mother dying. But a single cry would have put the life of every person in their hiding place at risk.

A total of 19,000 Jews, including a thousand children, were killed in Volodymyr-Volynsky. It was a real miracle that Henry and Ann survived those three rounds of killings. Although they had survived, they still faced a difficult road ahead. In March 1944, once they were able to leave the ruined ghetto, they joined a group of Polish partisans. When it became clear that the partisans did not want Jews, they fled and made their way on foot to the Soviet front. Hungry, dirty, infested with lice, covered with sores, and homeless, they were finally liberated by the Soviet army. Their first reaction was joy. It was an unbelievable feeling to be able to live without fear after years of hiding in attics, cellars, and cattle sheds.[96]

It should be noted that Ann Kazimirski appeared twice as a witness during the trials of the Nazis who had liquidated the Jews of Volodymyr-Volynsky: the first time was on 2 November 1971 in Düsseldorf, and the second, on 13 July 1982 in Dortmund (Germany), during the trial of Wilhelm Westerheide, the Gebietskommissar of Volodymyr-Volynsky, and his assistant Johanna Zelle.

During the first trial, Ann's husband Henry Kazimirski also testified that when he was passing himself off as a Pole and working as a dentist at the German clinic, he had access to information. He stunned the court with his testimony about Westerheide, who declared that Jews were not all that badly off because they had not suffered before being killed: "My men simply place Jews at the edge of the pit in such a way that they did not see who is shooting them. They are shot accurately from behind, and they fall into the pit." He had talked about this with Dr. Hecker, with whom Henry worked at the clinic.

The defendants were found guilty of murder and sentenced to prison terms ranging from three-and-a-half to nine years. But Westerheide, the chief organizer of these bloody events in Volodymyr-Volynsky, was not among them.

Unfortunately, Henry did not live to see the former Gebietskommissar put on trial.

There is another interesting detail to this story. It took Ann Kazimirski nine long years to receive the court's decision in this case, which was kept secret from the outset. During those years, her requests for information were denied on the grounds that she was a private

---

96 Kazimirski, *Witness to Horror*.

individual, despite her status as a witness in the case. It is probably no accident that Westerheide was found innocent by the court in Dortmund.

MOSHE KRIGSER RECALLS (TEL-AVIV, ISRAEL)[97]

My family was from Ustyluh. My father's name was Wolf; he was a photographer. My mother's name was Tova. Around 1937 our family moved to Volodymyr, where we lived on Ustyluzka Street.

The Krigser family, Ustyluh: Yitshak Krigser, his photographer son Joshua-Wolf and his wife Tova and their children Chava, Esther, Rachel, and Moshe. Everyone but Moshe perished in the Holocaust. Photo courtesy of Moshe Krigser.

With the arrival of the Germans we were chased into the ghetto, and we lived in all three ghettos. We managed to survive all the "actions." In the third ghetto, my parents and I lived in a house on Ustyluzka Street. There my father dug a hideout in the ground near the banks of the Luha River. When the last "action" began, all of us hid there and stayed there from 13 December to 1 January. My sister Eva

---

97 Interview with Moshe Krigser.

(Chava) was well known in the city, so when we came out, people who spotted us recognized her instantly. I remember the Poles throwing snowballs at her and shouting: "O! Eva—żydówka! Jeszcze żyje żydówka!" [Oh! Eva the Jewess! The Jewess is still alive!]. It was clear that we could not remain in the city, and we went to the village of Hanusyn, where we lived in a deep hideout built in a stable owned by a Pole. But on 24 February 1944, during an attack on the Polish colony by the Germans and Ukrainian policemen, the stable was set on fire. My parents and another married couple in the stable jumped outside and were shot. We heard these shots a few minutes after the stable caught on fire. A wall of the stable collapsed and blocked our exit. We could have stayed there, but when the Poles came and saw tracks leading from the hideout, they figured something valuable was buried there, and they began digging. When they heard our voices, they found us and told us to come out. The first to emerge was my sister Eva; she was recognized by the Pole Żylinski, who began to cross himself and pray. When I was leaving the hideout, I took only my father's tallis that I have kept as a memento all my life, and which I still have. We saw our dead parents and we had to bury them. Żylinski told us that we should head for the village of Bilyn, to the Soviet partisans.

My sister Esther was also killed during this attack. That is how I lost my entire family. My younger sister Rachel was shot in the village of Porytsk, where my parents had sent her to stay with relatives.

I was only fourteen at the time. We, very young boys, were taken into the partisan detachment "For the Fatherland," which was operating as part of Fedoriv's formation. My older sister Eva and I and her classmate Roza Delburd from Volodymyr were very lucky. A Jewish doctor from the large village of Rokytne, who was a member of the detachment, asked the command to take us in. There I was jokingly called the Jewish Moses. In the detachment I was issued a rifle, which turned out to be taller than me....I took part in combat actions. I was a demolitions man, and we took part in battles on the Prypiat River. My sister Eva also fought in the Kutuzov Detachment. And although it was difficult for us—there was war and death—in the partisan detachment, with weapons in our hands, we felt more confident and safer because there was hope, something that the ghetto residents, for whom the Germans had prepared only one fate—death—did not have.

I have combat decorations. In peacetime, veterans living in Israel were awarded jubilee medals from Russia and Belarus. It is too bad that Ukraine has forgotten about us....

Moshe Krigser (at left) and General Roman Yagel, former partisan, veteran of the Polish People's Army, and president of the Union of Fighters and Partisan-Invalids of the war against the Nazis, standing next to the eternal flame at Yad Vashem, Jerusalem. Photo courtesy of Moshe Krigser.

THE REMINISCENCES OF VOLODYMYR OKSENTIIOVYCH PATUTA (1929–2011, RESIDENT OF THE VILLAGE OF PIATYDNI)

In the summer of 1942, a ghetto was created in the city of Volodymyr-Volynsky. All the Jewish residents of the city and neighboring villages in the district were settled in one area, which was encircled by barbed wire. Everyone was ordered to wear yellow patches. They were sewn on the chest and back in order to distinguish Jews from other people. I remember that it was very humiliating for them to wear this mark.

There were also two Jewish families living in Mykulychi Druhi (today the village of Piatydni). They were intelligent people, who owned quite a large farm. In 1942, they too were moved to the ghetto. Soon the Jews began to be shot. The place of execution was near Piatydni. Nearly every day, a truck brought Jews to be shot. The fascists paid no heed to age, gender, or social status. The condemned had to dig their own trench. Then everyone was stripped naked and forced to lie on the bottom of the trench....One fascist fired at their heads. The next ones were laid on top in rows, face down on the people who had been shot, so that the bullets, hitting the bodies of Jews still alive, would finish off the wounded (if there were any) in the bottom rows. No one had any chance of remaining alive after such an execution.

Once the trench was filled with corpses, it was covered with earth. At the time, the elder of the village of Mykulychi assigned a certain number of village residents to fill up the trenches. I remember that they sent me, a twelve-year-old boy, together with my peers and older fellow villagers to those hellish jobs. Since the trenches were very wide, the earth did not reach the center. That is why slopes were created from the edges to the center of the trench. After a while the bottom of the slopes filled with human blood. At first, I did not understand what kind of puddles were gathering there. I threw a handful of earth and it made a plopping sound. It was blood....Believe me, it was a horrific sight....

When the Germans were leaving the execution site, the older people always asked hopefully: "Is there anyone alive?" But such questions were futile. I don't remember anyone surviving.

I was astonished by such a savage attitude to people. Before the execution, the condemned were stripped of everything: clothing and adornments, and women were made to unbraid their hair in the hope that some hidden gold or other valuables would be found in it. The clothing was sorted at once: old clothing was burned, and new clothing was loaded on a truck and taken away. Those who put up resistance or began to cry were brutally and hatefully beaten. During the execution, children were placed underneath their mothers, so that they would not take up a lot of space.

The Tragedy of the Jews of Volodymyr-Volynsky

After some time, the Germans altered the method of destroying Jews. After blowing up a piece of land, thus creating a huge pit, they placed the prisoners along the edges and shot them from behind. The bodies rolled to the bottom by themselves. Until late 1943, death pits and trenches covered areas of up to one hectare.

Refusing an assigned job meant risking the Germans' reprisals. People were afraid and they went [to their assignments].

These horrific scenes of brutality were firmly engraved in my memory. I always ask myself: "Why was it necessary to destroy innocent civilians?" (Village of Piatydni, May 2006).

Hanna Bohush, a resident of Piatydni, recalled the following: "I did not fill up the pit....We only went to look later....That first pit—it was terrible, there was blood there. It's easy to say this, but to see this with your very own eyes, to experience it....It would be better if such a thing were never repeated!"

In recalling the terrible tragedy that took place in the vicinity of Piatydni, it would be remiss not to mention that the Germans shot Ukrainians there too. This is recounted in the reminiscences of M. Bass:

> In the last and smallest of the three graves are many Ukrainians, because by then there were hardly any Jews left.
>
> In 1939–41 Yukhym Ustymovych Khorunzhy, who was born in 1897 and lived in the village of Zarichchia, where he completed four grades of the parish church school, was the deputy of Matii Stepasiuk, the head of the village council. In 1942, the inhabitants of the village of Zarichchia elected Yukhym Ustymovych as the village elder instead of Ilarion Kvit. He was honest and fair, and he tried not to send people to Germany [for forced labor—M.D.O.] or to supply food. On the orders of the German, Wens, and the chief of police, Novychenko, he was arrested by two *Volksdeutsche* [ethnic

Germans—M.D.O.]. He was arrested on Saturday, and on Monday he was shot together with Vasyl Kostiuk and Lukash, from the village of Chesnyi Khrest. A female resident of the town, Stepanyda Oleksiivna Hladkova, saw them being driven by car to Piatydni. She was a little girl at the time and was grazing cows next to the road.

There were five people in the car, and Vasia Kostiuk was sitting among them. "Vasia!" she yelled. He lifted his head and glanced at her. Prokopiuk and Khorunzhy were also in the car. According to partial data, sixty-two Ukrainians were shot in Piatydni.[98] This incident, in which a car was seen transporting people dressed in typically Ukrainian clothing to Piatydni, is also recounted by Volodymyr Patuta, a resident of Piatydni.

OFLAG "NORD 365"

There is another terrible place on the map of the city. "Nord 365" was a Nazi concentration camp for Red Army officers located on the outskirts of Volodymyr-Volynsky where 56,000 POWs were shot. As soon as this camp was established, Jews and commissars who were among the POWs were the first to be targeted for destruction, long before the rest of the prisoners were shot.

In his book *Captivity*, the historian Aaron Shneer cites materials held in the Yad Vashem* archives: "The search for Jews was carried out in the OFLAGs, (prisoner of war camps for officers) just like in the other camps. In Volodymyr-Volynsky, as a result of one selection alone, which was carried out in November 1941, 600 Jewish officers were discovered, herded into a shed, not given anything to eat or drink for several days, and then shot."[99]

---

98 Tsaruk, "Holhofa nad Luhoiu."
99 Yad Vashem archives, M-37/1176, fol. 6, cited in A. Shneer, *Plen: sovetskie voennoplennye v Germanii, 1941–1945* (Moscow: Mosty kul'tury; Jerusalem: Gesharim, 2005).

Some prisoners, eager to curry favor with the camp authorities, identified the Jews in their midst, while others took the opportunity to denounce prisoners of other nationalities as Jews.

Other documents list data indicating that approximately a hundred Jewish POWs were shot on 6 December 1941.[100] The execution took place outside the city.[101] And, even though they were not residents of Volodymyr-Volynsky, this fact underscores the Nazis' attitude and their priorities with regard to the question of cleansing the occupied territories of the non-Aryan population.

According to Nazi documents, which contradict all the stereotypes and despite all the prevailing circumstances, Jews in the ghetto were not passive observers of the events that were taking place. Aware of the situation in the POW camp, they tried to take part in efforts to liberate the captive officers. Here is a fragment from a document entitled "Announcement No. 12 from the Occupied Eastern Territories":

> In the district of Volodymyr-Volynsky we succeeded in neutralizing a partisan group that was planning an uprising in the city and the liberation of 8,000 captive Soviet officers from the local OFLAG. It was envisaged to carry out the operation first and foremost with the *assistance of the ghetto* [author's emphasis] (15,000 Jews) and numerous Bolshevik agents that are in the city.
>
> For this purpose, most officers have already armed themselves with homemade knives that they fashioned out of smashed helmets. As a result of the applied measures, the leaders of the plot were exposed: 36 Communists and 76 Jewish officers, among whom were several commissars. Special measures were used against the Communist agents as well as the 76 Jewish officers. One Jewish woman was arrested; a doctor who used her access to the POW camp for the purposes of espionage.

---

100 See *Mistsia skorboty*.
101 Raport zonderfiurera E. Kumminga, http://labas.livejournal.com/tag/ns.

The neutralization of this partisan group had a favorable impact on the attitude and moods of the population.

Berlin, 17 July 1942[102]

∽ ∽ ∽

In addition to the Soviet army and various partisan formations, the Jews of Volodymyr-Volynsky fought in the military formations of the Soviet Union's allies. Among those who emigrated from Poland before the war and waged an armed struggle against Nazism was Arie-Leib Kam (b. 1922). He was a member of the Chail Jewish Brigade and was killed in battle in 1945.

Arie-Leib Kam.[103]

There were some Jews in the OUN (Organization of Ukrainian Nationalists) and the UPA (Ukrainian Insurgent Army), but it is generally known that as a rule they were mobilized in the capacity of physicians. One of them, Shaya Varma (codename "Skrypal" [UPA codename Violinist], born in 1909, arrived in Volodymyr-Volynsky as a

---

102 RGVA, fond 500k, "Reichssicherheitshauptamt (RSHA: Reich Main Security Office, Berlin), list 1, file 775, fols. 273–80, 472–88, located at: http://www.9may.ru/unsecret/m10009001.

103 *Wladimir Wolynsk*, 560.

refugee from Poland after it was attacked by Nazi Germany, and he worked as a doctor in a village dispensary. He was mobilized to the UPA in May 1943, and by August 1944 he had treated nearly 200 injured insurgents and performed various complex operations. He was sentenced to a term of twenty years in the GULAG.[104]

Data on the presence of Jews in the ranks of the Ukrainian Insurgent Army are contradictory, as some researchers claim that Jews were prisoners of the UPA. Nevertheless, there are documented cases of Jews being saved by UPA detachments.

---

104 Gogun and Vovk, "Evrei v bor′be za nezavisimuiu Ukrainu."

The Catastrophe That Befell the Jews of Volodymyr-Volynsky District

Since Jews also lived in other areas of this district, they shared the fate of the Jewish residents of the city of Volodymyr-Volynsky, and therefore this topic cannot be overlooked.

The majority of the Jews living in Volodymyr-Volynsky District were herded into the ghetto in Volodymyr-Volynsky, but more than a hundred Jews were shot in the village of Verba. However, there are no data on the fate of three Jewish families—approximately twenty people—who lived in the village of Mohylno (today, the village of Zhovtneve, Volodymyr-Volynsky District), who are mentioned in the memoirs of Jadwiga Koziol.[1]

During the war, Hanna Bohush, a resident of Piatydni, lived in the village of Mykulychi. She knew the fate of the two Jewish families that lived in this village: they were all sent to the ghetto in Volodymyr-Volynsky and were never seen again.

In early July 1942 the Germans moved the 900 Jews who remained in the large village of Porytsk, along with approximately 900 people from neighboring villages, to a camp located in the village of Pereslavychi (situated today in Ivanychi District). They were all killed by the Nazis on 17 July near the village of Kuchkiv.

After Volodymyr-Volynsky, the largest Jewish town in the district was Ustyluh, situated twelve kilometers west of the city. According to various estimates, this town was home to around 3,200 Jews (thirty of

---

1   http://www1.yadvashem.org/yv/ru/righteous/poland/ziental.asp.

whom were Soviet activists), who were shot as early as July 1941. In March 1942, the Nazis created a ghetto, where they gathered over 3,000 Jews. In early September 1942, roughly 2,000 prisoners were shot.

According to various sources, the Jews of Ustyluh were shot in other locations in addition to Piatydni. One of the mass execution sites was the Jewish cemetery, which is now the schoolyard in Ustyluh.

Volodymyr Muzychenko by the gravestone, the only trace left of the 3,200 Jewish residents of Ustyluh. It was accidentally preserved in the park that now lies on top of the Jewish cemetery. During the Soviet era all traces of Jewish culture were wiped out, and a school and a kindergarten were built on this site. Every day children walk to school, treading right over these graves.

Moshe Krigser recalls:[2] "In Ustyluh I knew a doctor whose surname was Muzykansky. Right after the war, the residents of Ustyluh recounted that he and his family fled to a village along the Buh River. But they were captured there and killed. At the time, I was not able to find out who did this."

Volodymyr-Volynsky was surrounded by the Polish colonies of Bilyn, Hanusyn, Szedlisko, and Vorchyn, which were located within a radius of between six and fourteen kilometers from the city. It is no surprise that, in the atmosphere of hatred that was bred by the occupying regime, Polish insurgents killed Jews who were in hiding and had joined the Soviet partisans. Jews especially remember their 120 coreligionists who were killed in Vorchyn.

The Polish village of Vorchyn lay ten kilometers northwest of Volodymyr-Volynsky, situated next to Ukrainian villages, most of which had been burned down and abandoned. Based in the village of Bilyn, five kilometers north of Volodymyr-Volynsky, was the headquarters of the 23rd Polish Insurgent Garda Brigade. Soviet partisans from Fedoriv's large units from the Rivne region were also based in this area.

Some Jews from Volodymyr-Volynsky and Ustyluh went to Bilyn, where they joined the Polish forces. None of them knew that some Poles from the Narodowe Siły Zbrojne (National Armed Forces, NSZ)[3], the anti-Semitic part of the Polish right-wing, nationalist, and openly anti-Semitic National Democratic Party, also served in the Armia Krajowa (AK).

On 19 March 1944, leaflets appeared in Bilyn ordering all Jews to leave the village by 24 March and assemble in one of the Polish colonies that had been burned down by the Banderites. The Jews were assigned to two houses that had escaped destruction in Vorchyn.

There are two theories explaining the concentration of Jews. Shmuel Diamant, a member of the brigade, recalls that two Jewish boys left the village of Bilyn and were captured by the Germans. After

---

2   Translated from the Hebrew by David Shkolnik (Rehovot, Israel).
3   A Polish anti-Soviet and anti-Nazi paramilitary organization that was part of the Polish resistance movement during the Second World War.

interrogation, during which they made some statements, the Germans bombed the insurgents' camp.

Nachum Weisman, who arrived in Bilyn on 19 March 1944, was told by a Jewish woman that Jews had been ordered to leave Polish guerrilla territory because the Poles believed that they could transmit secrets to the Germans.

Eliahu Yakir, who was the division doctor and had visited divisional headquarters on many occasions, states that he never heard about any mass killings. However, he was aware that individual Jews were being killed. According to him, in early 1944 a subunit of the NSZ, whose troops were killing Jews, joined the division. The doctor personally rescued two Jews from their clutches.

However, from the division commander he had heard that, owing to a typhus epidemic, it was decided to gather Jews in the village of Vorchyn, which was on the edge of the district controlled by the Polish insurgents.

The announcements, which were read by various eyewitnesses, threatened that any Jews who failed to leave Bilyn would be shot. Indeed, once the deadline had passed, the Poles launched a roundup, going from house to house and shooting everyone they found.

The fate of the Jews who obeyed the order was equally tragic. A Polish Christian woman named M. Heist recounted: "Every day, Jews were being shot in Vorchyn. I did not believe that our Poles would be completing the work started by the Germans."[4]

In his reminiscences, Moshe Margalit writes:

> The Jews obeyed the announced order, ignoring the fact that it was quite odd, and moved to Vorchyn. On 19 March 1944 all the Jews in Vorchyn, approximately 120 people, were shot by the Poles, including Jews who were fighting in the ranks of the NSZ. One of them, whose surname was Tsuker, was from Ustyluh. He had stayed in Vorchyn even though a Polish

---

4 *Wladimir Wolynsk*, 208.

guerrilla from Volodymyr-Volynsky named Żylinski had warned him about the anti-Semitic moods of the Polish insurgents.

I do not know whether this massacre was carried out exclusively by the NDs (endeky)[5] from the NSA or with the participation of the 23rd Brigade.

Some Jews who refused to obey the order and were hiding in Bilyn were captured during roundups that were conducted in every Jewish house. They were shot on 24 March.

To this day, there are graves scattered throughout the forests in which entire Jewish families that tried to save themselves are buried. The fate of one such family is recounted by Nadia Dmytrivna Lysiuk (b. 1932), who lives in the village of Selysk, in an article written by a Ukrainian journalist:

This woman has a place in the forest that dates back to the war: there is a grave there. Fleeing from the Germans, a Jewish family built a dugout in the forest—a camp—and lived there. No one reported them to the German administration, even though many people knew about these unfortunates. But there were various kinds of people among the Ukrainians too.

That ill-fated day, Nadia and some other children were grazing a cow in the woods, and with her very own eyes she saw two armed men from the village of Zabolottia (near the village of Vierov [sic]) heading to the campsite. She knew the surname of one of them: Dzharyha. After some time she heard shots from there: the first, second, third.…As quickly as possible they [the children] drove the cow back home. Returning the following day with some adults, they saw that everyone who had been in the camp at that time was killed: the father and mother, Yosio and Pesia Karkh (or Karsh), their

---

5   Members of the National Democratic Party, Poland.

daughter, son-in-law, two small children, and a pregnant daughter-in-law. At the time, their son Helio, who had heard the shooting but did not go there because he already knew what was happening, was returning from Pysareva Volia. That is how he survived.

In the forest there, the residents of the village of Vierov dug a deep grave and buried the people who had been killed.

After the war, Helio Karkh lived in Volodymyr-Volynsky, where he worked as a rag-seller and trader. He owned a horse, on which he rode throughout the villages trading rags for various small goods. He also tended the grave. In the late 1960s Helio moved to Israel, and for some time the grave was neglected and became overgrown with grass and bushes, until Nadia Lysiuk began looking after it. She tidied and cleaned up the area, and poured fresh sand over the wide grave. She chopped down some branches in the woods, sharpened them, and made an enclosure, which she painted, and set up a bench. She sits there whenever she or a passerby comes, because the grave is near a forest path. Every time that she heads to the forest, she takes some candy and pastry to the grave—"lunch for the Jews," as she puts it. She worries that when she dies, there will be no one to look after it because it is far from the village.

Nadia Dmytrivna told me that one day she went to the forest, set out "lunch" on the grave, sat there for a bit, and then went deeper into the forest. All of a sudden, a large, gray bird appeared. It was flying after the woman, touching the trees with its wings. It accompanied her for a long time, until Nadia Dmytrivna began speaking to it out loud: "Go back to your people, I know the way." The bird screamed loudly, as though in a human voice, flapped its wings, and flew back. Nadia Dmytrivna considers this a sign of gratitude for honoring the grave that has been forgotten by all. She believes it may be the soul of one of those who were killed.[6]

---

6   A. Solodukha, "Pravedna stezhyna do lisovoï mohyly," *Slovo pravdy*, 31 August 2004.

Nadia Lysiuk at the Jewish grave.[7]

The village of Korytnytsia, which was a small town before the war, is situated on the Ukrainian-Polish border. There was also a Jewish community there, which numbered approximately 300 people. Nearly all of them were shot in 1942.

The entry in the *Russian Jewish Encyclopaedia* contains the following description of this village:

> In 1784, 77 Jews lived in the village of Korytnytsia, Volodymyr-Volynsky District; in 1847—384, in 1870—260 (40.1%), in 1921—279 (78.6%), and in 1931—350. Jews had lived in Korytnytsia since the sixteenth century. In 1628 there was a synagogue in Korytnytsia. In 1648 the Jewish community of Korytnytsia was destroyed by detachments led by B. M. Khmelnytsky. In the late eighteenth century there were two synagogues in Korytnytsia. The basic occupations of the Jewish population in the nineteenth and early twentieth centuries were trade and commerce. In 1913 the Jews of Korytnytsia owned six stores

---

7   Ibid.

and a tavern. In the 1920s and 1930s branches of various Jewish parties and organizations operated in Korytnytsia. The Jewish population of Korytnytsia was destroyed during the period of the Catastrophe.[8]

Fedir Mykhailovych Maziar (b. 1925), a resident of the village, recalls:

> I was born and lived my whole life here. There were about twenty-five Jewish homes; they had a lot of children.
> They were all tailors, shoemakers, horse traders. They had their own oil-press. Itsko the Jew had a shop where he sold salt and gas. Next door lived the Jew Tuvii; he had five or six children. He was a tailor. But for the most part they were poor. Our Jews were good people. I had great pity for them.
> One family, which had six children, fled to the woods, but they were killed there too. The only survivor was their daughter, who left during the evacuation; afterwards she returned and worked at the Zahotzerno [Grain Procurement Office] in Ustyluh. After the war she returned and reburied her family members in the general cemetery. Then she moved somewhere in the Vinnytsia region.
> Only three people were saved. One was called Viktor, the second was Srul, and there was a child with them. They had a hideout somewhere near Kladniv, and at night they would come to beg for bread and potatoes. Later they lived in Volodymyr. They moved someplace afterwards.
> My brother had a wife with a dark complexion, and when the Germans were rounding up Jews to kill them, they took her. But the soltys (village elder) saw this and told them that she was not a Jew, and she was released.

∽ ∽ ∽

---

8 *Rossiiskaia Evreiskaia Entsiklopediia*, vol. 5, s.v. http://www.rujen.ru/index.php/КОРЫТНИЦА

Paraskoviia Ivanivna Dobryniuk (b. 1917), a resident of Volodymyr-Volynsky, who lived in the village of Korytnytsia during the war, recounted the following:

> The village was large; in fact, it was comprised of three villages that had been merged. The Jews of Korytnytsia lived in a small area that was in the center of the village. They were mostly merchants. One of them sold horses; he had a straw-cutter.
>
> There were two shops: one sold groceries, and the other sold various domestic articles. They had a pharmacy. But they also owned farms, on which they raised cattle and poultry. Thus, they had plots of land, where they mowed hay and grazed cattle. They lived amicably and helped each other. You could always obtain credit at a shop because people knew each other well, and there was trust. One was quite wealthy: he had a tar factory, where he produced pitch.
>
> When the Germans came, they killed the Jews. There were two spots where they killed them. One was near the DZOT [earth and timber pillbox—M.D.O.], which was to the left of the road leading to the village of Kladniv. But where the other one was, I don't know exactly; somewhere in a field....
>
> I was traveling from Torchyn to Korytnytsia, and I saw many Jews being driven on trucks to Piatydni.

Before the war, Korytnytsia was a small town with shops, a synagogue, and a Jewish cemetery. But after the Jews were shot by the Nazis, it went into a decline, and today this village is practically dying out.

The mass grave of Korytnytsia's inhabitants, which was a pit from a dismantled defensive structure—the DZOT—is now located past the control zone, and nothing marks it as a burial site. At the present time there is no access to this place because the grave is located on the territory of a border post, behind border structures. Special permission is required to enter.

During the occupation years, from July 1941 to October 1944, the Nazis and their accomplices liquidated the Jewish community of Ukraine: over one and a half million people. Facts about this genocide emerged during the course of liberating Ukraine from the Nazis, thanks to the work of extraordinary commissions to investigate Nazi crimes. Open trials of Nazi war criminals and their accomplices took place in Kharkiv in 1943, Kyiv in 1946, and in other Ukrainian cities in subsequent years. The killers got their just deserts.

Once the war ended and soldiers began returning from the fronts and temporary places of evacuation, civilian life resumed. That was when the scale of the catastrophe became evident. The well-known writer Vasily Grossman wrote these painful words:

> There are no Jews in Ukraine. There is silence, quiet. The people have been destroyed.... This is not the death of people during a war with weapons in their hands, who have something left at home—a family, a field, songs, traditions, history. This is the destruction of a people that lived together with the Ukrainian people, working together with them, shared joy and trouble in one and the same land.... No one can name all the places where the mass killings of Jews took place in the fall of 1941 and the summer of 1942.... There was a massacre everywhere.... The fascists killed Jews because they were Jews.

This tragedy became known as the Holocaust (Hebrew, *Shoah*), derived from the ancient Greek word meaning "sacrifice by fire." The plan to destroy the Jews was described in Hitler's notorious book *Mein Kampf*, which, under the guise of disseminating information, is still being circulated among pro-fascist politicians to this very day. This speaks clearly to the fact that humanity has still not drawn the right conclusions about what happened.

MOSHE MARGALIT RECALLS[9]

(B. 1930, a retired pensioner living in the city of Givatayim, Israel.)

---

9 Interview with Moshe Margalit recorded by Volodymyr Muzychenko.

My father's name was Judah, he was a merchant; he sold lumber and wood. My mother's name was Tali; she was a housewife who was born in Volodymyr, like her parents. I had three sisters: Sosia, Rachel, and Chana, and two brothers: Chaim and Mordechai. Our family lived in a house at 11 Rylovytsia Street (today: Lutska Street).

Moshe Margalit. Photo dated 14 June 1939. From Moshe Margalit's family archive.

Every Saturday, my father and I went to pray at the synagogue on Lutska Street near Shulman's mill. I attended two schools. One year, together with my male cousin, whose surname was Kornfeld, I attended a school with Polish as the language of instruction. We were the only two Jews in the class. We sat at desks at the back of the room, and the teacher who taught us never once asked me [to answer a question], even though I raised my arm. Later I studied at a Jewish school located in a building that now houses the infectious diseases hospital on Shukhevych Street. My cousin lived in the village of Zymne, and on Saturdays I often went to his house. This was the only Jewish family in Zymne. They owned land and cows, and they were engaged in farming; the translation of their very surname was "wheat field."

I remember an incident that the entire street talked about for a long time. Among the Jewish refugees who had arrived in the city after the Germans invaded Poland was a tall, red-haired man with a beard. He had a horse and wagon with which he collected glassware, metal, and all sorts of things that he delivered as raw materials.

He rented a room on our street and, like all of us, he spoke Yiddish, attended the synagogue, and read the Torah. One day he was detained by soldiers, who brought him to our street in order to verify his identity. We all vouched amicably for him, declaring that we knew him. In the first days of the occupation, a German officer came to see us, asking if we knew that old man and where he was. When we admitted that we did not know where he was, the officer laughed and said: 'He is right in front of you.' It so happened that the entire street had protected a German spy, and more than likely he was not the only one among the refugees from Poland.

My older brother Chaim was a socialist sympathizer, but I don't know if he was a Communist. After the city was captured by the Soviet Union in 1939, he became an important director in the city, in charge of trade. When the war began, a military vehicle that was being used to transport children from the city orphanage was sent for him and my sister, who was a teacher at the children's shelter (she was fluent in the Ukrainian language), and the soldiers suggested that my brother and sister go with them, saying they had enough gas for thirty kilometers. He got into the vehicle, but my mother ran outside and did not let him leave. She was afraid that something would happen to him, because you could hear shooting and constant explosions from the bombardment. The soldiers were advising all the men to flee, but they all refused.

Bombs were falling on the city and planes were firing on roads. Later, however, my mother, two sisters, and I tried to catch up with the Soviet troops, but the Germans beat us to it, and on the evening of 24 June we were forced to return to the occupied city.

Volodymyr-Volynsky: The family of Moshe Margalit, 1938. Standing from left: Moshe's brothers Mordechai and Chaim. Seated from left: Moshe's father Iuda Margalit, Moshe, his mother Tali, and younger sister Chava. Photo from Moshe Margalit's family archive.

During the occupation, I took notes of what I saw. For this I used sheets of paper that I managed to find, even pages from books. After the war, when I asked a female acquaintance to hide these notes in her house, she turned me down flat and advised me to hide them inside the wall of an abandoned house, which I did. Eventually I recopied them on clean paper, and when I left for Palestine, I gave my diary to the Volyn committee in Israel. It was subsequently published in the book *Pinkas Ludmir*.

An atmosphere of permanent fear soon descended on the city; fear for one's life. Right after the city was captured, in prison cells the

Germans discovered the corpses of prisoners who had been shot by NKVD troops. Throughout the city, the Germans hung announcements about this in the Ukrainian and Polish languages and invited everyone 'to come and see what the Jewish NKVD has done.'

A few days later, when the unidentified corpses were starting to decompose, the Germans brought in a few Jews whom they ordered to dig a pit and bury the bodies of the people who had been shot. I do not know where they were buried. If we are dealing with a large number of people who were killed near the prison (1,000 or more), then they could not have been Ukrainians or Poles, because they were never held in prison long, but were deported to Siberia, since there was not much room there [in the prison]; I think there was room for 150–200 people. And on 22 June 1941, the NKVD simply did not have the time to dig pits; they had barely managed to escape the advancing Germans. That is why they killed the prisoners right in their cells. If the NKVD did kill its ideological opponents in the prison courtyard, then this was done before the outbreak of the war.

On 5 July, the police carried out a roundup of Jews, capturing 150 young men. It was claimed that they were needed to perform labor. But no one ever saw them again. All of them were killed in the prison courtyard, but mostly without the use of firearms, because few shots were heard. The killings were carried out by the Germans.

A second roundup took place on 31 July, during which nearly 200 people were captured. Of course, these are approximate figures. At present it is impossible to determine the exact number, and the Germans and the police did not keep such records. Also, people were occupied with other matters.

A third roundup took place during the night of 30 August 1941. Taken away with the men were several women who wanted to go with their husbands, explaining their wish by the need to prepare meals for them. They too disappeared. One day, some Jewish painters among the captured were taken for work in the prison, where they saw piles of bloody clothing, but the guards ordered them to keep quiet about what they had seen.

During the last roundup of Jewish men, my father and my brother Mordechai were captured, but Chaim hid with some neighbors in a hideout. I was only a young boy and nobody bothered me. When my brother Chaim saw that a German roundup was approaching, he grabbed a newspaper and headed straight for the pogromists, as though he were going to the toilet. They let him pass, taking him for a Ukrainian. When the Germans entered the house and realized that these people were Jews, they became very angry and set out in pursuit of him, but he managed to hide in some straw. Searching for Chaim, the Germans found my father, dragged him into the yard, and began beating him. Seeing this from the hideout, Chaim ran out and said to them: 'Why are you beating an old man, what did he do to you?!' Then they began to beat Chaim, and when he was covered in blood, they wanted to shoot him, but reacting to the hubbub, some Ukrainian neighbors ran up and began pleading with them not to kill him, and they succeeded. One of our Ukrainian neighbors knew German well, I don't remember how, and one of these Germans showed off his rifle to her, with which he had already shot fifty-seven Jews, and Chaim would have been his fifty-eighth if they [the neighbors] had not stopped [him]. It is true that we did not believe him at the time; we thought he was simply boasting.

My father and brother were taken away for heavy forced labor. My mother and I brought them food and we saw them being beaten. My mother begged the guards to release my father, but they said that it was the SS and they were powerless right now and had to keep their mouths shut. Eventually, however, my mother somehow managed to get the Germans from the convoy to release my father; it was a Sunday.

Mordechai recounted that they could not sit down in the cell because there were so many people. He was lucky enough to survive the executions....

One night, the guards opened the doors to the cell and ordered all those on whom the lantern light fell to come out. They were led to the prison courtyard, where there were two lines of Germans with various objects in their hands: shovels, crowbars, metal rods, axes.... They began prodding the prisoners to "run the gauntlet" between these two ranks of executioners, who beat the unfortunates wherever their blows landed. The majority fell down from these blows.... Mordechai was short and he managed to survive this punishment, which is why he and a few other lucky people were ordered to toss into the pit those who were unable to stand up, including people who were still alive. They were buried that way.... There were no shots; obviously, the Germans did not want to attract the attention of the women who were standing near the prison gates even at night, waiting for their husbands and children. Shouting coming from behind the wall was an ordinary phenomenon.... This took place throughout the entire night. At the end of this horrific massacre, Gebietskommissar Westerheide himself appeared in our midst. He asked how many had been killed and he was told 250 Jews. He said, "That's enough," and left.

The survivors were returned to the prison bunks, and in the morning they were driven out to work, after which they were released. That was when we learned what had happened to those who had been captured during the roundups. This was the Friday before Yom Kippur. After this the roundups stopped, but at that time no one suspected what awaited us....

During the first days of the occupation, the Germans opened the bread shops and began to sell it [bread] for Soviet currency, as I recall. A loaf of bread cost three rubles. There were two lineups next to the shop: one for Christians and the other for Jews. For every ten Christians it was permitted to sell one loaf to the Jews. Even if there was no one next to the shop, Jews had to wait until ten Ukrainians or Poles arrived. One such shop was on Lutska Street near Shulman's mill. Next to it was a military gendarmerie, and one gendarme constantly made sure that there was enough space among the people in the lineup for another person.

If people clustered together, they were dispersed and beaten with staves. Some people were reselling bread at triple the price. One Ukrainian woman, our neighbor, the one who knew German, worked for the Germans at such a shop, and every day she brought us a loaf of bread. At that time this was the only thing we had to eat. We paid her, and when my parents tried to pay more, she refused categorically: "How can I take money from you when you are sitting here hungry?!" Later, after the first pogrom in the ghetto, I was hiding on its territory, and this woman brought me some food, in exchange for which I would throw items over the fence from the abandoned buildings. There were many valuable articles; the Germans had not managed to take them away, and it was forbidden to enter the ghetto. I entered the houses and destroyed everything I could lay my hands on, so that the Germans would not get them.

Since the railway tracks in the Soviet Union and German differed in terms of width, for passage along Lutska Street a place was organized for transporting aviation bombs for their further transshipment by railway to the front. The bombs weighed 100 kilograms each or more. The transshipment was done manually. Throughout September, Jewish men were taken every day to perform this labor. They were fed only once a day. Those who could not cope with the heavy work were forced to dig a pit, ordered to lie down in it, and then shot. Sometimes people were buried alive.... When the laborers started running away, they were locked inside the prison after work. I was often in that little area where they were stacking the bombs unloaded from the train cars. Odd as it may seem, it was very easy to reach this place. To this day I cannot forgive myself for not blowing up this stock—all it would have taken was one grenade....

One day, I was walking through the city and saw three Soviet prisoners of war being guarded by a German. I was carrying a basket of apples, and when they saw them they began calling to me and begging me. The apples did not belong to me, but if I had said for whom they were meant, nothing would have happened to me. I gave each of them an apple. When he saw this, the German began shouting at me and ordering me to take them back, and although I was sorry for those people, I had to take them back, which I was able to do....

During the First World War, a wounded German officer of Jewish background was being treated in the city. Unfortunately, I don't remember his name. He had married a local German woman and settled down here. In 1941, when the city was captured by his former countrymen, they did not even take into account that he had spilled his blood at the front for Germany, and he was sent to the ghetto. True, his family was permitted to remain in the Aryan part of the city. His wife and children went to the ghetto to visit and bring food to their husband

and father. When the pogrom happened, his sons were sent from the ghetto, and the father was dispatched to Piatydni along with the other captives.

Within the Judenrat was a Jewish ghetto police force of around 120 men. Some of them, seeking to curry favor with the Germans, beat Jews; they often beat me and my sister. When the Jews of the city were being shot, the Germans used some of these scoundrels as an auxiliary labor force to place the dead bodies into the pits. But they did not participate directly in the shootings; the Germans never supplied Jews with weapons.

On the order of the Gebietskommissar, 250 men were selected to be sent to Kyiv for forced labor, including those with health problems. My brother Chaim was also taken. It was Sunday morning. But by Monday evening everyone was released, after having been kept in overcrowded cargo train cars without food and water. Rumors were circulating that this had happened because partisans had blown up the railway track.

I often saw Gebietskommissar Westerheide and his assistant [Johanna] Zelle in the city. They arrived in the city and the ghetto dressed in civilian clothing, but they had pistols and were on horseback. They ordered the ghetto prisoners to build a small bridge on the banks of the Luha River, and every day in the summer, at the same hour, they would come there to fish off the bridge or from a boat. They really enjoyed this recreation, and it lasted a long time until one time someone on the opposite bank fired on them.

Eventually, there were hardly any young people left in the city: the Jews had been shot, and the majority of Ukrainians and Poles had been deported as slaves to Germany, even teenagers who looked older because they were physically well developed and tall. After the second "action" I survived by walking around the city and begging people for a scrap of bread or a potato to eat. Usually these were elderly Polish women who had fled the pogroms in the countryside. They too were starving. I was not afraid of the Germans; they could not tell a Jew from a Pole or a Ukrainian, but I was afraid of the policemen—Poles and Ukrainians—who could tell that I was a Jew by my accent, and local people could also have known me by face. When the Germans asked me something, I made out that I did not understand, even though I understood German well, and they left me alone. When I had to ask something, I did not go up to a Pole or a Ukrainian, I went to a German; it was not as risky. Whenever I walked along a street, I tried to walk abreast of Germans because it was safer that way; no one would bother me then; that's why I avoided walking on side streets, but walked mostly along the central one, where there were a lot of Germans.

I was only twelve years old, but fear and the hungry life in the ghetto and cellars killed all my trust in people. I did not trust a single person; I did not believe that there were good people on earth. But one day, when I was in the city center during the wintertime, I asked a German something and then fainted from hunger and physical exhaustion.

I was helped up by a nicely dressed young man who was with a girl. He asked me why I had fallen, but I was afraid to answer him. Then he said in Ukrainian: 'Don't be afraid, let's go; good people will help you,' and he held me close in his arms until I regained complete consciousness and was able to stand. That time, after a lengthy chunk of life lived in horrible conditions, disillusionment in people, for the first time I understood that there are still good people on earth."

[Recounting these events, Moshe could not hold back his tears and he wept. He said that he is forbidden to talk about those days because the resulting agitation has a very bad impact on the fragile health of this 80-year-old man.]

"On Monday, 31 August, my older brother Chaim and I went to see a friend with whom he had worked during the period of Soviet rule. The friend had two very beautiful twin daughters. They discussed the possibility of an action the next day, since the ghetto had been surrounded and non-local policemen had arrived. We went to hide in the rabbi's house, where there was a hiding place on the second floor. There were people there with a small child, and my brother said that it was not necessary to stay there; the child might betray everyone. We went to another building.

It was located in the western part of the ghetto, not far from the western gates of the ghetto; there was also a hiding place, where we spent the entire night, but everything was quiet. Besides us, the Liberman couple and a woman with two children were hiding there.

Toward morning my brother said that the Germans would not be killing children in the daytime, so we left the house. I decided to go home; I really wanted to sleep. On the way I ran into a friend of mine. I saw a lot of policemen—dozens; they were not just from Volodymyr. Suddenly, the policemen opened fire on people who had gathered near the *Arbeitsamt* (the Judenrat institution that sent people out to work) in order to obtain work in the morning. Frightened, I ran back to the hiding place, followed by others, which resulted in a large gathering of people. A child began to cry.

Out of fear for their lives, the people wanted to kill it in order to save themselves, but the mother did not allow it. Searching for the missing people, policemen came to the house and began knocking on the walls. They heard the child's crying and began shouting: 'There are Jews here!' They began smashing the wall with axes and after breaking through, they began beating the people and chasing them out of the hiding place.

They chased out my brother together with the others. During the attack the policemen shot me in the arm and I played dead. They shouted in broken German that there was only a dead boy left. There were many things in the house; a wealthy Jew had lived there. The policemen found valuables there, and they began putting them inside their clothing. Searching for gold, they poured out a sack of peas onto me, and I fainted.

I came to because a cat was licking the blood off me; I pushed it away. Outside you could hear Germans talking. One of them said that today was Saturday, so I realized that I had lain there for five whole days. I had to get out of there: I was very thirsty. In one house I found several eggs and a bottle of liquid, but my hands were shaking so much from weakness that the eggs got smashed. I began drinking from the bottle, but it turned out to be gas. I realized why they had taken me for a dead person when I saw myself in a mirror. My whole face was covered in blood from the wound on my arm. I still managed to find a piece of bread that had been gnawed by rats. I ate it, ignoring the rat smell....

When I entered a house in search of water, from upstairs I heard someone's voice; it was calling to me from the attic, where a man was hiding. I shared the last of my bread with him, and he let me stay with him. Climbing into the attic, we raised the stairs up with us.

His name was Yosyf Smoliar. He had been captured at the very beginning of the action and sent to Piatydni with the first group. There, a German soldier took him and a few other men aside and ordered them to strip naked the people who had been brought to be shot. The Germans did not trust the policemen, believing that they would steal. After the shooting they sent Yosyf and the dead people's belongings to the "red school." After the articles were unloaded, they wanted to drive him back to Piatydni, but Smoliar waited until the policemen looked away and he ran away as fast as he could. He realized that they would never let him leave alive again.

We hid together until the end of the pogrom. It was a large building with an area of 200 meters, opposite the prison. The sound of shots being fired and cries often came from there. Before the action I saw the prison guards: they were policemen.

After the liquidation of the ghetto, I hid in the city center, in one of the Jewish buildings of the former ghetto, which was occupied by a family of Poles, Leon and Zosia Garczynski and their son Casik. This family was from the village of Khmelivka, from where they had fled when the Ukrainians began attacking the Poles. At the time, Poles who were fleeing the Ukrainians were allowed to occupy abandoned Jewish homes. Between the time I began hiding at the Garczynskis on 15 December 1943 and the liberation of the city, I never left the hideout. After all my terrible tribulations, it was better for me there. The Garczynskis took care of us, sharing everything they had with us. We ate mostly potatoes and soup. In Khmelivka they had a nice farm: two horses and a cart and some pigs. Once a week Leon traveled in secret to his farm and brought back food. Once for New Year's, Leon even had meat, which was an extraordinary luxury at the time.

Hiding with me were a woman named Polina, whose husband and two twin sons had been killed by a policeman, and a physician named Azriel Shampan, who had been the director of a hospital in

Poland before the war. When the war broke out in 1939, Azriel fled to Soviet [Ukrainian] territory, to Lokachi, where he worked as a doctor. When the war began, a German officer was seriously wounded during a battle against Soviet troops, and he was brought to occupied Lokachi, where the help of a doctor was sought. They were told about Azriel. When the officer died after being given an injection, the Germans became incensed: 'What kind of doctor are you? Maybe you're not a doctor! Show us your papers!' And then it was determined that he was a Jew....

They accused him of doing something deliberately so that the officer would die, and ordered a soldier to shoot him. As Azriel was being led into the woods, the doctor, who was fluent in German, begged the soldier not to kill him. He [the soldier] told him to run away to the forest while he shot into the air, pretending to escape. After his escape, Azriel came to Khmelivka, to the Garczynski family, where he hid from the first days of the occupation, and later, when they were escaping from there, they moved him to Volodymyr, even though they themselves were in danger. Practically the entire street knew that a Jew was hiding at the Garczynskis; they were Poles, but no one betrayed us.

After the war, I found Azriel in Tel-Aviv, and he was in constant contact with our rescuers. Thanks to his efforts, in 1993 Leon and Zofia Garczynski were awarded the title "Righteous among the Nations." They were illiterate villagers who did not know how to read or write, but, as it turned out, this does not determine the measure of a person. Azriel Shampan died at the age of 98.

Leon Garczynski said that in the summer of 1944, shortly before the city was liberated, many times he saw Soviet POWs under convoy dragging corpses out of the prison courtyard, stacking them behind the wall, and burning them on bonfires. I do not know how many of them there were or who these murdered people were.

We only left our hiding place two days after the city was liberated—on 22 July 1944. We did not know that the city had already been liberated by Soviet troops. I was dressed in rags, and soldiers on the road who spotted me thought I was mentally ill, but when we began speaking Yiddish, they thought we were Germans and were ready to shoot. Then we began speaking Russian to them: "Don't shoot, we are Jews!"...

The Catastrophe That Befell the Jews of Volodymyr-Volynsky District

Jewish child survivors after the city's liberation, 1945. Seated from right: Reuven Mibab; David (surname unknown); Yosef Raisfeld (brother of Eliezer); a girl who had lost her parents and lived with the Mibab family; Itsyk Kiper, brother of Menashe Kiper; Peretz Mibab, brother of Reuven Mibab. Standing from right: unidentified boy who was saved by a Ukrainian family; Itzhak Berger, brother of Yaacov Berger (Harari). Photo courtesy of Moshe Margalit.

Moshe Margalit

After I arrived in Palestine, for a long time I could not talk about the Holocaust. You may wonder why. The point is that when I talked about what had happened to the Jews there, people did not believe me and looked at me as though I were mentally ill. Normal people could not imagine that something like that could have happened. Even my own sister did not believe me! My memories of Volodymyr were so painful that I tried to forget everything that I had experienced there, and I even avoided telling my own children about it. For some time I did not admit that I had been born there. It was only later that the whole world began to realize the scale of the crime that had been committed by the Nazis and their accomplices.

At the war criminals trial where I appeared as a witness, Gebietskommissar Westerheide (b. 1908) recounted his life. He had lived with his father in northern Africa. After his father died, he returned to Germany, where he worked in a textile plant. In 1927, he met some members of a branch of a Nazi organization, the name of which is translated as "Steel Helmet." He did not have any special education. In 1937 he enlisted in the army and was a Sub-Officer [*Unteroffizier*]. By this time he was already personally acquainted with Rosenberg, Germany's minister of ideology,[10] who in the first week of the war offered him the post of Gebietskommissar in Volodymyr-Volynsky. And although Westerheide refused, he insisted that this was an order of the party. That is how Westerheide ended up here. He stated that during the first "action" he was absent from the city, but even if that were true, it does not mean that these killings could have been prepared without his knowledge, participation, and direction, like the other two "actions" as well.

Zelle personally killed Jews, and Westerheide systematically organized the mass killings and directed this process, but it was impossible to prove anything because those who had witnessed this were already dead by that time. Obviously, this allowed the court to hand down a decision about their innocence. Only horrible memories remained,

---

10 Alfred Rosenberg was one of the main authors of key Nazi ideological creeds, including the Nazis' racial theory, persecution of the Jews, and *Lebensraum*. In July 1941 he was appointed Reichsminister for the Occupied Eastern Territories.

which were transmitted from person to person and lived on in the memory of relatives and friends."

MYKHAIL (MOTL) BASS'S ACCOUNT

I was born in 1926 in the Polish city of Volodymyr-Volynsky; this was Polish territory at the time. My father's name was Eli (Illia); he was a believer and a highly educated person; he taught Hebrew at the Talmud-Torah, whose building is still standing today, and he was a member of the Mizrachi organization. He followed all the Jewish traditions, attended synagogue, and prayed. His mother's name was Zlata (née Pomerantz). She was a housewife, like the majority of women in Jewish families. I had three sisters: Shulamit, Pesl, and Sarah.

We lived on Sukenych Street, which led to the wall in the vicinity of Pidzamche Street. All this was the Jewish quarter with wooden, one-story houses.

Mykhail Bass lives in the city of Holon (Israel). From the Bass family archive.

Located on Ivan Franko Street (formerly Copernicus Street) were the youth organizations Hashomer hatsair and Brit-ha-Chayal, of which [the latter] my uncle was a member. On Pidzamche Street was a club that belonged to the Akiba youth organization, which I attended. We heard lectures with Zionist content there, and played table tennis. The TOZ [collective farm] organization was located on Shukhevych

Street, the present site of the infectious diseases hospital. There were two Jewish baths with mikvahs in the city: one on Kovelska Street, where the new marketplace is today (the building was reconstructed as a store), the second on Shevchenko Street (former Koliiova Street), which is now the building of the ZhEK [Housing Office]. Before the war a third was being built; today this building houses the editorial offices of the newspaper Slovo pravdy [The Word of Truth].

I remember well the beginning of the Great Patriotic War,[11] when the Germans bombed the city center on the very first day, and by Monday the Jewish wood houses, which surrounded the rampart of the old town, had practically all burned down, including our house. Our family was left homeless, wearing just the clothes in which *we were standing.*

*The city was o*ccupied by the fascists. A German hospital was set up in a building at 10 S. Bandera Street, and the Gestapo headquarters were at 17 Ustyluzka Street. Roundups of Jews began in the first days. Mostly men were captured; they were killed in the courtyard of the prison behind the rampart.

The ghetto began to be built in April 1942. Part of the city was enclosed by a barbed-wire fence three meters high, and there were two gates: the east one on Lutska Street and the west one on Ustyluzka Street, at the corner of Soborna Street.

The ghetto contained not just Jews from Volodymyr; with me were also people from Porytsk and the surrounding villages. There was starvation from the very beginning. You risked your life clambering through the fence and bartering your remaining possessions for potatoes and other vegetables.

A Judenrat was organized, which was in charge of dispatching Jews to perform labor for the Germans. The last head of the Judenrat, L. Kudysh, was killed by the Germans at the very beginning of the third "action."

At first I worked on laying the Berky-Vinnytsia cable, and then I was sent with four other boys to groom the horses of the SS men and the mounted police.

---

11   The Soviet nomenclature for the Second World War—*Translator's note.*

In August 1942, a group of Jews was sent to dig pits outside the city. No one knew why this was being done; there were rumors that they were for us, but how could one believe this?

The first "action" to destroy the Jews began on 1 September. People were loaded onto trucks that were standing near the western gate of the ghetto. The first to be destroyed were the Judenrat and the Jewish police that controlled order in the ghetto; they were no longer needed.

My family and I hid in an attic. The pogrom lasted fifteen days, but they did not find us. By a miracle I succeeded in fleeing to a village to a Ukrainian acquaintance, who sheltered me for some time; I helped him around the farm. But my parents remained in the ghetto.

The second "action" began on 13 November 1942. During this second action, my parents and sister Sarah hid in the ghetto, in the very center of the city, in a two-story building owned by the Jew Lymonnyk (today a monument to soldiers and partisans stands in this place, which is the main square of the city), but they were discovered and, as people told me later, they were shot around 3:00 p.m. on 26 November 1942 on the premises of the prison; they had been told this by the person who had done this: a German officer of the Field Gendarmerie whose surname was Schach. My sisters Shulamit and Pesl managed to escape.

The only Jews who remained alive were those who had a specialty that was useful to the Germans; they were issued an *Ausweis* (identification) and resettled in a third ghetto. A new Judenrat was created. Death awaited us every minute in the ghetto. People had nothing to eat; they could not endure and died of hunger and cold before the eyes of their relatives.

My sisters were in the third ghetto because they were seamstresses. In December 1943, I visited them and stayed the night, but that very night the Germans carried out another pogrom, the third "action" to liquidate the Jews. That is how I became trapped. My sisters hid in the cellars, and I, along with other Jews, spent eleven days in the hideout until 24 December. The conditions we found ourselves in were horrible, and it was only the desire to live that compelled us to stay there practically without food and water. It was very damp, and condensation accumulated on the floor; to quell our thirst we sucked it through a handkerchief. Darkness, cramped conditions....When I could no longer endure this I decided to leave and, not knowing what awaited me, I made my way outside. I realized that I could be captured at any moment and this would be the end of my life.

I found shelter and hid in a Polish colony in the vicinity of Bilozovshchyna, a hamlet on the outskirts of the city, near Kovel, with the family of a Ukrainian named Mykola Oberuk; his wife Kasia was a Pole. My two sisters came here on 1 January 1944, and in January 1944 I left this place and ended up with Polish partisans, pretending I was a Pole. That is how I was lucky enough to survive all three pogroms and live to see the city liberated.

In June 1944, our unit merged with Soviet army units, and I was mobilized at once. I witnessed the victory over the Nazis near Prague, although the war did not end for me here. Our unit was deployed to the east, where it fought in the war against Japan.

My mother had three brothers, all of whom perished. One of them was taken into the Polish army in 1939; he ended up in German captivity and was sent to a Jewish camp, where he died. The two other brothers were killed in Piatydni....

It was only in 1948 that I returned to my native city, where I worked all my life in commerce; for many years I was the director of the main department store.

In 1979 Aron Babukh, who had also survived the Holocaust, and I appeared as witnesses at the trial of Gebietskommissar Westerheide and J. Altvater, which took place in the FRG [Federal Republic of Germany]. To obtain our testimony, we were invited to the prosecutor's office in the city of Lutsk. It is a crying shame and highly unjust that the court did not find them guilty of the mass killings of the Jews of our city.

In December 1994, I left for Israel to live with my daughter Tetiana, but I cannot live without this city and every year I come here, where everything is near and dear to me. This is where my other daughter, Zoia, and my grandchildren and great-grandchildren live."

Righteous Among the Nations

Whosoever saves a single life, saves an entire universe.
Mishnah, Sanhedrin, 4:5

Rescue those who are being taken away to death; hold back those who are stumbling to the slaughter, Oh hold them.
Proverbs 24:11

Despite the prohibition and mortal risk to their lives, many Ukrainians and Poles hid Jews who were doomed to die. Without a doubt, they are the same kind of heroes as those who fought with weapons in hand, because every minute they were risking not only their own lives but the lives of their children and families.

There are cases of rescuers paying with their lives for their efforts to save Jews. Volodia (Vladek), a resident of the village of Ostrovok, lived alone. He sheltered a family of Jews for an entire year. By the spring of 1944, the SD took away the Jews and the owner of the house.[1]

After the war, rescuers were awarded the title of "Righteous Among the Nations" (Hebrew, *Chasidei Umot ha Olam*). Israel's parliament awards this title to people who saved Jews during the Holocaust. The awarding of this title is a very complicated procedure requiring weighty evidence and eyewitness statements. That is why,

---

1 Tsaruk, "Holhofa nad Luhoiu."

unfortunately, few people have earned the right to receive this title. Not everyone who was saved during the Holocaust lived to see victory, and not all people who were rescued later managed to find their rescuers. Not all rescuers lived long enough to be found.

Ukraine has the fourth-largest number of Righteous Among the Nations—after Poland, the Netherlands, and France, although it might very well hold first place. It was not possible to study this question in the Ukrainian SSR or any of the other Soviet republics; in these places the Holocaust was deliberately ignored. Associating with foreigners, one risked being persecuted by the KGB. Thus, Ukrainian Jews who had immigrated to the West could not freely visit their fatherland and find their rescuers. These titles began to be awarded in Ukraine after the Iron Curtain fell in 1991, by which time not many participants of those events were still alive. Before that year, only a handful of such titles had been bestowed.

Ukraine has the title of "Righteous of Ukraine," which is conferred by the Council of Nationalities of Ukraine on the basis of eyewitness testimonies and documents.

In contrast to those who collaborated with the occupiers (unfortunately, there were some), the Righteous Among the Nations and the Righteous of Ukraine represent the true face of the Ukrainian people. Without a doubt, they are its finest representatives.

Among those who have received this high honor are several residents of the city who offered assistance and shelter to the doomed Jews of Volodymyr-Volynsky. They are:

Mykola Mykhailovych Vavrysevych, his wife Maria Adamivna, and their sons Mykhailo and Mykola;

Oleksandr and Solomeia Diachuk and their children Pavlo and Maria (Otsaliuk);

Klavdiia Danylivna Polishchuk;

Leon and Zofia Garczynski;

Anatolii and Kateryna Lipiński and their children Iryna and Rostyslav;

Omelian Petrovych and Ustymiia (Epistymiia) Vakulivna Fisiuk;

Olha Pylypivna and Serhii Tykhonovych Miaskovsky and their children Halyna (Filatova) and Yurii;

Franciszek and Hanna Strojvons;

Bronisława Ziental and her daughter Irena (Yakir).

These Great Individuals deserve to have the stories of their feats described in greater detail.

This is what the Vavrysevych brothers, Mykola and Mykhailo, recounted: "One day our mother Maria Vavrysevych was walking past the ghetto enclosure, in the vicinity of today's School No. 1. From behind the barbed wire, a Jewish woman spoke to her; obviously, she knew her because she called her by name. She asked her to take her middle daughter to her house. "We will all die here. Take her, she is blonde, she looks like a Ukrainian girl, let her be a living monument above our common grave!"

The Jewish woman was poorly dressed; next to her stood two little girls and both of them were weeping bitterly, probably realizing that they were seeing each other for the last time. The mother passed the little girl through the barbed wire into Maria Vavrysevych's outstretched hands. "Goodbye, our Fania!" wept the mother and the sisters.

Maria took the little girl by the hand and moved quickly away from the fence. The little girl Fania was twelve years old. She began living with our family like an adopted daughter. One day, German officers came to the owner of the house. The housewife prepared lunch, and Fania brought the food to the table for the officers. They did not recognize that she was a Jew.

From time to time, fugitives from the ghetto came to the Vavrysevych house and asked for shelter. Five of them were in the cellar for seven days, and seven others lived in the house until the city was liberated from fascist occupation.

Mykola Vavrysevych recalls:

> Our house was large; we dug a hideout under the house, which was divided into two sections. Leading to this hiding place was an entrance from an unoccupied room; there was only a large cupboard. In order to enter, you had to push it aside and raise

the carefully camouflaged doors; the first compartment of the hiding place was in there, and from there you could reach the second one. That is where they hid.

One day a policeman came to our house; he probably had some suspicions, or a denunciation had reached him, and he asked if he could live there. My parents realized that they would raise suspicions if they refused, so they agreed. On some pretext we left him alone in the house because we realized that he would want to search it, and when we returned, the policeman said that he had changed his mind. It is difficult to imagine what was going through the minds of the people who were in the hiding place, afraid to breathe, while the policeman was rummaging through the house and studying the empty room with the entrance to the hiding place.

Mykola and Maria Vavrysevych rescued twelve people. Eleven other Jews were given assistance, which helped save their lives.

This is the complete list of the Jews who were rescued by the Vavrysevych family, according to data compiled by Yad Vashem: Leon Berger; Avraam Roiter; Tonia Zuberman; Chenia Stein; Shoshana Bergman (Stein); Klara Roiter; Frida Weinberg; Nechama Singer Ariel; Ida Ivri; Ivri (first name unknown); Ivri (first name unknown); Weinberg (first name unknown); Arie Hemulka; Irka Roiter; Rachel Singer; Elia Borenstein; Klara Borenstein; Raia Borenstein; Reizl Stein; Beila Rokhvarger; Roza Rokhvarger; Berberova (first name unknown); and Henek Berberov.

Later, all these people immigrated to various countries, and their subsequent lives followed different paths. Rukhtsia Singer lives in Brooklyn, New York, where she is a doctor, and Aron Borenstein lives in Australia. The following reside in Israel: Freida Migdal; Leon Berger, who became a writer; Motel Zuberman, Arie Hemulka; Tonia Zuberman; Avraam Roiter; and Klara Roiter. Unfortunately, there is no information on the subsequent fate of some of the other people who were rescued. The rescued individuals remember their rescuers, correspond with them, and invite them to visit. If some of the rescued are no longer alive, it is their children who correspond. They do not forget and are helping.

Thanks to the efforts of the Jewish Council of Ukraine and the foundation "Memory of Babi Yar," on 27 January 2010, International Holocaust Remembrance Day, President Viktor Yushchenko of Ukraine signed the decree "On Conferring State Awards of Ukraine." The decree states that Righteous among the World and Righteous of Ukraine are to be awarded medals "For Bravery," third degree, "for bravery and self-sacrifice demonstrated during the years of the Great Patriotic War in rescuing individuals of Jewish nationality from the fascist genocide, preserving the memory of Holocaust victims." Among the ten residents of the Volyn region who received these medals are the Vavrysevych brothers, Mykola and Mykhailo.

Mykola Mykhailovych Vavrysevych (1891–1978) and his wife Maria Adamivna. Photo courtesy of Mykola Vavrysevych.

Mykola Mykolaiovych Vavrysevych. Photo courtesy of Mykola Vavrysevych.

Certificate of honor awarded to Mykola and Maria Vavrysevych and their two sons Mykhailo and Mykola.

Article in the New York Times *published on 28 November 1997 about the Vavrysevych brothers' reunion with Nechama Ariel in the USA.*

At the reception held at the Ukrainian Consulate in New York City in 1997. Second from left: Mykola Vavrysevych; second from right: Mykhailo Vavrysevych; in center: Ambassador of Ukraine to the United Nations Hennadii Udovenko. Photo courtesy of Mykola Vavrysevych.

The Vavrysevych family kept Mykola's writings, including the text of a play that he wrote in 1944, after the city was liberated. It is called *The Fascist Ghetto*, and even though this is a literary work first and foremost, it also features a description of events based on the accounts of its direct participants, the prisoners of the Volodymyr-Volynsky ghetto.

In the introduction, the author writes that before the city was liberated, the Germans tried to cover up the traces of their crimes by blowing up the mass graves in Piatydni. He also talks about the Jews from the last ghetto, who were shot in an area situated four kilometers from the city, near the village of Falemychi; their bodies were burned in that place. As far back as 1944, Mykola Vavrysevych had begun insisting on the need for the Soviet state to honor the memory of the innocent victims, but it took forty-five years for this to happen, and then only under pressure from the international community.

The medal awarded to Mykola Vavrysevych, recognizing him as Righteous Among the Nations.

KATERYNA PETRIVNA LIPIŃSKA

The Lipiński family lived in the vicinity of Ustyluh, where the Luha River flows into the Buh. They owned quite a large farm.

Henry Orenstein describes the story of his rescue by Kateryna Lipińska in his book:

> Soon we realized that we were near Lipińska's, whose son I used to tutor; Sam and Felek knew Mrs. Lipińska, too. It was almost daybreak. We had to find a place to hide for that day, and so we cautiously entered the Lipiński yard. The house was on the edge of a property of about two and a half acres, with vegetable and flower gardens in front. Farther down was a barn with a cow, and a stall where Mr. Lipiński kept a horse. On the opposite side of the path, facing the stall, was a haystack. Behind it was a fruit garden with raspberry bushes and other fruit trees and bushes. The hay was packed tightly between four poles about twelve or thirteen feet high, which formed a square, each side seven or eight feet long. A tile roof rested on top of the four poles, and a ladder leaning against the hay led to the top of the haystack.... We climbed the ladder to the top of the stack and wearily lay down on the hay.
>
> Soon we saw Mrs. Lipińska come out of the house and walk toward us. She was a woman of about forty with blue eyes, light brown hair, and a round, pleasant face. Cautiously I called out: "Mrs. Lipińska!" She was startled but calm. "How many of you are there?" she asked. Father, Sam, and Felek raised their heads so that she could see the four of us. She nodded, and told us to be very quiet and not come down, because the SS and the Ukrainian police were searching all over town for Jews. She said she would come back later, and went into the barn.
>
> At least she hadn't thrown us out; probably she would let us stay until nightfall. But we were worried about her husband,

whom the Germans had appointed mayor of Uściług; to what extent was he cooperating with them?

In mid-morning Mrs. Lipińska left the house. A few hours later she returned, went into the house, and came out to us carrying a bag full of food: potatoes, soup, bread, butter, and milk. This we had not expected; what a wonderful woman! She came back to collect the dishes and warned us again to be very careful. Her husband and children must not see us, she said. Her children might say something to their friends, and her husband might not be willing to run the frightful risk of having Jews found on their property.

No wonder. In the afternoon a sound truck drove by, blaring out a warning: Anyone caught hiding Jews, or helping them in any way, would be summarily shot. If he or she had a family, they also would be killed. It took a very special person to run this kind of risk. Mrs. Lipińska knew very well that she was endangering not only her own life, but also the lives of her son, daughter, and husband.

Those were wild times, savage, merciless. It meant nothing to the SS to take a life, Jewish or gentile. The order was "Kill all Jews," and anybody who stood in the way was eliminated as a matter of course. Nevertheless, Mrs. Lipińska never hesitated. It was clear to us that she was prepared to do whatever was necessary to save us, regardless of the risk.[2]

Until 30 September 1942, the Orensteins hid in the haystack, and Kateryna Lipińska gave them food and water, and took care of them as best she could. Meanwhile, she had made contact with the Orensteins' relatives in Hrubeshiv, where no pogroms had taken place yet, and she organized their passage across the Buh River. For some reason, the Germans were controlling the old border that led to the Buh. The first attempt to cross the river failed, and a second attempt was possible only ten days later, when every minute of their stay at the Lipińskis could

---

2 Orenstein, *I Shall Live*, 96–97.

have been fatal. Leiba and his son Felix ended up in a camp in Poland and were shot, but the two brothers, Sam and Henry, survived and later immigrated to the USA. Sam died in 1990. Henry, who lives in the township of Verona, New Jersey, is an entrepreneur, inventor, and self-made millionaire.

The Lipiński family also rescued Matilda Topolia-Hertel, who also lives in the USA, as mentioned earlier.

On 14 May 1989, a tree was planted in honor of the Lipiński family on the Mount of Remembrance in Jerusalem, in the Avenue of the Righteous established at Yad Vashem, the World Center for Holocaust Research, Documentation, Education and Commemoration, and a plaque was installed with the inscription, "Ekaterina Lipinskaja, USSR (Poland)." A commemorative plaque in their honor was installed on the Wall of Honor. Since Mrs. Lipińska was in poor health, the medal was sent by mail to her. It bears the following inscription: "Whosoever saves a single life, saves an entire universe," which appears as the epigraph at the beginning of this chapter.

Kateryna Lipińska and her daughter Iryna, Righteous Among the Nations. Photo courtesy of A. Kupriichuk.

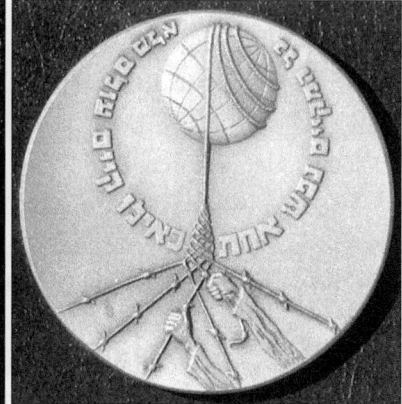

Kateryna Lipińska's medal recognizing her as Righteous Among the Nations.

Memorial plaque near the tree planted in honor of Kateryna Lipińska, Righteous Among the Nations, Jerusalem (Israel). Photo courtesy of A. Kupriichuk.

The cover of Henry Orenstein's book I Shall Live, in which the author inscribed a dedication in Polish to his rescuer: "Dear Mrs. Lipińska! Thank you for everything that you did for us. Hugs and kisses, Henek."

Henry Orenstein and Matilda Topolia-Hertel next to the tree planted in honor of the Lipiński family, Jerusalem (Israel). Photo courtesy of A. Kupriichuk.

From 29 April to 6 May 1991, Mykola Vavrysevych, Jr. and Kateryna Lipińska's daughter Iryna were in Israel as part of a twenty-three-person Ukrainian delegation invited by Yad Vashem and the foundation "Remembrance of the Victims of Fascism in Ukraine." As members of the delegation, they met with the president of Israel, who thanked them for saving Jews and wished them health and happiness and peace for independent Ukraine. The delegation visited Israel's parliament, the Knesset, where the guests were greeted on the occasion of Ukraine's independence. "You will be wealthy because you like to work, like we do," the Israeli MPs declared.

Henry Orenstein, who was quite well-off and thus able to provide material assistance to the Lipiński family, did so wholeheartedly. However, receiving packages from abroad was a risky proposition in Soviet times, and the KGB carefully monitored individuals who had contacts with foreigners. This explains the publication in the newspaper *Slovo pravdy* of a lengthy article, in which the well-informed author enumerated the contents of the packages that had been sent to this family of rescuers. The article also condemned Iryna, a schoolteacher by profession, for discrediting Soviet teachers. Naturally, Iryna lost her job as a result of the article. A key role in this was played by someone's jealousy, because few Soviet citizens—including the wives of Communist Party officials—had an opportunity to acquire beautiful, Western-made clothing. This tense situation greatly affected Iryna's health. She became ill, and her illness later hastened her premature death.

THE ACCOUNT OF HALYNA SERHIIVNA FILATOVA (MIASKOVSKA), RIGHTEOUS AMONG THE NATIONS[3]

My family lived in a house that is still standing at 32 Pavlov Street. I lived with my mother Olha Pylypivna Miaskovska and my brother Yurii. The Ukrainian and Polish police forces as well as the German gendarmerie all functioned in the city at the same time. The latter

---

3   Interview with Halyna Filatova recorded by Volodymyr Muzychenko.

cooperated in turn with one or the other, depending on the villages that they planned to loot: they attacked Ukrainian ones with Polish policemen, and for attacks on Polish ones they took Ukrainians with them. People are saving their lives, but they are confiscating food, poultry, and cattle for meat; if it is convenient, they set fire to the nearest house. However, practically from the very first days the occupiers singled out Jews from among the local population and enclosed them in a specially created ghetto. At first they drove them out to work, and later—to be shot.

The name of the Jewish girl who was hiding in our house was Pepa [Paulina] Cohen. She and her family had been hiding in a house owned by a family whose surname was Kudril, which moved to Poland after the war. They were storing all their precious belongings in the house. Very likely, the Kudrils' desire to get their hands on them spurred them to denounce them to the Germans. By some miracle our Pepa was saved.

They were taken away in the winter. At that moment she came out of the house to go to the toilet, where she waited while her parents were being led out. She came to our house to hide straight from Sahaidachnyi Street, where her family was living. My mother took her in not for any reward, not for money, but because Christian custom dictates this. There was a commandant's office operating in our house, and the girl lived in the cellar. She only came out at night, once everyone was asleep, in order to wash, change her underclothing, and do some laundry. From our house she was able to make her way to Poland and then to Israel. We received a letter from her saying that she was alive and had gotten married. She said that she very much wanted to help us because her conscience was bothering her that she could not repay us with anything. She suggested that we take what remained in the Kudril house, and the piano that had been left behind in the home of the Voitovskys, who lived near Kryva Street. Mama told me to write back to her saying that we had not sheltered her for material gain, but had acted as Christians because she needed help. May the Lord recompense us for that. And she ordered me not to tell anyone about this act. I tried to keep this promise, but a medal arrived out of the blue."

In 1988 Halyna Filatova and her brother Yurii, who lives in Kyiv, were recognized as Righteous Among the Nations. This title was posthumously awarded to their mother Olha Miaskovska.

On 26 September 2008, Ukraine's president signed the decree "On Conferring State Awards of Ukraine," naming those who were recognized as Righteous among the Nations and Righteous of Ukraine—a total of 171 individuals. Among those awarded the medal "For Merit," third degree, is Halyna Filatova. This extraordinarily modest woman donated her medal to the local history museum in order to preserve the memory of those terrible times. Furthermore, she says that the efforts to save the Jewish girl were all her parents' doing. Today her medal is part of the museum's collection.

That period was very complex, and the impact of settling political and territorial "accounts" on the lives of ordinary people is generally known. Halyna Filatova did not have a carefree childhood, as it was marked by the kinds of problems with which Ukrainian adolescents are completely unfamiliar today. As a thirteen-year-old girl during the occupation, Halyna, who had already snatched her father away from a machine gun aimed by an SS soldier who wanted to shoot an innocent man for no reason whatsoever, could not be—and was not—an indifferent observer when faced with the prospect of saving completely innocent people.

Regrettably, Halyna Filatova died in July 2011, before this book was published.

The distinctions awarded to people recognized as Righteous among the Nations and Righteous of Ukraine are, in fact, a gesture of recognition of their feats on the part of our state. It is a pity that such awards are not accompanied by any material benefits. After all, former ghetto prisoners are equated with combatants and receive appropriate benefits. Those who rescued them risked no less, and hence they too deserve state support and should obtain status equivalent to that held by combatants.

Olha Pylypivna Miaskovska, her husband Serhii Tykhonovych, and their daughter Halyna. Photo courtesy of Halyna Filatova.

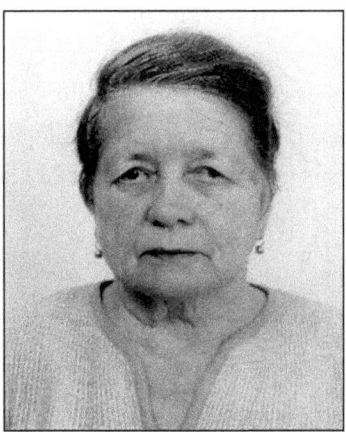

Halyna Serhiivna Filatova (née Miaskovska) (b. 1928).

Pauline Kamm (née Cohen), who was saved by the Miaskovsky family. Photo courtesy of H. Filatova.

OLEKSANDR AND SOLOMEIA DIACHUK[4]

The family of the Christian Evangelical couple Oleksandr and Solomeia Diachuk lived in the village of Sviichiv in the district of Volodymyr-Volynsky. It was a large family with eight children. In March 1943 Hitel (Gitel) Tabak from the village of Oziutychi turned to them for help. This is how their daughter Maria Otsaliuk described these events:

"One day, when I was tending a flock of geese, a beautiful young girl came to our house and asked if my mother was at home. After learning that she was, she asked me to call her, but my mother was tired and told her to come inside the house. Sending the children out, she spoke with her, and when we were getting ready to attend a Christian gathering, she proposed bringing her to the stable, where it was safer; there was a place to hide. That woman, whose name was Gitel, had her

---

4 Interview with Maria Otsaliuk recorded as part of the project "I dai u vichnosti nove im'ia [And Provide a New Name for Eternity]," ATM (Volodymyr, 2007).

family with her: her son Zelik and daughter Roza; there was a man with them: altogether four people. That's how they ended up with us. There was enough food because we had a farm and a field. They helped out on the farm, and in the evenings we shut ourselves up in the house and talked, read, and studied the Holy Scripture. We felt that God would save us.

Maria Oleksandrivna Otsaliuk (née Diachuk), Righteous among the Nations, lives in the USA.

One day they were in the barn when we were not at home, except for my older brother, who suddenly saw some Germans approaching with policemen. My brother was writing something and, holding the pencil, he went into the yard to see them. They asked: "Are there Jews here?" My brother said that he had to tap that pencil on his hand to conceal his trembling hands, but he answered with a question: "Are there any left?" to which they replied that they wanted to look for themselves.

They went and searched the place where we had been hiding them earlier; when my mother had a premonition, she moved them to a different place.

Afterwards they continued to live with us for a long time, more than a year. A hideout was constructed in a pit dug behind the barn, the entrance to which was strewn with leaves, and was invisible. That is how they were saved."

The Diachuk family saved six people: Shymshon Gruber, Semor Tabak, Chaim-Zelig Tabak, Reizl Tabak, Natan Frankfurt, and Gitel Tabak.

On 28 November 2000, Yad Vashem honored Oleksandr and Solomeia Diachuk and their son Pavlo by recognizing them as Righteous Among the Nations. On 27 January 2003 this distinguished title was also conferred on their daughter Maria Otsaliuk.

Oleksandr and Solomeia Diachuk.[5]

---

5   http://www1.yadvashem.org/.

FRANCISZEK AND HANNA STROJVONS AND BRONISŁAWA ZIENTAL AND HER DAUGHTER IRENA YAKIR (NEE ZIENTAL)

The Catholic peasants Franciszek and Hanna Strojvons lived in the village of Vladyslavivka, which was situated twenty kilometers from the city of Volodymyr-Volynsky. During the Nazi occupation, Mr. and Mrs. Strojvons were around thirty-five years old and they were raising three children.

Franciszek and Hanna Strojvons with their son Jan (standing) and daughter Lialia (sitting on Franciszek's lap), Volodymyr-Volynsky, mid-1930s.[6]

In October 1942, Franciszek Strojvons came home with four Jews from Volodymyr-Volynsky: Dr. Tuvia Levit and his wife Rachel, and Dr. Isaak Grinberg and his brother Hryhorii, a lawyer. He had just met them the day before and decided to help these persecuted Jews. After concealing them underneath a layer of straw in his wagon, Franciszek succeeded in bringing them to his house. The couple's

---

6 http://www1.yadvashem.org/yv/ru/righteous/poland/ziental.asp.

home consisted of one room, adjoining which was a pigpen. Next to this was a threshing floor, where a hiding place was made for the Jews under the straw. This is where the Levits and the Grinbergs spent the winter of 1942–43. Despite their terrible poverty, the Strojvons shared their last piece of bread with their secret guests. In order not to starve to death, Hanna was forced to comb through other people's fields for potatoes and beets.

In the spring of 1943, armed Ukrainians began launching attacks on the Poles. People living in villages and hamlets were at particular risk, so Franciszek took his family and "his" Jews and moved to Volodymyr-Volynsky. Unable to find lodgings in the city and having no money to survive, the Strojvons couple was soon forced to go to their relatives in Hrubeshiv, and the Jews had to find another refuge.

Dr. Levit turned for help to Irena Ziental, a young Polish woman who was a nurse in his hospital. Irena instantly agreed to help, and the next day she brought the Levits and the Grinbergs to the home of her parents, Bronisława and Stanisław Ziental. Spotting certain signs, Dr. Tuvia Levit guessed that the Zientals were already hiding Jews, and his guess was confirmed one day when he went down the hatchway into the cellar, where he encountered his acquaintances: Dr. Marian Keitelman and his wife Tilia, Dr. Bernard Torbechko, Froim and Sarah Shrah, and the Pekler couple. All of them had ended up at the Zientals' house at various times and under different circumstances. Bronisława Ziental cooked for everyone, carried out buckets of feces, and took care of them even though she had a sick husband at home who also required attention. Recalling this time twenty years later, she said: "When my strength flagged, I forced myself to think about all the horror that the Jews had experienced in the ghetto, and I would feel better instantly at the thought that I could save at least a few people."

In early 1944 Irena Ziental went to the forest to join the partisans. Her parents moved westward, following in the footsteps of their older daughters. The Strojvons, who had returned from Hrubeshiv, moved into the Zientals' house, where twelve Jews were still living in the cellar. They took care of the people in hiding, who remained there until the city was liberated on 20 July 1944.

After the war, Irena Ziental married a Jewish doctor named Eliahu Yakir, who had spent all the years of the occupation working in the open, passing himself off as a Pole. The couple adopted Eliahu's twelve-year-old niece Miriam, who was saved by a Ukrainian Orthodox priest, Rev. Ihnatii Hrohul, in the city of Dubno. In 1949 they immigrated to Israel, along with Irena's mother Bronisława, who was widowed in 1944.

On 26 November 1968, Yad Vashem conferred the title of Righteous Among the Nations on Franciszek and Hanna Strojvons, Bronisława Ziental, and her daughter Irena Yakir.[7]

Yosyp Ptashnyk, his wife, oldest daughter Nadia (b. 1922), and their three other children lived in the village of Shystiv. For more than a year and a half this family hid two young Jewish couples in a hiding place that could be entered from the barn: the first names of one of the couples are Aba and Mundyk. After the liberation, the NKVD arrested Nadia for allegedly working with the Ukrainian Insurgent Army, and the Ptashnyk family were slated for deportation to Siberia. But the Jews whom they had saved went fearlessly to the NKVD and declared: "How could they have been working with the Ukrainian Insurgent Army, when we were living with them for more than a year and a half and didn't notice anything?" Thanks to their corroborative statements and persistence, the NKVD was forced to release Nadia and stop harassing the Ptashnyk family.[8] There is no information on their subsequent fate, but it is known that they left the country.

The peasant Petro Zasadko lived in the village of Zymno with his wife Olena and daughter Maria (b. 1923). During the second German action, Petro received a visit from a Jew named Froim and his two sons

---

7   Ibid.
8   Tsaruk, "Holhofa nad Luhoiu."

Moishe (b. 1933) and Itsek (b. 1938). They were from Hrubeshiv, but Petro knew them. At night they dug a hideout together with the homeowner. They fashioned an entrance to it from the barn. Then they made an entryway from this hideout into another one and from that one to a third. For more than a year and a half, the father and his sons lived in these three small, damp hiding places until the arrival of the Soviet army. Shortly after the liberation, the Jews moved to Poland, to the city of Hrubeshiv. Froim got married and all traces of him vanished.[9] Unfortunately, Petro and Olena Zasadko have died. It is not known why all contact with the rescuers was lost.

After my articles on the tragic fate of the city's Jews appeared in the press, I was contacted by a resident of our city named Halyna Oleksandrivna Kovalchuk (née Kozlovska, b. 1933). She told me that in 1941–43 a Jewish doctor named Blokh, together with his daughter Frida and son Yurii, were given shelter in her family home (by her father Oleksandr Ivanovych Kozlovsky; and grandfather Yevdokii Ivanovych Stepaniuk), located in a hamlet near the village of Ponychiv in the district of Volodymyr-Volynsky. Before the war, they had lived in a two-story house that still stands today next to the Dormition Cathedral. After some time, her father led the doctor and his children across the Buh River into Polish territory.

After the war (1956–58), Halyna's family received a letter from the Australian Red Cross, informing them that the Jews whom they had rescued were searching for them and wanted to establish contact with them. The letter frightened the Kovalchuk family because the father had just returned from the Stalinist labor camps, and they were afraid of being persecuted by the KGB. Halyna's parents burned the letter and never mentioned another word about this. After reading my published articles, in 2007 she began trying to locate the people whom her parents had saved.

---

9   Ibid.

When I became interested in this question and tried to obtain some information from the long-time residents of this street, I found out that this doctor had visited Volodymyr-Volynsky, where he tried to find his rescuers, but with no success. He even spent the night in the house adjacent to his former home. Unfortunately, he has not been able to locate them.

My articles sparked a reaction from another city resident, Yevheniia Stepanivna Hapko (née Sheptytska). During the war, she lived with her parents, Maria Fomivna and Stepan Antonovych Sheptytsky in the colony of Zaslavska, situated north of Volodymyr-Volynsky. This is her account:

> We had a hideout, and the entryway to it—from the barn—was covered with manure. The barn housed a cow and a horse. The hideout was strewn with straw and covered with sacking. Five Jews—two men and three women—took shelter there. I was a little girl and curious about everything. I would crawl down there; my father would let me down into the hideout. I would sit on their laps. They all lay next to each other. An elderly woman lay near the entryway; next to her were Abram and his wife—I don't remember her name; then Sura [Sarah] Maier, whose father owned a bakery in Volodymyr-Volynsky. There was also Leibko, the brother of Abramov's wife. My mother knew them well. In the daytime they sat in the hideout and came outside only at night. They would come into the house to wash and eat supper. Large pans of food were cooked in our house; my mother often baked bread. In the daytime my father brought food to the hideout for them. It was a very terrible time. The Germans and Vlasovites were swooping down from house to house. One time we saw a taxi coming from the intersection of Dubnytska Street, which drove into our yard: they were Germans. There was so much fear....We

thought they would find the Jews and kill us all. But the Germans took a slaughtered pig and drove off. I don't remember how many Jews stayed with us. When Soviet partisans appeared in Bilyn, they ordered the Poles and Ukrainians to stop killing each other and the Jews. By now it was very dangerous for the Jews in our house; the city was nearby. Early one morning, my father drove them by wagon to Bilyn, where it was safe now. After they left, a woman and a little girl ran to our house asking us to hide them. Mama gave them some bread and showed them the way to Bilyn.

When the Soviet troops liberated us from the Germans, my father and other men were taken to the front. That woman who had come to us with her little girl came to see us and thanked my mother very much for giving them the right advice. They were saved in Bilyn.

Maria Fomivna Sheptytska. Photo courtesy of Ye. Hapko.

Stepan Antonovych Sheptytsky. Photo courtesy of Ye. Hapko.

After the war my father, who was Polish, did not come back home but remained in Poland. Abram, who had sheltered in our home, signed over his house in Poland, in the city of Zamość, to my father. Abram left for America or Israel.

THE ACCOUNTS OF LIUDMYLA STEPANIVNA YEVTOSHUK AND HALYNA ZINOVIIVNA NAZARUK (VILLAGE OF PIATYDNI, DISTRICT OF VOLODYMYR-VOLYNSKY)[10]

During the Great Patriotic War, our grandfather, Omelian Petrovych Fisiuk, who was born in 1903, lived in the village of Khrypalychi, in the district of Volodymyr-Volynsky. He had a wife who was two years younger than he and three children ranging in age from one to fifteen. They farmed: they owned a cow and some pigs, and worked the land; they had vegetable gardens. They were not wealthy and lived modestly. Grandad was literate and he was a church elder; he was tall and physically strong. After the war, when the villages were being enlarged, their house was transferred to the village of Khrypalychi.

Omelian Petrovych and Epistymiia Vakulivna Fisiuk

Grandad recounted that during the war they sheltered Jews who had escaped from the Germans in an effort to escape death. This was in the fall of 1942, after the Jews were shot in Piatydni. One night, someone knocked on our window. When Grandad came outside, he

---

10 This interview was recorded by Volodymyr Muzychenko in August 2011.

saw a man whom he knew well. His name was Lipa Mendelson, and he owned a little shop in downtown Volodymyr. Our grandfather and grandmother were friendly with the Mendelson family: they delivered milk to them in Volodymyr and took payment in kind.

Lipa begged him not to turn him away. He asked for shelter for himself and his three children, and Grandad hid them in the hay in the barn, although this was risky for the entire family. The man swam across the river and brought the children on his back, one by one. They were three boys: the oldest was sixteen and his name was Itzhak (Itsyk); fourteen-year-old Mordechai (Motel); and eleven-year-old Viktor.

We do not know how they managed to escape. The only thing we know is that his wife, the mother of the children who were in hiding with him, was shot together with other Jews in Piatydni during the first pogrom in the ghetto. When their family went into hiding, they quickly ran out of water. The wife wanted to drink badly and, unable to endure her thirst, she went outside. That was when she was captured. She was never seen again.

In the morning Grandad went to the barn, and Lipa asked him for something to eat. Grandad gave them food bit by bit because he was afraid that they would die, they were that worn out by hunger. The children asked for more, but Grandad increased the portions only gradually because he was afraid for their lives.

One day, Omelian Petrovych and Lipa dug a hiding place in the cowbarn, with an exit to the street, in such a way that it was invisible to strangers. Then Omelian made a trapdoor that concealed the entryway to the hideout and scattered snow over it. They hid there for seven whole months.

One day, a German vehicle drove into our yard, and some Germans headed straight for the barn. The Germans were shouting: 'Jude, Jude!' Grandad became so afraid that at first he could not utter a single word. Then, getting a grip on himself, he began saying over and over again that there was no one here. The hiding place was well set up, and they did not find our Jews. Such searches, during which the Germans used metal rods to poke through hay and the soil in yards and barns, took place periodically in other farmyards in the village.

We fed our fugitives by dropping food down into the pit in which they sat. We shared everything that we had with them: potatoes, milk. Once it became colder, Grandad would take the children into the house for the night. These children were so well trained that at the slightest sign of danger they would hide at once. My grandmother was a seamstress, and she sewed clothing for those boys out of old things. That is how they lived in my grandfather's family. Lipa stayed in the hideout the entire time, until the village was liberated by Soviet troops. All of them survived. Lipa and Mordechai settled down in Israel, Itzhak in the USA, and Viktor in England.

After the village was liberated, the front had receded, and the shooting had died down, Lipa left the hideout and thanked Grandad Omelian very sincerely, said goodbye, and went off with his children to seek his fortune.

For a long time my parents did not have any contact with them. When I was in seventh grade, a letter arrived from Lipa, which began with the following words: 'My dear rescuers!' All subsequent letters began with these words. Unfortunately, these letters were not saved. Lipa sent us packages and helped as much as he could. But Grandfather Omelian did not talk about this with anyone; those were uncertain times.

After my grandfather's death, the correspondence stopped, but after some time we were tracked down by his [Lipa's] middle son Mordechai, and since then we have kept in touch with them, mostly by telephone.

In August 2011, Mordechai Mendelson and his family visited Ukraine, including Volodymyr-Volynsky. They prayed at the memorial erected at the site of the mass grave in Piatydni, where his mother lies among the thousands of other innocent victims. He also paid a visit to the family of Omelian Fisiuk's grandchildren. There was a warm reunion marked by embraces and tears.

As a result of everything that he [Mordechai] had experienced, a negative image of most Ukrainians had become imprinted on his consciousness, but this visit changed his attitude. He said: 'After we lost our entire family and so many innocent people perished, and my father, brothers, and I hid in the earth like mice, afraid of people, and not daring to come up to the surface, today, now that I have come here, I see interest and attention paid to me. Very likely much has changed here.'

After Lipa Mendelson's visit to Ukraine in 2012, the news came that Omelian and Epistymiia Fisiuk had been recognized posthumously as Righteous Among the Nations."

Mordechai Mendelson's family with the grandchildren of his rescuers in Volodymyr-Volynsky. Third from left: Halyna Nazaruk; next to her are Mordechai Mendelson and Liudmyla Yevtoshuk.

HERASYM AND NASTIA NESTYRUK (VILLAGE OF PODRUDZE; TODAY: OKHNIVKA)—RESCUED: YOSYF-TZVI EIZENBERG, CHANA EIZENBERG, HERSCHEL ROH, LEAH ROH

The Evangelical Christians Kyrylo and Marta Nestyruk lived in the village of Podrudze with their son Potap. The only Jewish family that lived in Podrudze before the war was the family of Yosyf-Tzvi Eizenberg. The Eizenbergs were friends of the Nestyruks, and their friendship deepened the year that Eizenberg loaned some money to Nestyruk.

The Eizenbergs were allowed to remain in their house until the fall of 1942, but they were forced to sew yellow stars on their clothing, and they were very afraid of leaving the confines of their home.

After learning of the mass destruction of Jews, Eizenberg and his family fled to the forest. Shortly afterwards, they returned to their house, and Yosyf-Tzvi began considering to which of his Ukrainian friends he could turn for shelter. At first he searched for a hiding place in his former clients' homes, but these quests were unsuccessful.

Then, on New Year's Eve 1941-42, it was decided that Eizenberg and his older daughter, thirteen-year-old Chana, would leave in search of shelter, while his wife and their two younger children would remain at home and wait. That rainy night, Yosyf-Tzvi and Chana saw their loved ones for the last time.

While the father and his daughter were looking for a place to shelter, the mother and two children who had remained at home were captured and shot. Meanwhile, Yosyf-Tzvi and Chana, in keeping with their prior arrangement, headed for the Nestyruks in order to prepare a hideout for themselves in a storeroom.

They hid there for several days, and then Kyrylo Nestyruk brought them to the woods, to a little house that he had built for them with his own hands. The orphaned father and daughter hid in this tiny house for a long time. In order to protect his Jewish friends from the cold, Nestyruk brought them sheepskin coats, and to protect them from wolves, he gave them staves. He supplied them with food, and sometimes he brought his son Potap, who was Chana's age.

During one of these visits, Potap spotted two suspicious-looking people hanging around the Aizenberg's house. They became afraid and decided to move their friends to the house of Potap's grandfather, Herasym Nestyruk.

Herasym and his wife Nastia also lived in the village of Podrudze. As of September 1942, Herschel Roh and his sister Leah, who were from another village, were hiding in their house. In order to conceal them, Herasym built a hideout in his barn. Aizenberg and his daughter were concealed in this hiding place, even though it was very cramped.

In the spring of 1944, the Nestyruks heard a rumor that the Germans would soon be arriving in the village. One night, Herasym drove the four people in his care into the woods and built them a campsite, where they hid until the danger passed.

Then the brother and sister returned to Herasym's house, and Kyrylo Nestyruk once again took Yosyf-Tzvi and Chana into his house. Until the liberation in 1944, they hid in the small storeroom adjoining the Nestyruks' house, where the householders had once kept chickens.

During this entire time, Kyrylo's wife Marta took an active part in saving the Jews. The Rohs soon left their hiding place and went to the woods, where Herasym helped them build a mud hut. Despite their difficult material circumstances, Herasym and his wife continued to feed Herschel and Leah Roh until the liberation and, whenever necessary, brought them fresh clothing. After the liberation, they immigrated to the USA. In the 1990s, they reestablished contact with Potap Nestyruk.

On 19 January 1995, Yad Vashem recognized Kyrylo and Marta Nestyruk, their son Potap Nestyruk, and Herasym and Nastia Nestyruk as Righteous Among the Nations.[11]

YERMOLAI AND YEFIMIIA LIASHCHUK AND THEIR DAUGHTER NADIA NIFAK (NÉE LIASHCHUK)

Yermolai and Yefimiia Liashchuk were farmers who lived in the village of Khotiachiv. In 1941, when the German authorities temporarily allowed the Jewish population to perform labor for local residents, Yermolai befriended Esther Vorzel, who lived in nearby Ustyluh.

The Liashchuks hired Esther to work in their fields and around the farm. As payment, she received enough food to feed herself and her family that was living in the Ustyluh ghetto. On 31 August 1942, all the Jews were ordered to return to the city, from where they were brought to the ghetto in Volodymyr-Volynsky.

---

11 http://www1.yadvashem.org/

Esther met her sister Leah, who was working in the neighboring village, and together they went to the assembly point for Jews. En route, a local resident warned the girls that the Germans were planning to kill all the Jews the next day, and, horror-struck, they returned to the Liashchuks' house.

Yermolai and Yefimiia took pity on the sisters and built them a hideout in the hayloft. In early 1943, they were joined by their brother Feivel. They remained hidden until April 1943, when one of the neighbors noticed Feivel helping Liashchuk on his farm.

Then Feivel, Esther, and Leah decided to return to Ustyluh, where there was a Jewish work camp. The first to return was Feivel, but when his sisters came to the city the next day, they were told that he had been captured and shot.

The Vorzel sisters decided to return to the Liashchuks, who concealed them in the same hiding place. When searches of this locale became more frequent, the girls were moved into the field, where they hid inside haystacks. While Esther and Leah hid in the field, every night the Liashchuks, mainly fifteen-year-old Nadia, would bring them food and everything else that they needed.

When the front line came very close, Liashchuk hid the Vorzel sisters once again in his house, where they remained until the Red Army liberated these territories in June 1944.

In the late 1940s, the Vorzel sisters left Ukraine and later immigrated to Israel. In 1990, they reestablished contact with Nadia Liashchuk, whose parents were no longer alive.

On 22 January 1992 Yad Vashem recognized Yermolai and Yefimiia Liashchuk and their daughter Nadia Nifak as Righteous Among the Nations.[12]

∽ ∽ ∽

The Righteous Among the Nations in Volodymyr-Volynsky include the Czech couple Wojtech Kovar and his wife Mari, who

---

12 Ibid.

rescued Anna Dub. This high distinction was conferred on them on 25 June 2000.

This title was also bestowed on Maria Lytvynova and her daughter Helena Dvorovska, who saved Netel and Pola Borenstein.

∽∽∽

In communicating with long-time residents of the city, I reached the conclusion that we are not aware of all cases of Ukrainians and Poles saving Jews. The situation was not that straightforward. This is how I. Vozniuk, who worked for the police in those days, describes the events that were taking place during this period:

> On the corner of the street near our house lived a Jew named Pinchas. When the Germans came to take them to the ghetto, his wife jumped into the well and stayed there, despite being all bruised up. My parents had dug that well together with their Jewish neighbors on the boundary between our two properties. Later my mother and a [male] cousin dragged her out (and organized other people's help), although she asked people not to let it be known that she was hiding there. My mother washed her in her house, and later [the Jewish woman] left us and hid in the raspberry bushes in a neighbor's yard. My mother brought her food there. Then she went away somewhere. People said that this woman's daughter survived and left.

It is known that Teklia Ustymivna Vozniuk, a resident of the village of Zarichchia, hid five Jews in her house. She revealed this to the journalist Yakov Tsaruk, who later spoke with one of the rescued individuals (who later immigrated to Australia) in Novovolynsk.

∽∽∽

The Jews have a symbol known as *Etz chaim*, which means "tree of life." The Jewish symbol of life is the tree. Thus, it is no accident that trees are planted in the Avenue of the Righteous at Yad Vashem in Jerusalem in honor of those individuals who rescued even one Jew. Next to every tree is a marker inscribed with the name of the rescuer, e.g., "Lipińska, Kateryna, Ukraine," "Vavrysevych, Mykola, Ukraine." Nearby is the Wall of Honor, on which are memorial plaques inscribed with the names of families that saved Jews.

The search for and recognition of people who merit the title Righteous Among the Nations continue to this day. Upon the presentation of eyewitness testimonies, this title is conferred even posthumously. Their memory is sacred to the Jewish people.

A very interesting case of a Jew being saved, which is connected with the city of Volodymyr-Volynsky, is described by Alan Slepo in his fact-based, Russian-language short story "Syn trekh narodov" (A Son of Three Nations[13]). In it the author describes how one August day in 1941 a German captain-intendant (quartermaster) named Ludwig Türner, who was responsible for the timely delivery of food to the front, was traveling from Rivne through Manevychi. By the side of the road near the temporary Jewish camp he saw a naked little boy who was half-dead. Realizing the risk he was taking, he picked up the Jewish boy and brought him to the home of a peasant woman named Olha Peredun. He told her that the little boy was a *Volksdeutscher*, left her several cases of German food and money, asked her to take care of the child, and promised to come back for him. When the unconscious boy came to, she realized who he was. His name was Samuil Alper.

She raised him like her own son together with her daughter Oksana, and gave him a new name: Petro Peredun. Türner kept his word, and after sustaining a severe injury and recovering in a hospital in 1943, he managed to find them in Volodymyr-Volynsky, where the woman had moved after their village was burned down and its inhabitants expelled for collaborating with the partisans.

---

13 Jewish, Ukrainian, and German.

Ludwig Türner requested an audience with Colonel Lemke, the military commandant of Volodymyr-Volynsky, and with surprising ease obtained his permission to bring out his adopted child who, as he claimed, was a Volksdeutscher whose parents had been killed by the partisans. He gave the boy a third name, Günther Türner, and took him to Munich, where, concealing the boy's origins, he raised him until the victory over the Nazis. For years he kept in touch with Olha Peredun and did not let the boy forget his parents' names in the hope of finding them. But, as was determined subsequently, his entire family—his parents Moishe and Golda Yakivna Alper, his sister Rivka, and grandfather Shlomo—perished in the Nazi concentration camps. Many years later, in 1961, Samuil Alper/Petro Peredun/Günther Türner, who was a chemical engineer, member of the West German Olympic team, and a frequent participant and prizewinner of international biathlon competitions, met with his second mother, Righteous among the Nations Olha Peredun, and her daughter Oksana, whom he regarded as his sister. That year he took part in the European biathlon championship in Leningrad.[14]

REMAINING TRACES OF THE CITY'S JEWISH COMMUNITY

There are still some buildings in the city that have a direct connection to the history of its Jewish community. Located on Lutska Street are a house that once belonged to a Jew named Sokuler, who was well known in Volodymyr-Volynsky; the synagogue next to Shulman's mill; the building that once housed the Jewish club; the synagogue on Pidzamche Street; a building on D. Halytsky Street whose wall is decorated with the Etz chaim symbol; and others.

---

14 Alan Slepoi, "Syn trekh narodov," http://pepovez.brinkster.net/html/son138.htm.

The synagogue next to Shulman's mill, 81 Lutska Street. Before the war there was a Star of David on the building instead of the emblem of a canning factory. Photo: Volodymyr Muzychenko.

The building housing the Akiba Jewish youth club and the synagogue on Pidzamche Street. Photo: Volodymyr Muzychenko.

The Etz chaim (Tree of Life) after restoration. Photo: Volodymyr Muzychenko.

A building decorated with the Etz chaim symbol at 22 D. Halytsky Streeet. Photo: Volodymyr Muzychenko.

The Jewish men's school at 17 Ustyluh Street. Photo: Volodymyr Muzychenko.

The Jewish school at 1 Soborna Street. Photo: Volodymyr Muzychenko.

The Beit-Yaacov Jewish women's school at 9 Drahomanov Street. Photo: Volodymyr Muzychenko.

Rabbi's house at 24 D. Halytsky Street. Photo: Volodymyr Muzychenko.

A copper cup used for netilat yadayim (ritual washing of the hands) found in the city. From the private collection of antiquities owned by M. Matusevych.

EVERYDAY JEWISH ARTIFACTS DISCOVERED IN THE CITY

Fragment of a Torah scroll.

A matsevah (gravestone).

A matsevah.

A hanukiah (candelabrum with nine branches), which is lit for the feast of Hanukah*.

A box for storing etrog*, a citrus fruit used in the rituals of the festival of Sukkot (lit. "booths").

Unfortunately, this is practically all that is left of the city's community, which once numbered more than 20,000 people. Nonetheless, articles associated with Jewish culture periodically surface in the homes of private individuals, and they are very popular among sellers and buyers of antiques.

Wall of Honor at Yad-Vashem, Jerusalem.

Jewish Natives of the Volodymyr-Volynsky Area Abroad

The first émigrés from Volodymyr-Volynsky began moving to Palestine as early as the late nineteenth century. Bloody pogroms and the turbulent period of 1919–20 led to an increase in the number of Jews leaving the city. Among the pioneers of this movement were the members of the Hehalutz organization, who began building houses and roads among hostile Arabs. In the 1920s and 1930s, they created *kibbutzim* and agricultural settlements called *moshavim*, laying the foundations of the future state of Israel in the land of their forefathers.

Homesick for their dear Volynian land, they created associations uniting their fellow Volynians. Among the first to be founded in 1935 was the Ludmir association; the Ustyluh association was created in 1943.

According to various data, of the 22,000 Jewish natives of Volodymyr-Volynsky, between eighty[1] (individuals who were hidden by local residents, took shelter in hideouts they built themselves, or joined partisan detachments) and 140[2] Jews survived (together with those who were drafted into the Soviet army in 1939–41 and after the city was liberated in 1944–45, survived the war, or were sent to the east).

Immediately after the city was liberated, the surviving males were drafted into the Soviet army. According to the terms of an agreement on repatriation signed by the Soviet Union and Poland on 6 June 1945, the majority of the survivors moved to Poland and later to Israel, the USA, Australia, and other countries in the West.

---

1   *Wladimir Wolynsk.*
2   *Rossiiskaia Evreiskaia Entsiklopediia*, vol. 4.

According to the agreement signed between the Polish Committee of National Liberation and the Soviet government, people of the Jewish and Polish nationalities could leave Ukraine only if they had lived under Polish rule prior to 17 September 1939. Between 10 October 1944 and 15 September 1946, 30,408 people moved to the territory of Poland.

One of them was Menachem (Mikhael) Kochubes, who was severely wounded on the first day of the war but survived; after the war, he settled down in the Polish city of Łódź. Israel was the destination of Menashe Kiper, Moshe Margalit, Moshe Kirgser, and Yaacov Golansky, who in various years headed the Committee of Volodymyr-Volynsky Natives and other institutions.

The mass emigration of Jews from the USSR was damaging the reputation of the Soviet state, but despite the government's stubborn opposition to the large-scale emigration of Jews from the USSR—members of the Soviet intellectual elite—on 25 March 1957, under pressure from the Polish government in Warsaw, a second, similar treaty was signed between the USSR and Poland, allowing other family members to emigrate as well. The repatriation of Jews to Poland at this time was the only way to reach Israel, where they could build their own state in the land of their ancestors and be masters in their own land. That is how the Jews of Volodymyr-Volynsky ended up far away from their native city.

Today, fewer than twenty Jews from Volodymyr-Volynsky who survived the Holocaust are still alive. They live mostly in Israel and the USA, but inexorable time is taking them away one by one.

The Jews of Volodymyr-Volynsky have always loved their native land—the country of Ukraine. This is where their ancestors were born and raised; where they worked and where they are buried. This is where their families perished. Those who managed to survive by immigrating to their historical Fatherland of Israel before the war still have an abiding love for their native city of Volodymyr-Volynsky, which they built together with the Ukrainians and Poles. They continue to love the Volynian land, where they left behind all their families and friends. Moshe Margalit says he is a resident of Israel only in the daytime: in his dreams, during the hot Israeli nights, he still walks the narrow streets of Volodymyr-Volynsky, where he recalls every stone and his near and dear ones, those whom he befriended and with whom he coexisted.

In 1945, Jews from Ukraine's Volyn region living in Israel began issuing a trilingual periodical collection of reminiscences and documents entitled *Yalkut Wolyn* (Volyn Almanac), which appeared in Yiddish, Hebrew, and English. The last—fifty-seventh—issue of the almanac was published in 2005.

In 1963, the head of the Union of Wolyn Jews in Israel, A. Avaticha, and her fellow activists resolved to establish a base for Volhynian Jews, which would serve as the spiritual center of Volynian associations and unions throughout the world, a place to collect and store historical documents and reminiscences—the cultural heritage of the Volynian Jews.[3] This idea received support from communities based in New York and Los Angeles (US), and Montreal (Canada). At a conference, the Committee of the Wolyn Center was transformed into the New York Federation of Wolynian Jews. The idea to build a center fostered the unification of Volynian Jews into the World Federation of Wolynian Jews. Today, the federation unites organizations based in Israel, the USA, and Canada, and maintains periodic contact with the Federations of Wolynian Jews in Australia, Argentina, France, the UK, and Brazil.[4]

It was decided to build the Palace of Wolynian Jews in the city of Givatayim, near Tel-Aviv, whose municipal authorities donated a plot of land for its construction. The foundation of the future center was solemnly laid on 12 October 1965, in the presence of more than 700 members of Israeli and American Volynian associations, and the building was officially opened on 4 May 1969.[5]

The building was called Heichal Yahaduth Wolyn (Hebrew, "The Palace of Wolyn Judaism"); it is also called informally Beit Wolyn,

---

3 L. Kogan, "Vsemirnyi Soiuz volynskikh evreev: Zametki po evreiskoi istorii," http://berkovich-zametki.com/2009/Zametki/Nomer5/LKogan1.php.
4 See the following articles: Ia. Elbirt, "Federatsiia v korotkikh shtrikhakh," *Yalkut Wolyn*, no. 43 (1988): 38–39 (Yiddish); M. Gakman, "Volynskaia Federatsiia v Los-Andzhelese," *Yalkut Wolyn*, nos. 53–54 (1997): 77; Ia. Elbirt, "Federatsiia v N'iu-Iorke," *Yalkut Wolyn*, no. 35 (1978): 45.
5 E. Mandel' and R. Brener, "40 let Dvortsu 'Volyn'," *Yalkut Wolyn*, nos. 55–56 (1998): 11.

meaning "Volyn House." Located at 10 Korazin Street, the building has a hall that accommodates 380 people, as well as a 100-seat auditorium and a library. The first floor has seventeen rooms dedicated to the Jewish communities of Lutsk, Volodymyr-Volynsky, Liuboml, Olyka, Ustyluh, and Lukiv, all of which were wiped off the face of the earth. Some of the rooms are dedicated to two or three communities.[6] Old photographs displayed on the walls of the rooms and the exhibition hall reflect the unique lives and mores of Jewish towns in Ukraine. Yad Vashem is the co-owner of the Palace.

The Palace of Wolyn Jews is both a museum and a cultural-educational center where Volynian Jews regularly gather to reminisce about Ukraine's Volyn region, which remains their native land. The Ukrainian poet Vasyl Symonenko was correct when he wrote:

> Son, you can choose everything in the world,
> But you cannot choose your Fatherland.

Every year, prayers for the souls of family members and countrymen who perished in the Holocaust (*hazkarot*) are held at the Palace, which also hosts meetings of the Union of Wolyn Jews in Israel and congresses of the World Federation of Wolynian Jews. The first congress took place in 1983, and subsequent ones were held in 1985, 1988, 1991, and 1992.

The main purpose of the Palace's work is to preserve and honor the memory of family members and countrymen who were killed during the Holocaust in the Volyn region. When quite a few former residents of the Volyn region were still alive, mourning meetings were held every year to mark the dates of the mass shootings that took place in various locations according to the Jewish calendar. For Volodymyr-Volynsky this date is the sixteenth day of Kislev (13 December), the day marking the start of the final "action." For Ustyluh, the date is the eighteenth of Elul (1 September).[7] But with the inexorable passage of time, the

---

6   "V Federatsii volynskikh evreev v Amerike," *Yalkut Wolyn*, no. 20 (1965): 31.
7   "V zemliachestvakh Izrailia: Torgovitsa, Goshcha [Hoshcha]," *Yalkut Wolyn*, no. 20 (1965): 31–32; "Organizatsiia Ustiluga," ibid., 34.

numbers of Holocaust survivors are dwindling. The Palace also hosts the commemoration of the joint day of mourning on the twenty-seventh day of Nisan (April), known as Yom HaShoah—Holocaust Remembrance Day. Every year, the members of the federation gather to honor the memory of their relatives who were buried all over the Volyn region in pits resembling the one in Piatydni. On this day, millions of Jews throughout the world read Kaddish, the memorial prayer for the dead. Of the 1.5 million victims of the Holocaust in Ukraine, 102,500 were killed in the Volyn region.

Unable to be present on such days at the mass graves of their loved ones in their Ukrainian Fatherland, the members of various associations of Volyn Jews gather at monuments erected in Israel. In the Chamber ("Cellar") of the Holocaust on Mount Zion in Jerusalem, former residents of the Volyn region have installed memorial marble plaques, on which are inscribed the names of cities and towns in Volyn.

Zippora (Feiga) Weinstock-Zaar (at left) at the commemorative ceremony in the community building in the city of Givatayim (Israel), 14 April 2007. Photo courtesy of Zippora (Feiga) Weinstock-Zaar.

In the land of Israel, a number of commemorative markers have been unveiled to honor the memory of those who remain forever in the Volynian soil. These include an obelisk in Jerusalem and memorial markers on Mount Zion and Mount Eshtaol. Strangely enough, nothing about these monuments is known in Volodymyr-Volynsky.

On 2 September 1997, a monument to Jewish partisans and fighters of Volyn was erected next to the Palace of Wolyn Jews. Around a thousand people attended the unveiling, including the Ambassadors of Ukraine, Poland, and Belarus.[8] The monument is comprised of three sections: a four-meter-high marble stele depicting a Soviet partisan; a ten-meter-high marble wall with the Soviet partisan hymn inscribed on it in Hebrew, Yiddish, and English; and a glass wall near the entrance to the Palace, on which are inscribed the names of approximately 900 partisans and fighters who were killed in battle or died after the war. On Holocaust Remembrance Day, wreaths are laid here.

Commemorative marker on Mount Zion in Jerusalem. The inscription states: "For the holy Jews of the city of Ludmir who perished at the hands of the Germans and their accomplices."[9]

---

8 Sh. Ziskind, "Vsemirnyi Soiuz volynskikh evreev v 1987–98 gg.," *Yalkut Wolyn*, nos. 55–56 (1998): 7.

9 *Wladimir Wolynsk*, 603.

Stone on Mount Eshtaol, near Jerusalem, with a commemorative plaque dedicated to the Jews of Ludmir, erected by the members of the association of Jews from Volodymyr-Volynsky in Argentina.[10]

Inscription on the obelisk: "In memory of the twenty thousand men, women and children of Wlodzimierz Wolynsk, Poland, innocently and cruelly slain at the brutal hands of the Nazi invaders 1939–1945."[11] Located in Elmont (Nassau County, New York State), Bet David Cemetery, Section A, Block 3. Erected in 1958. Published with the permission of the Museum of Family History.[12]

---

10 Ibid., 604.
11 Ibid., 606.
12 http://www.museumoffamilyhistory.com/hm-vv-bd.htm.

*The building of the Heichal Yahaduth Wolyn in Givatayim, Israel.
Photo: Volodymyr Muzychenko.*

*Monument to Soviet Jewish partisans of Volyn next to the Beit Wolyn building in Givatayim, Israel. The inscription on the monument states: "In memory of Jewish partisans and combatants from Wolyn, 1939–1945."
Photo: Serhii Muzychenko.*

A wall with the names of Wolyn towns and cities where Jews were killed during holocaust. Photo: Sergei Muzychenko.

Model of the Great Liuboml Synagogue in Beit Wolyn. Photo: Serhii Muzychenko.

In the room dedicated to the city of Volodymyr-Volynsky: a model of the monument to Holocaust victims in the village of Piatydni.
Photo: Serhii Muzychenko.

Photographic stands in the room dedicated to Volodymyr-Volynsky.
Photo: Serhii Muzychenko.

Jewish Natives of the Volodymyr-Volynsky Area Abroad

Moshe Krigser (at right), head of the committee of Jews from Volodymyr-Volynsky. Photo: Serhii Muzychenko.

Menashe Kiper (second from right) and Moshe Margalit (third from right) during a meeting of the committee of Jews from Volodymyr-Volynsky. Photo courtesy of Moshe Margalit.

Soirée attended by members of the Federation of Wolyn Jews in New York.

Memorial in the Village of Piatydni

For every single man is a world which is born and which dies with him; beneath every gravestone lies a world's history.
Heinrich Heine

Monument to the victims of the Holocaust in Piatydni.

The centuries-old village of Piatydni is located on the left bank of the Luha River. Across the river is a meadow situated on a sandy plain, where thousands of innocent people found their eternal rest. Not a single one of these people was killed in battle bearing arms against an enemy. All of them were civilians, people who had prayed, grown grain, built their city, and created a life for themselves, their families, and future generations. All of them wanted to live.

The first monument to appear on the site of the mass shootings in Piatydni was erected by Jewish survivors in 1944. In 1971, thanks to the efforts of A. Zhornytsky, a new monument, prepared in secret, was surreptitiously installed one night. According to other data, this monument was erected in 1967.[1]

In the late 1980s, thanks to the concerted efforts of various individuals and human rights organizations, attention began to be paid to mass grave sites in the USSR. One of those who took an active part in these efforts was the president of the World Federation of Wolynian Jews, Jack (Yaacov) Elbirt, who was born in Lutsk. After the site of the mass graves was excavated during earthwork done in the district of Volodymyr-Volynsky, P. Sahaniuk, the representative of the president of the USSR for that district, issued a directive, as a result of which three huge burial mounds were erected, and the surrounding terrain was leveled and tidied up.

On 17 September 1989, a commemorative obelisk to the victims of fascism was erected near the site of these mass graves. This grand monument, which stands in the middle of a field, reminds every visitor of the national sorrow and sufferings in this land.

The creators of the monument are the Lviv-based sculptor Pesach Flit; architect Andrii Rudnytsky; and author of the text Aleksandr Lizen (Isroel Lizenberg, 1911–2000). It was built out of colored concrete resting on a polymer base the color of ashes, in the form of a twelve-meter-high, cone-shaped candle. The diameter is 3.5 meters at the base and 1.5 meters at the top.

---

1 *Kholokost na territorii SSSR.*

Memorial in the Village of Piatydni

The obelisk dominates the surrounding landscape and emphasizes this commemorative site. It stands on a hillock approximately 300 meters north of the Ustyluh–Volodymyr highway. Images of murdered people are depicted in relief: young and old people as well as children. The composition is crowned with the figures of a mother and child, a symbol of eternal life and the continuation of the human race. The two figures seem to be telling their descendants: "It was not just innocent people who were killed in this spot. A nation was killed here." Engraved on the monument are inscriptions in three languages: Ukrainian, Russian, and Yiddish:

Let us pause, let us be silent for a moment.
We solemnly, passionately swear
That we shall never forget your torments.
Inevitable punishment for all executioners.

25,000 Soviet citizens were killed here in 1942–1943 by the fascist occupiers.

People, stop for a moment of silence,
And make a solemn promise, devoted and strong as steel,
That you will never ever forget our torments,
And will never allow this to happen again.[2]

From its elevated spot, the monument—a symbol of eternal sorrow—gazes into the distance. It seems as though an inextinguishable candle of memory for the executed people is growing out of the earth. The area around the obelisk is laid out with pieces of crushed red brick symbolizing soil soaked in blood.

During the unveiling ceremony, the right to cut the red ribbon was granted to the former ghetto prisoner M. Bass; Ya. A. Zhornytsky; war veteran M. V. Rekunovych; and first secretary of the municipal party committee S. V. Lesyk.

---

2 Translated from the Yiddish by Broina Pest.

The participants of the mourning meeting were addressed by Mrs. B. D. Zeligzon, who said:

> I would like to list everyone by name, but death took away the list. The installation of a monument to the martyrs of the Jewish ghetto became possible only in the perestroika years. And in this we see internationalism at work. We thank the residents of Volodymyr-Volynsky for the work that they put into its construction, and the employees of the Lviv artistic-ceramic factory, who embodied the project of the talented sculptor P. B. Flit and the architect A. M. Rudnytsky.

The first monument at the site of the mass shootings in Piatydni, 1944.[3]

---

[3] *Wladimir Wolynsk*, 537.

Memorial in the Village of Piatydni

At the unveiling of the monument, 17 September 1989. Photo: I. Dziola.

The mass graves in the village of Piatydni. Photo: Volodymyr Muzychenko.

Grave no. 1. Photo: Volodymyr Muzychenko.

Grave no. 2. Photo: Volodymyr Muzychenko.

Grave no. 3. Photo: Volodymyr Muzychenko.

The sculptor Pesach Flit recounted: "For two years I worked on this project together with the architect Andrii Markovych Rudnytsky. I too went through this.... My entire family perished in the same way near Kamianets-Podilsky, in the same kind of pit as here. That is why I tried to put my soul, my feelings, and my sorrow into every stroke."[4]

The mass graves are located 300 meters to the north of the obelisk. The geographic coordinates of the memorial complex are 51°8 24°14. This place is listed in the state registry of locally important historical sites and granted the status of Monument Protection No. 640 (decision of the Volyn oblast executive committee no. 267-r, 25 August 1986).

By the 1990s, the site of the mass graves had turned into an illegal garbage dump. Some local residents had carted away the sand from the burial area and even from the actual burial mounds for their own construction needs, and when the snow melted, human bones washed out of the soil.

After Ukraine's Ministry of Defense transferred the plot of land on which the memorial is located to the land reserve bank of the Piatydni village council (59 hectares), some of these lands were transferred from the holdings of the "Volynsky" military Soviet farm to the Volodymyr-Volynsky city council in order to create a gardening cooperative. Today the northern part of the cooperative's holdings is directly adjacent to the area of the mass shootings. The likelihood that they occupy part of the memorial zone cannot be excluded. Some land is also being cultivated south of the memorial column—between the pillar and the highway heading to Ustyluh (8 hectares).

In 2008, biolocation (dowsing) was carried out on the initiative of the Office of the American Union of Council for Jews in the former Soviet Union, which helped pinpoint the location of the burial sites more accurately. The results showed that shootings had also taken place in other areas near the monument.

"I don't know if it is worth mentioning that the monument is located some distance from the graves, but it is crucial to tidy up these hillocks of bones. We have to put our heads together and figure out how

---

[4] V. Fedoryshyn, "Vshanuvannia pam'iati zhertv fashyzmu," *Slovo pravdy*, 20 September 1989.

to do this. A nation is judged according to its attitude to the past, to history," Ia. Tsaruk wrote in an article published in 1991. In the past twenty years, despite passionate declarations, nothing has been done.

Unfortunately, the three mass graves, in which lie thousands of innocently murdered residents of the city and the district, are not cordoned off and do not have proper markers such as gravestones or memorial slabs. As a result, the area of the burials gradually became littered, and it is only thanks to the cooperation of the government agencies in the district of Volodymyr-Volynsky and the Jewish community's work to inform the public that this site is being maintained in the proper fashion today. Several incidents of vandalism took place in the spring of 2010: some graves were ransacked. When appeals to the forces of law and order in this connection were completely ignored, the unknown vandals, who went unpunished, carried on with their black deeds. In 2011, more areas near the mass graves showed signs of digging. Someone must think there are valuables buried there. The vandals are still oblivious to the fact that everything, including life itself, was taken from the unfortunates who are buried there. The Nazis, who robbed and shot naked Jews, did not leave anything behind for today's marauders.

It is unfortunate that even in this case the local authorities stubbornly refuse to view these acts of vandalism as crimes. A criminal case was never launched despite numerous requests from the community and articles that appeared in the press.[5] In their view, digging up graves that are part of a historical heritage site is not a criminal act. The authorities also ignored the insult to the memory of those who perished there, the spiritual pain of their loved ones, the destruction of society's moral values, and the damage being done to the reputation of the Ukrainian state in the eyes of the international community.

---

5   See V. Muzychenko, "Khto zupynyt' maroderiv?" *Volyn'*, 17 May 2011; K. Pavliuk, "'Uzakonenyi' vandalism: i na tomu sviti ne prysnyt'sia," *Misto vechirnie*, 12 May 2011; V. Muzychenko, "Viina tryvaie," *Khadashot*, no. 6 (June 2011).

Memorial in the Village of Piatydni

The memorial to the victims of fascism in Piatydni, mass grave number 1. The unknown vandals tried to mask the traces of their exploratory digging, April 2011. Photo: Volodymyr Muzychenko.

The graves in Piatydni are not the only resting places of Holocaust victims in the district of Volodymyr-Volynsky. Not all mass shooting sites are being properly maintained and registered by local authorities. One should not forget about the hundreds of Jews who were killed in the prison that was located behind the thick wall, or about the site of the shooting and burning of nearly 2,000 prisoners of the third ghetto, which took place in the vicinity of the village of Falemychi (today the site of the local sugar factory treatment plant). The time has come to speak out about these horrific places, which are not marked on the map of the city.

Only after numerous cases of looting these graves did I receive permission to install the memorial signs there. The plaques—which I planned and produced—were installed on all three graves, a project carried out together with the members of the Jewish communities of Volodymyr-Volynsky and Lutsk.

After installing the memorial plaques on the graves of the Holocaust victims, August 27, 2014. Left to right: A. Voytzehovsky, V. Kozak, R. Bogatyrsky, S. Shvardovsky, V. Muzychenko, A. Kovalchuk, B. Garber.

സ സ സ

One often hears the question: Why did this happen? Many books have been written on this topic, and there are various answers to this question. One of them is the absurd idea that the Holocaust happened because the Jews had turned away from God. Perhaps the people who turned away from God were the executioners who created this horror in the first place and those who provided the ideological justification for it.

We have no right to forget what happened in Piatydni in 1942–43. We should preserve this place for our descendants if we truly wish to ensure that nothing like this will ever happen to them. It should be fully protected and maintained by the state. The road to this spot should not become overgrown. The more people know the truth about the tragedy that befell the Jews of this city, the more chances we have of creating a truly democratic society, in which the supreme value will be not the belief in some idea but human life.

Safeguarding Memory

Those who do not remember their past are not worthy of their future.
Maksym Rylsky

Most of the members of the small Jewish community in Volodymyr-Volynsky, who are members of the Lutsk Congregation for Progressive Judaism, are not natives of the city, but they have never been indifferent to the history of their people. They are doing everything possible to preserve it, the author of this book included.

The brochure that the city council published on the eve of the city's millennial celebration does not mention a single word about its Jewish residents, their parents, or their grandparents who lived in Volodymyr-Volynsky and contributed to its growth, and who for a certain period of time constituted the majority of the population. Neither is any mention made in a history article that was posted on the official website of the city council. This is not just. The memory of these people should be preserved.

"The Jewish cemetery, which was damaged during the German occupation, was destroyed during the period of Soviet rule. Only the graves in Piatydni remain, a site worthy of being commemorated as both a historic area and in remembrance of the 25,000 residents of the city and district who were killed in a savage fashion, as a lesson to future generations and a constant reminder of the horrors of fascism," wrote Moshe Margalit.[1]

---

1   http://www.yivoencyclopedia.org/search.aspx?query=ludmir.

Unfortunately, most of the city's residents who were born after the war do not know about the terrible tragedy that occurred there in 1942–43.

After many years of silence stemming from certain political and ideological approaches to this topic, thanks to initiatives put forward by the city's Jewish community the memory of this page from the history of the city, the tragedy of Piatydni, is being gradually restored, and the public is becoming informed about these events.

A number of articles have been written on this topic. Two documentary films have been produced by local television stations: *Cry, Mama*, about the tragedy that befell the city's Jewish population, and *Give New Life to Eternity*, about the Righteous Among the Nations who live in there. In 2008, the Lutsk Congregation for Progressive Judaism helped organize an exhibition of documents and posters recounting the history of the Holocaust in the Volyn region and the city. This year, a scholarly-practical conference of local history teachers took place in the city, whose proceedings were used to carry out various pedagogical activities designed for students attending educational institutions located throughout the city. The history of the Jews of Volodymyr-Volynsky has become a topic of reports prepared by students, wall news papers, and research. In 2010, an exhibit of artifacts and documents, as well as a lecture read before an audience of schoolchildren, was organized in collaboration with the local history museum. Several Righteous Among the Nations took part in these activities, recounting their experiences during the war. Lectures featuring state-of-the-art visual aids, including photographs and audiovisual materials, were held in 2010 and 2012 at the Medical and Technical College.

Despite the economic hardships besetting the young Ukrainian state, funds were obtained in 2009—thanks to the support of Ukrainian parliamentarian Viktor Oliinyk—for the purpose of registering the memorial complex consisting of the monument and burial sites in Piatydni as a historical and cultural heritage site.

With the assistance of local government bodies, maintenance work is carried out on the site from time to time. Cleanup projects have taken place with the participation of pupils from the elementary school in Piatydni, who were supplied with the necessary tools.

For many years this place was virtually forgotten. Today, however, commemorations of the victims of the worst crime against humanity, the Holocaust, have become an annual event. For the last six years, mourning meetings have been held at the monument and the mass graves of the innocently slaughtered victims in the village of Piatydni. These gatherings are attended by Ukrainian officials and church leaders of various faiths. It is important to note that young people have begun attending these gatherings. This is commendable because the crime, the victims of which were Jews, was a crime against humanity, and only the memory of this tragic event, transmitted to the younger generation, will help mankind avoid anything similar in the future. Therefore, this sad date, the first of September, which marks the beginning of the mass shootings in Piatydni, should be marked on the calendar of statutory measures instituted by the city council (because residents of Volodymyr-Volynsky comprised the preponderant majority of the victims), the district administration, and the district council (since the memorial is located outside the city limits).

Thanks to the Va'ad of Ukraine and the Euro-Asian Jewish Congress, on 22 June 2010, the Day of Remembrance for Victims of the War, an information billboard was ceremoniously erected next to the monument to the Holocaust victims in Piatydni. It contains information about the site and, more importantly, about the mass graves that are located in the vicinity of the monument.

A place should be set up in the city to commemorate those of its residents who perished during the Holocaust. It would only be just to install a memorial plaque or board on one of the buildings that were once owned by Jews in honor of people who made a significant contribution to the development of the city and who were killed only because they were Jews. It would also be prudent to restore the original historical name of Roksoliana Street, which prior to the war was called Old Jewish Street (Staroievreiska), where the large choral synagogue was located and which was populated mostly by Jews. It would be an act of justice and a show of respect for the memory of these people.

The goal of safeguarding the memory of the Jews of Volodymyr-Volynsky is served by books that have been published abroad, such as the bilingual (Hebrew and Yiddish) work *The Volodymyr Notebook: A Collection of Materials on the History of the City's Jews and Eyewitness Memoirs of the Period of the German Occupation* (1962); Moshe Margalit's personal narrative *Yaldut be-lehavot* [A Childhood in Flames, 2000], the diary of a Jewish ghetto prisoner spanning the period from the beginning of the Nazi occupation to December 1943; Ann Kazimirski's memoir *Witness to Horror*; Susan Gold's Holocaust memoir *The Eyes Are the Same*, and other publications. Ukrainian translations of these books would shed much light on this important page of the city's history.

Meeting held at the monument in the village of Piatydni, 2006. Photo: I. Dziola.

At the unveiling of the information billboard in 2010. Photo: K. Pavliuk.

After the commemorative meeting in 2008 held at the monument in Piatydni. From left: Petro Horbachevsky, pastor of the Church of Seventh-Day Adventists; Volodymyr Muzychenko, head of the Jewish community of Volodymyr-Volynsky; Mordechai Shlomo Bald, Chief Rabbi of Lviv and Western Ukraine; Rev. Mykola Hynailo, a Ukrainian Orthodox priest; and Ihor Rubin, religious studies lecturer at the Ukrainian Humanities Institute (Kyiv).

Prominent Jews Born in Volodymyr-Volynsky

It is not important what the goyim say, it's important what the Jews do.
David Ben-Gurion

The following prominent Jews were born and raised in Volodymyr-Volynsky:

Bardach, Janusz (Natan) Markovich (b. 28 July 1919, Odessa, d.?, Iowa City, USA); his mother Ottilia (née Neuding) was born in Odessa.

Janusz Bardach.

In 1972 he joined the Faculty of Otolaryngology, University of Iowa, in Iowa City (USA) and later headed the Department of Plastic and Reconstructive Surgery of the Head and Neck. His entire family was shot in Piatydni. Janusz Bardach was a well-known writer and the author of *Chelovek cheloveku volk: Vyzhivshii v GULAGe* [Man Is Wolf to Man: A Survivor in the GULAG] and the foreword to Nathaniel Deutsch's book *The Maiden of Ludmir: A Jewish Holy Woman and Her World*.

Bardach, Juliusz (b. 3 November 1914, Odessa, d. 26 January 2010, Warsaw). Brother of Janusz Bardach, he was a distinguished Polish scholar specializing in state building and law in Central and Eastern Europe, professor, holder of honorary degrees (doctor honoris causa) from the universities of Warsaw, Vilnius, and Łódź, and a corresponding member of the Polish Academy of Sciences. Dr. Bardach studied at the Kopernik Gymnasium of Volodymyr-Volynsky.

Bardach, Juliusz Meirovich (b. 1827, d. 1904, Odessa). Educator, philologist, author of philological works on the ancient Hebrew and Aramaic languages.

Bardach, Yakov Iuliovich (b. 1857, d. ? Odessa). Son of Juliusz Bardacz, bacteriologist, privat-docent of Novorossiisk University.

Cheskis, Avrom (b. 1879, d. 1935, Moscow) was a journalist and professor who received a traditional Jewish religious education. His first literary articles (in Hebrew), written from Marxist positions, were published in 1902 in the newspaper *Ha-Dor*. He joined the Bund Party in 1903. He was a delegate to the Second Congress of the Russian Social-Democratic Workers' Party, which took place in London in 1903. That same year, he moved to France. In 1912–14 he collaborated with a French socialist publisher and the newspaper *Die Sozialistische Tribüne*. After the February Revolution of 1917, he returned to Russia, where he worked actively in the Bund and became one of the founders of a people's university in Kyiv (1918). He was published in the periodical *Komunistishe veg* (The Communist Way, Homyel, 1919) and *Komunistishe fon* (The Communist Banner Kyiv, 1919–20). Beginning in 1920, he taught historical materialism in the Jewish Department of the Communist University in Moscow. His articles were published in the newspaper *Der emes* and the central press. He is the author of the following Yiddish-language books: *Jean Jaurès: Life and Works* (Katerynoslav, 1918), *Ludwig Feuerbach* (Moscow, 1922), and *Lessons on Historical Materialism* (Moscow, 1924).

Helmond, Shmuel Izrailevych (b. 1907, d. 1941, Vasin, Kirovohrad oblast, Ukraine), was a poet. After graduating from a pedagogical institute in Ukraine, he taught in Zhytomyr and Odessa. He made his poetic debut in the Moscow-based Jewish youth journal *Yungwald* in 1924. His articles later appeared in central Jewish newspapers, magazines, and almanacs, including the Moscow almanac *Sovetish*. In 1926 he published his first book of poetry—the poem *Trypillia*. He is also the author of the collection *Jungt in Land* (Youth in the Country, 1931), the poems "Elektre in Step" (Electricity in the Steppe, 1935), and other works. In the 1930s he lived in Odessa, where he taught in a Jewish school and was active in the city's sociopolitical and cultural life. On 23 June 1941 he volunteered to fight at the front, receiving the rank of Junior Lieutenant, and was killed in battle.

Hershtansky, Demian Iosyfovych (b. 1854, d. 1936). Priest, deputy of the Second State Duma of Russia, member of the Polish Sejm, 1922–1927.

Liuksemburg, Anatolii Izrailevych (b. 1891, d. 1961, Mukachiv, Ukraine). Impresario, founder and director of the Yiddish theater Gezkult, 1929–1948.

Nuger, Abram Petrovych (b. 1896, d. 1994, Nazareth Illit, Israel), actor and director, began his theater career in 1917, when he joined a traveling Yiddish theater group. In 1922–24 he worked at the Idishe Folksbiene Theater in Kyiv, whose directors were the actors Ya. T. Libert and I. Rakitin. In 1925 he joined the Kharkiv-based company of the All-Ukrainian State Yiddish Theater. In 1928 he was one of the directors of the Kharkiv branch of the State Yiddish Theater. By 1934 he was one of the leading actors of the Kyiv branch of the State Yiddish Theater, where he worked until its closure in 1950.

Abram Nuger in the role of Bobe Yakhne, the witch.

Abram Nuger was blessed with extraordinary musical and improvisational talents, and was the continuer of the *Purim-shpiler* (jester) traditions of the Yiddish theater in the Soviet Union. His main roles were Kuneleml (in *Kunelemlekh*) and Bobe Yakhne (in *The Witch*) (the director of both these productions was Abraham Goldfaden Abram Goldfadn); Nakhmen (in Ya. B. Reznik's film *The Recruit*); Covielle (in *The Bourgeois Gentleman* by Molière); Harpagon (in *The Miser* by Molière; dir. B. Nord); Hershele Ostropoler (in the eponymous play by Moshe Gershensohn); Tevye the milkman (based on the eponymous story by Sholem Aleichem); the Actor (in Isaak Dunayevsky's operetta *The Free Wind*); Sultanbek (in the Azerbaidzhani musical comedy *Arshin Mal Alan* [The Cloth Peddler] by Uzeyir Hadzhibekov); Herh fon Deber (in the play *Ich leb!* [I Live!] by Moyshe Pinchevsky), dir. M. Goldblat of the Kyiv State Yiddish Theater, 1944. Nuger directed the following plays: *Tevye the Milkman* (Sholem Aleichem); *Nashestvie* (by Leonid Leonov); *Hershele Ostropoler* (Moshe Gershensohn); *Energiia* (Energy by A. Kahan; codirected with E. Dinor); *Chaim Boitre* (Moyshe Kulbak); *Professor Mamlok* (Friedrich Wolf); and others. He was the director of the variety show *Vsegda s vami* (Always with You) by S. Tal.

More detailed information on his life is featured in the book *Abram i Sheva: Dve zhizni i odna sud'ba; Vospominaniia docheri evreiskikh akterov*[2] [Abram and Sheva: Two Lives and One Destiny], which was written by his daughter Yanna Nuger and published in Israel in 2009. His poetic works include "The Grandfather and Granddaughters," "The Ballad of Mikhoels"[3] (translated from the Hebrew by Israel Rubinchyk), the song "Mikhoels," and the tale "The Eagle and the Rooster." He wrote the scenarios for the musical numbers "The Chimney-Sweep" and "A Mother's Heart," as well as for the musical monologue *The Comedian*.

Rozmarin, Aharon (b. 1896, Ustyluh, d. 1977, Ramat Gan, Israel), journalist. Born into a Hasidic family, he received a traditional Jewish religious education. He immigrated to the USA in 1920. In 1927–1931 he studied at the universities of Berlin and Würzberg, where he obtained a doctorate. In 1931 he returned to the USA and in 1971 he moved to Israel. His first articles—historical sketches about the Khazars, the Falashas, and Moroccan Jews—were published in the English-language press; his articles also appeared in German-language Jewish periodicals. Within a short period of time he switched to Yiddish, and his articles were then published in Yiddish-American newspapers. He was on the staff of the newspaper *Amerikaner* and served as the editor of the weekly newspaper *Der Id* (The Jew) in New York from 1954 to 1957. In Israel his articles appeared in Hebrew and Yiddish. He is the author of the books *An entfer: tsu der polemik arum dem Idishen teologishen seminar* (The Answer, 1943), *Die Shehnkayt fun Identum* (The Beauty of the Jews, 1947), *Li-khvoyd Shabes: Gedanken oyf ale sedres* (In Honor of the Sabbath, 1949), and *Gedank un hokhme* (Thought and Wisdom, 1955, New York). Aharon Rozmarin also compiled the two-volume *Tanakh entsyklopedye* published in New York in 1964–67.[4]

---

2   Maks Veksel'man, "Pamiat' serdtsa," http://izrus.co.il/weekly__news/810.html.
3   Solomon Mikhoels (1890–1948) was a famous Soviet Jewish actor, the artistic director of the Moscow State Yiddish Theater, and a prominent leader of the Jewish community in the Soviet Union. In 1942 he was appointed chairman of the Jewish Anti-Fascist Committee. He was murdered on the orders of Stalin, his death disguised as a hit-and-run car accident.
4   *Rossiiskaia Evreiskaia Entsiklopediia*, vol. 4.

Shelomoh Gotlieb of Karlin (b. 1740, d. 1792), was the founder of a dynasty of Hasidic rabbis, philosopher, tsadik, rabbi, and author of Torah commentaries entitled *Shema Shlomo*.

Werbermacher, Khane-Rokhl (b. 1815?, d. 1892, Jerusalem), was the only female tsadik in history, who was known as the "Maiden of Ludmir."

Addenda

Table 3: Population of Jews (with Sources Indicated)

Year and Source	1662[1]	1764[2]	1765[3]	1784[4]	1790[5]	1799[6]	1801[7]
Number of Jews	318	1401	1,237 (1,327[8])	340	630	1,834 (1,849[9])	1946
Total						2,910	
Percentage of Population						63	

Year and Source	1805[10]	1847[11]	1857[12]	1861[13]	1863[14]	1884[15]
Number of Jews	1,942, (1,977[16])	3,930	3,672	6,122	3,953	6,456
Total	2,615			8,636	5,900	
Percentage of Population	74.3			70.89	67	

---

1 Lukin, "Volodymyr Volyns'kyi."
2 *Wladimir Wolynsk.*
3 *Rossiiskaia Evreiskaia Entsiklopediia*, vol. 4.
4 *Elektronnaia Evreiskaia Entsiklopediia*, http://www.eleven.co.il/article/10945.
5 *Rossiiskaia Evreiskaia Entsiklopediia*, vol. 4.
6 Deutsch, *Maiden of Ludmir.*
7 *Rossiiskaia Evreiskaia Entsiklopediia*, vol. 4.
8 *Evreiskaia Entsiklopediia Brokgauza-Efrona*, http://encyclopediya.ru/brockhaus-efron-jewish-encyclopedia/slovnik/03-5.html
9 *Rossiiskaia Evreiskaia Entsiklopediia*, vol. 4.
10 Deutsch, *Maiden of Ludmir.*
11 *Rossiiskaia Evreiskaia Entsiklopediia*, vol. 4.
12 Ibid.
13 *Elektronnaia Evreiskaia Entsiklopediia*, http://www.eleven.co.il/article/10945.
14 *Rossiiskaia Evreiskaia Entsiklopediia*, vol. 4.
15 Ibid.

Year and Source	1886[17]	1892[18]	1897[19]	1910–11[20]	1912[21]
Number of Jews	6,502	6,389	5,869 (5,837[22])	7,060	7,156
Total		8,185	9,883	15,622	
Percentage of Population		78	59.3	45	

Year and Source	1921[23]	1931[24]	1934[25]	1937[26]	1939[27]
Number of Jews	5,917	11,985 (10,665[28])	10,406	12,000 (11,554[29])	17,000
Total	11,623	23,500	27,117	30,000	37,000
Percentage of Population	50.9	51 (43.5)	38.3	(39)	45

---

16 Ibid.
17 Ibid.
18 *Entsiklopedicheskii slovar' Brokgauza i Efrona*, vol. 12, 642.
19 Wladimir Wolynsk; *Elektronnaia Evreiskaia Entsiklopediia*, http://www.eleven.co.il/article/10945; *Rossiiskaia Evreiskaia Entsiklopediia*, vol. 4.
20 *Rossiiskaia Evreiskaia Entsiklopediia*, vol. 4.
21 Ibid.
22 Kuz', "Zakhidna Volyn' v tsyfrakh.
23 *Wladimir Wolynsk*.
24 Tsynkalovs'kyi, *Kniazhyi horod Volodymyr*.
25 Ibid.
26 *Wladimir Wolynsk*.
27 Ibid.
28 *Rossiiskaia Evreiskaia Entsiklopediia*, vol. 4.
29 Ibid.

Addenda

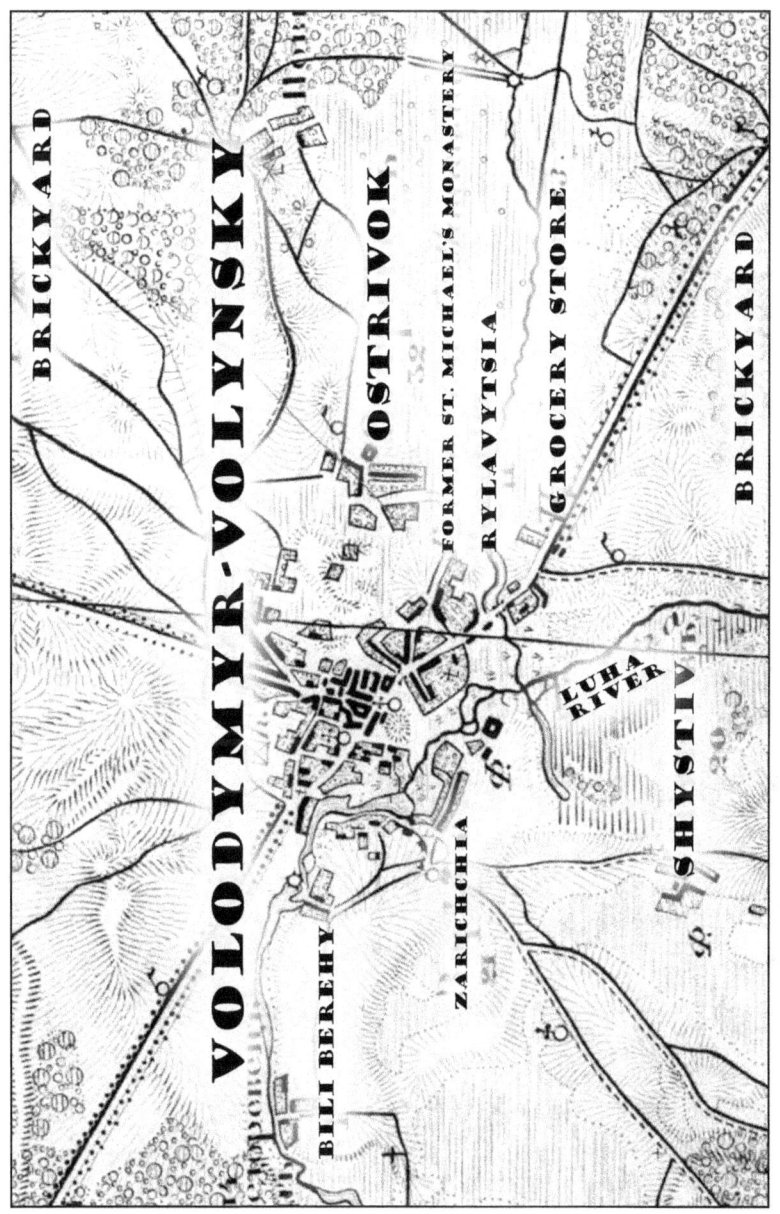

Map of Volodymyr-Volynsky and surrounding villages, published in the Russian Empire, 1867.[30]

---
30 http://oldmaps.org.ua/all/lutsk/1100-Volodimir-Volinskii__Rosiya__1867.

The area circled in the upper left corner is Volyn province containing Volodymyr-Volynsky.

Glossary of Terms

Aron ha-kodesh (Hebr., "holy ark")—a special cabinet in which Torah scrolls are kept in the synagogue.

Av—the Hebrew month corresponding to August.

Bet ha-Midrash—"house of interpretation," a place where Jews gather to study the Torah, listen to the midrash, i.e., discussions and interpretations of the Torah.

Betar—Zionist organization whose name is formed from the Hebrew acronym for Berit Yosef Trumpeldor (Joseph Trumpeldor Alliance). It was named in honor of Yosef Trumpeldor, legendary leader of the Russian Zionists, officer of the Russian army, holder of the Cross of the Order of St. George, and hero of the Russo-Japanese War. Trumpeldor's life was devoted to the armed struggle for the creation of a Jewish state in Eretz-Yisrael (the Land of Israel). In 1920 Trumpeldor was fatally wounded in a battle near the village of Tel Hai in Galilee. His last words, "It is good to die for our country!" became a symbol of Israeli patriotism. The members of Betar were among the organizers behind the Warsaw Uprising in the Warsaw ghetto and fought in subunits of various countries' armed forces. Among them are Heroes of the Soviet Union.

Bima—the pulpit used by the cantor in a synagogue.

Eretz Yisrael—the Land of Israel.

Etrog—a citrus fruit (citron) that is mandatory for the feast of Sukkot, which is celebrated in early autumn.

Gaon—wise man.

Ghetto—derived from the Venetian dialect, "ghèto nuove," meaning "new foundry," which existed in Venice in 1516. The foundry gave rise to a district where the Jews were subsequently ordered to live. During the Second World War, Jews were forcibly herded into ghettos prior to their destruction. The word has a distinctively negative connotation.

Ha Halutz—Jewish youth movement of the twentieth century to train members to settle in Palestine.

Halakhah—the general term for Jewish law. In the narrower sense, it refers to the authoritative and ultimate resolution of a private matter. The word means "the path that one walks"; it is the correct upholding of the commandments in any situation under all circumstances. Halakha is aimed at forming a person's conduct, and it designates ethical obligations and religious acts. It examines all aspects of people's lives and their attitude to one another and to God. Thus, it not only regulates religious life in the narrow sense of this concept, but also encompasses the sphere that is regarded by non-Jewish scholars as the sphere of morals and ethics as well as civil and criminal law.

Hanukah—Jewish holiday commemorating the victory of the Maccabees over the Greco-Syrian tyrant Antiochus IV. This festival marks the rededication of the Holy Temple in Jerusalem and of the Menorah, the ritual olive oil of which had been profaned by the Syrians. Hanukah marks the end of an unsuccessful attempt to destroy Judaism, which posed both an internal and external threat: the influence of Hellenistic culture was so great that some members of Jewish communities preferred to assimilate completely in order to be accepted as Greek citizens. The resistance of the Maccabees and their allies to assimilation, no matter how attractive a prospect, helped preserve Judaism. The history of Hanukah is the history of the Jewish people's age-old struggle to remain Jews in a non-Jewish world. During each day of this festival, which is dedicated to the miracle that occurred with the container of olive oil that ended up lasting an entire week, the nine-branched Hanukah candelabrum—the *Hanukiah*—is lit, one candle per day.

Hasidism (Hebrew, "pious")—a religious branch of Judaism that emerged in Ukraine in the eighteenth century and within several dozen years attracted a mass following. The founder of Hasidism, Ba'al Shem Tov, insisted on the priority of sincere faith. He preached that the main thing is not intellect and wisdom but the feelings and emotions of the faithful; love and care for the ordinary, uneducated Jew; and love of people regardless of their merits and qualities. He taught that the best way of communicating with God is through prayer, which is expressed with joy; this allows the person to "sunder" the ordinary laws of the universe and to create a miracle in the world of everyday existence. He preached joyful service to God; everything that a person needs is to take pleasure in life through holiness and purity. According to the founder of Hasidism, the nature of evil is not absolute but relative; evil is not the opposite of goodness but its lesser degree. The *tsadik* plays an important role in Hasidism.

Hebrew—the Jewish language.

Heder (Hebr., "room")—a school for boys. In small towns or cities, the heder was often one room in a teacher's house.

Kabbalah (Hebrew, "receiving")—mystical tradition of Judaism connected with the meaning of the Creator and creation, the Creator's role and goal, the nature of the human being, and the meaning of life. The history of Kabbalah may be traced back to Babylonian times, but its perfected form emerged during the Middle Ages. Kabbalah is based on the works *Yetsirah*, *Bahir*, and *Sefer Zohar*, and the writings of Ari (Rabbi Itshak Luria Ashkenazi, also known as Arizal). Judaism views Kabbalah as the fourth and highest level of understanding of the Torah, therefore it is customarily believed that the study of Kabbalah may be initiated only by those who have passed all the preceding levels: those who have studied the written Torah and the oral Talmud.

Kaddish—Jewish prayer for the dead.

Kahal, kehila—a Jewish community; the organ of self-rule overseeing relations with a local government administration.

Korytnytsia—a small Ukrainian town (today a village situated fifteen kilometers north of Volodymyr-Volynsky), which had two Eastern-rite churches and a Roman Catholic church. It was home to more than 300 Jews and a synagogue that was built in 1915.[1]

Kosher (Hebrew, *kashrut*, "acceptable")—a set of Jewish dietary laws that regulate the use of food products and the manner in which they are prepared. Only meat from animals that both chew their cud

---

1 http://wolyn.ovh.org/ippw/005.htm.

and have cloven hooves and which are slaughtered according to the proper ritual is considered kosher; fish with scales and fins are also considered kosher. Kashrut requires the separation of meat and dairy products, including separate dishes for these foods.

Lokachi—Today a district (raion) center of Volyn oblast, Ukraine. In 1765 this village was home to 907 Jews (Regesty, 1; Liczba, 1765). Following the revision of 1847, the Jewish community of Lokachi numbered 1,150 people. According to the 1897 census, the village had a population of 2,309, of whom 1,730 were Jews.

Magid (Hebrew, "preacher")—In Eastern Europe, magids most often traveled through cities and towns, receiving compensation for their activities. Many communities had their own permanent magids, who were supported by the community. Some magids enjoyed great popularity, and their sermons were published in as books. This title was accorded to some Hasidic leaders (e.g., the Great Magid of Mezhyrich, the Magid of Zolochiv, et al.).

Matsevah—a gravestone in a Jewish cemetery.

Midrash—This term has two meanings: 1) Penetration to the deep content of Torah verses in order to understand their spirit; 2) The revelation of the meanings of words and expressions in a text; "explanation," "translation," "interpretation" of the Torah in a language that would be comprehensible to a broad circle of people; an explication or commentary that reveals certain semantic levels of the Torah. Midrash was also used as a way of interpreting biblical stories that goes beyond simple distillation of religious, legal, or moral teachings, filling in many gaps left in the biblical narrative regarding events and personalities that are only hinted at.

Minyan (Hebrew, "tally," "number")—The quorum of ten adult Jews (older than thirteen) necessary for a formal religious service.

Mitsvah (pl. *mitsvot*; Old Hebrew, *tsivva*, "to command," "to appoint," "to announce")—A Jewish commandment. In everyday language the word means a good deed; a charitable act. According to ancient tradition, the Torah contains 613 commandments, of which 365 are prohibitive and 248 are prescriptive.

NDs (National Democrats, popularly known in Polish as *endecy*)—Members of the People's Democratic Party, an anti-Semitic right-wing party in Poland, which supported the expulsion of Jews from the country. The party leader was Roman Dmowski (b. 1864, Warsaw, d. 21 January 1939). During the Second World War, armed insurgent brigades of the Polish armed forces (NSZ), derived from a radical secession from the National Democrats, took part in the killings of Jews.

ORT (*Obshchestvo rasprostraneniia truda sredi evreev* [Organization for Rehabilitation through Training])—Founded in the Russian Empire in 1880 to promote vocational training of trades and agriculture among impoverished Jews.

Porytsk—Ukrainian village; renamed Pavlivka in 1951. Following the revision of 1847, the "Porytsk Jewish Society" numbered 1,100 people. According to the census of 1897, Porytsk had 2,264 residents, 1,316 of whom were Jews.[2] Today it is part of the Ivanytsia District.

Rabbanit—Female rabbi.

Rabbi (also rebe, rav, ravi, rabi)—All variants of this word denote a a Jewish sage, a scholar of the Torah and the Talmud. A rabbi is the religious and spiritual leader of a Jewish community, teacher, and mentor. In order to acquire the title of rabbi, a person must undergo complex examinations and then obtain the *semicha* (rabbinic ordination). The main tasks of a rabbi are to act as a spiritual mentor, resolve halakhic questions that may emerge, and settle disputes.

Rosh Hodesh (Hebrew, "new head")—The first day of each month according to the monthly Jewish calendar.

Seder (Hebrew, "order")—Jewish ritual feast that marks the beginning of the Passover holiday.

Shabbat—The Sabbath; the most important ritual observance in Judaism.

Shavu'ot—a harvest festival that begins seven weeks after Passover; it also commemorates the revelation at Sinai and the giving of the Torah. It lasts two days (in Israel, one day).

Shulhan 'arukh (Hebrew, "set table")—The halakhic code (the most authoritative legal code of Judaism), written by the Sephardic rabbi

---

2   *Evreiskaia Entsiklopediia Brokgauza-Efrona*, 1908–1913, http://encyclopediya.ru/brockhaus-efron-jewish-encyclopedia/slovnik/03-5.html.

Yosef Karo (Yosef ben Efraim?) (b. 1488, d. 1575). It is based mainly on the rulings of Spanish authorities, and to this day it is regarded as the most widely accepted compilation of Jewish law. It was first published in Venice in 1565. The reason behind its general acceptance is the inclusion in this work of both Sephardic and Ashkenazic customs and positions. This was the result of happy circumstance: When Yosef Karo was compiling his code, the same type of work was being planned by the Polish rabbi Mosheh Isserles (Rema'). Initially, Isserles was saddened by this circumstance, but the question was resolved. The *Shulhan 'arukh* was published as a compilation, in which the positions of Rabbi Karo (according to Sephardic traditions) are followed by the supplements and glosses of Rabbi Isserles (in accordance with Ashkenazic traditions). Volume 1: *Orach chayim*, laws governing prayer and feast days; volume 2: *Yoreh deah*, various norms (*tsedakah* [charity], Torah studies, and culinary matters); volume 3: *Even HaEzer*, laws governing marriage and divorce; volume 4: *Choshen mishpat*, Jewish civil law.

Sub-kahals—Settlements with a small number of Jewish inhabitants, which did not form an independent kahal, as they were considered part of the territorially proximate community with regard to taxation and administrative affairs.

Synagogue (Greek, "gathering")—Jewish prayer building or place where Jews pray to God. According to Hebrew religious rules, a synagogue may be any structure that has been ritually sanctified.

TOZ (Towarzystwo Ochrony Zdrowia Ludności Żydowskiej w Polsce [Society for Safeguarding the Health of the Jewish Population])—Jewish health organization founded in Poland.

Tallit—Prayer shawl worn by Jewish men.

Talmud-Torah—Elementary-level religious school for boys.

Tanakh—The canon of the Hebrew Bible (in the Christian tradition, it corresponds nearly fully to the Old Testament). The word "Tanakh" is an acronym based on the initial letters of the first three chapters: T (for "Torah"), N (for "Neviim," the Prophets), and (K for "Ketuvim," the Sacred Writings).

Tanya (also known as *Likutei amarim*, Compilation of Teachings)— The main book of Hasidism; regarded as the principal work of the "Old

Rebe," Rabbi Shneur Zalman (b. 1746, d. 1813; 5505–5573, according to the Hebrew calendar), the founder of Habad Hasidism.

Tefillin (also called phylacteries; Hebrew, *batim*, "little houses")—Set of two small, black leather boxes that contain parchment fragments of the Torah. They are attached to the body by straps made of the hide of kosher animals: one is attached to the left arm (opposite the heart), and the other above the forehead, between the eyes. Tefillin are worn by Jewish men every day for morning prayers, except on the Sabbath and holidays. The sacred nature of the tefillin is second to the holiness of a Torah scroll.

Torah—The first five books of Moses (the Pentateuch). For public readings in synagogues it is permitted to use only a manuscript form—parchment scrolls—that have been specially copied by an educated individual, *i.e. a sofer* and blessed. For domestic use, a printed version may be used.

Treyf—Non-kosher foods whose use is not permitted by the law of kashrut, e.g., meat that is not permitted for use or which has been rejected for certain reasons (e.g., disease) after a special inspection procedure.

Tsadeket—Female tsadik.

Tsadik—A righteous man; spiritual leader of a Hasidic community; teacher and preacher (a person with a direct connection to God); a sage.

Ustyluh—A city in Volyn oblast, located eight kilometers west of Volodymyr-Volynsky. Following the revision of 1847, the "Ustyluh Jewish Society" numbered 1,487 people. According to the census of 1897, the city had a population of 3,590, of whom 3,212 were Jews. Today it is part of Volodymyr-Volynsky District.

Va'ad (Hebrew, "committee")—System of Jewish autonomous self-rule; a diet. The va'ad resolved questions pertaining to the internal life of the community, relations among the district va'ads, and questions relating to religious life; it also acted as a court of law. The va'ad was responsible for making sure that all Jews on the territory of Poland and Lithuania paid their taxes to the government.

Va'ad Arba Aratsot—A va'ad comprised of the leaders of four regions of Poland.

Western (Wailing) Wall (Hebrew, *HaKotel HaMa'aravi*)—The remnants of the wall of the Temple Mount in Jerusalem, which existed for 420 years and was destroyed by the Romans during the Great Judean Uprising in the year 68. The Western Wall is a remnant of the western part of the temple's external wall, discovered during the reconstruction of the temple by Herod the Great. It is one of the most sacred sites of Judaism.

Yad Vashem (Hebrew, "A Memorial and a Name")—The name is derived from the words spoken by the prophet Yeshayahu: "And to them will I give in my house and within my walls a memorial and a name [a "yad vashem"] ... that shall not be cut off" (Isaiah 56:5). Israel's official memorial to the Jewish victims of the Holocaust established in 1953. It operates the World Center for Holocaust Research, Documentation, Education and Commemoration and pays tribute to the Righteous Among the Nations, who, risking their lives, rescued Jews during the Second World War. Located on Har Hazikaron (Mount Herzl) in Jerusalem.

Yeshiva ("sitting," "meeting")—A higher religious institution dedicated mainly to the study of the Talmud. During a certain period of time, yeshiva had legislative and court functions. In the latter centuries it was also the place where scholars were trained to become rabbis. The *yeshivot* (pl.) produced the spiritual leaders of the Jewish people and fostered the creation of the intellectual elite. An indefinite period of study at a yeshiva opened the doors to knowledge for those who sought to penetrate the essence of the ethical and theological teachings of Judaism.

Yom Kippur—Day of Atonement, a Jewish holiday that falls on the tenth day of the month of Tishre, which ends ten days of atonement. This day is regarded as the holiest and most solemn day of the year; its main ideas are atonement and reconciliation. According to religious laws, all work is forbidden on this day, as well as consuming food and drink, washing, using cosmetics, wearing leather footwear, and engaging in sexual relations.

Zohar (Hebrew, "splendor," "radiance")—The foundational work of kabbalistic literature.

Bibliography

(English-, German-, Hebrew-, Polish-, Russian-, Ukrainian-, and Yiddish-language Works)

Almanacs, Encyclopedias, and Encyclopedic Dictionaries

Elektronna Ievreis'ka Entsyklopediia, http://www/eleven.co./il/article/14439 (Ukrainian)

Elektronnaia Evreiskaia Entsiklopediia, http://www.eleven.co.il/article/10945 (Russian) *Encyclopaedia Judaica*, Second Edition. 22 vols. New York, NY: Macmillan Reference USA, 2003.

Entsiklopedicheskii slovar' Brokgauz i Efron v 12 tomakh: biografii, vol. 12. St. Petersburg: Brockhaus-Efron, 1892. (Russian)

Evreiskaia Entsiklopediia Brokgauza-Efrona, 1908–1913, http://brockhaus-efron-jewish-encyclopedia.ru/

Oren, Y., M. I. Zand and Samuel Ettinger. *Kratkaia Evreiskaia Entsiklopediia*. Jerusalem: Keter, 1976-<1992>. (Russian)

Rossiiskaia Evreiskaia Entsiklopedia, http://rujen.ru (Russian)

Spector, Shmuel, Geoffrey Wigoder, and Yad Vashem. *The Encyclopedia of Jewish Life before and during the Holocaust*, vol. 3. Jerusalem: Yad Vashem; New York: New York University Press, 2001.

The Yivo Encyclopedia of Jews in Eastern Europe, http://www.yivoencyclopedia.org

Yerusholaymer Almanakh 28 (July 2008), Jerusalem.

Documents (Archival, Annotated)

"Doneseniia s zaniatykh vostochnykh oblastei no. 12," Russian State Military Archive [Rossiiskii gosudarstvennyi voennyi arkhiv, RGVA], f. 500k "Glavnoe upravlenie imperskoi bezopasnosti

(RSKhA)," (Berlin), op. 1, d. 775, l. 273–80, 472–88, http://www.9may.ru/unsecret/m10009001 (Russian)

State Archive of Volyn Oblast, Ukraine [Derzhavnyi Arkhiv Volyns′koï Oblasti, DAVO], R-1049, op. 1, spr. 1, ark. 37, 46. (Ukrainian)

"Sudebnyi prigovor nad zhidami, kotorye brosali kamniami v episkopa Vladimirskogo Meletiia Khrebtovicha i v sviashchennikov, sovershavskhikh krestnyi khod v gorode Vladimire. 22 maia 1590 g.." In *Arkhiv Iugo-Zapadnoi Rossii* (AIuZR), pt. 1, vol. 1, *Akty, otnosiashchiesia k istorii pravoslavnoi tserkvi v Iugo-Zapadnoi Rossii (1481–1596 gg.)*, edited by N. Ivanishev. Kyiv: Universitetskaia tipografiia, 1859. (Russian)

Volodymyrs′kyi grods′kyi sud: Podokumentni opysy aktovykh knyh, vyp. 1 edited by H. Boriak and L. Demchenko. Kyiv: Tsentral′nyi derzhavnyi istorychnyi arkhiv Ukraïny, 2002. (Ukrainian)

Journal Articles

Bar-Itzhak, H. "The Legend of the Jewish Holy Virgin of Ludmir: A Folkloristic Perspective." *Journal of Folklore Research* 46, no. 3 (September/December 2009): 26 –92.

Bulos, Ibn Az-Zaïm (Pavlo Khalebs′kyi). "Podorozh patriarkha Makariia (uryvky)." *Dzvin*, no. 9 (1990): 119–24. (Ukrainian)

Elbirt, Ia. "Federatsiia v N′iu-Iorke." *Yalkut Wolyn*, no. 35 (1978). (Yiddish)

_____. "Federatsiia v korotkikh shtrikhakh." *Yalkut Wolyn*, no. 43 (1988). (Yiddish)

Gakman, M. "Volynskaia Federatsiia v Los-Andzhelese." *Yalkut Wolyn*, nos. 53–54 (1997). (Yiddish)

Kulik, Aleksandr. "Evrei Drevnei Rusi: istochniki i istoricheskaia rekonstruktsiia," *RUTHENICA*, no. 7 (2008). (Russian)

Mandel′, E., and R. Brener. "40 let Dvortsu 'Volyn′.'" *Yalkut Wolyn*, nos. 55–56 (1998). (Hebrew)

Shiber, A. "Monument v pamiat′ o evreiskikh partizanakh i boitsakh Volyni." *Yalkut Wolyn*, nos. 55–56 (1998). (Hebrew)

Tsynkalovs′kyi, O. "Materialy do arkheolohiï Volodymyrs′koho povity," *Zapysky naukovoho tovarystva im. T. H. Shevchenka* 154 (1937). (Ukrainian)

"V Federatsii volynskikh evreev v Amerike." *Yalkut Wolyn*, no. 20 (1965). (Yiddish)

"V zemliachestvakh Izrailia: Torgovitsa, Goshcha." *Yalkut Wolyn*, no. 20 (1965). (Hebrew)

Ziskind, Sh. "Vsemirnyi Soiuz volynskikh evreev v 1987–98 gg." *Yakut Wolyn*, nos. 55 –56 (1998). (Hebrew)

Articles in Books

Nadol′s′ka, V., and L. Miroshnychenko. "Z istoriï ievreis′koï obshchyny Volyni." In *Mynule i suchasne Volyni: Oleksandr Tsynkalovs′kyi i krai; Materialy IX naukovoï istoryko-kraieznavchoï konferentsiï*. Lutsk: Nadstyr'ia, 1998. (Ukrainian)

Newspaper Articles

Deineka, Iu. "Beznevynni zhertvy." *Volodymyr vechirnii*, September 6, 2007. (Ukrainian)

Fedoryshyna, V. "Vshanuvannia pam'iati zhertv fashyzmu." *Slovo pravdy*, September 20, 1989. (Ukrainian)

"Holos svidka." *Radians′ka Ukraïna*, May 15 1982. (Ukrainian)

Ianovych, B. "Holokost na Volodymyrshchyni." *Slovo pravdy*, September 2, 2008. (Ukrainian)

Ivaniuk, L. "Do ievreis′kykh mohyl nesut′ kaminnia." *Slovo pravdy*, September 7, 2006. (Ukrainian)

Marhalit, M. "Hirka pam'iat′ P'iatydnivs′kykh mohyl." *Slovo pravdy*, January 12, 2006. (Ukrainian)

———. "Istoriia ievreïv Volodymyra-Volynskoho." *Volodymyr vechirnii*, August 17, 2006. (Ukrainian)

Mosoruk, N. "Znovu do mohyl nesly kaminnia." *Slovo pravdy*, September 16, 2008. (Ukrainian)

Muzychenko, V. "A pro pokhovannia zabuly." *Volodymyr vechirnii*, September 1, 2005. (Ukrainian)

———. "Konferentsiia: Pro istoriiu i trahediiu ievreis′koï obshchyny." *Slovo pravdy*, October 9, 2007. (Ukrainian)

———. "Kozhen pravednyk povynen otrymaty nahorodu vid derzhavy." *Slovo pravdy*, February 5, 2009. (Ukrainian)

———. "Ne znalo misto trahediï zhakhlyvishoï." *Slovo pravdy*, August 27, 2009. (Ukrainian)

———. "Khto zupynyt′ maroderiv?" *Volyn′*, May 17, 2011. (Ukrainian)

Nesteruk, Liubov. "P'iatydnivs′kyi 'Babyn iar.'" *Volyn′*, August 9, 2007. (Ukrainian)

Palaievs′ka, T. "Kvity ta kaminnia v pam'iat′ pro zakatovanykh." *Volodymyrs′kyi ekspres*, no. 38 (September 2008). (Ukrainian)

Pavliuk, K. "Orden i spokiina sovist′ Halyny Filatovoï." *Slovo pravdy*, January 22, 2009. (Ukrainian)

———."'Uzakonenyi' vandalizm: i na tomu sviti ne prysnytsia." *Misto vechirnie*, May 12, 2011. (Ukrainian)

Sharan, T. "P'iatydnivs′kyi 'Babyn iar.'" *Volodymyr vechirnii*, September 18, 2008. (Ukrainian)

Solodukha, A. "Pravedna stezhyna do lisovoï mohyly." *Slovo pravdy*, August 31, 2004. (Ukrainian)

Stemkovs′kyi, V. "'Babyn iar' na Volodymyrshchyni." *Volyns′ka hazeta*, October 11, 2007. (Ukrainian)

Tsaruk, Ia. "Holhofa nad Luhoiu." *Slovo pravdy*, July 10, 12, 18, 20, 24, 26, 27, and 31, 1991. (Ukrainian)

———. "Chornyi stovp dymu." *Slovo pravdy*, April 23, 1994. (Ukrainian)

"Volodymyrs′kyi bloknot na ivryti." *Slovo pravdy*, August 3, 2006. (Ukrainian)

Electronic Materials

http://www.aleph.org/IsraelTrips.htm

http://alefsfarim.com/ettinger/ocherki__po__istorii__evreyskogo__naroda/1-22.htm (Russian) http://www/haaretz.co.il/hasite/spages/449208.html PAGE NOT FOUND (Hebrew)

http://www.iajgs.org/cemetery/ukraine/vladimir-volynskiy.html

http://www.ictv.ua/wasp/ua/facts/detail.php?sec=213&id=635635

http://www.nazireich.net/forum/viewtopic.php?t=4139&sid=15d85fff3edfb223bcea255fa625c48b PAGE NOT FOUND

http://www.oldmaps.org.ua/all/lutsk/1100-Volodimir-Volinskii__Rosiya__1867

http://www.sztetl.org.pl/?a=showCity&action=viewtable&cat__id=16&city__id=1314&id=12973&lang=en__GB

http://www.yadvashem.org/yv/ru/righteous/poland/ziental.asp (Russian)

http://yivo1000towns.cjh.org

Bar-Asher, Shalom. "Yitshak ben Shemu'el ha-Levi," http://www.yivo-encyclopedia.org

Gogun, A., and A. Vovk. "Evrei v bor'be za nezavisimuiu Ukrainu," http://lib.oun-upa.org.ua/gogun/pub07.html (Russian)

Gorodetskii, C. "Evreiskaia starina 1909 g.," http://www.lechaim.ru/ARHIV/172/deva.htm (Russian)

Kolodny, D. "Celebrating the life of the Maiden of Ludmir," http://www.aleph.org/pdf/MaidofLudmir.pdf

Kral', Kh. "Pravnuk," http://www.judaica.kiev.ua/eg9/eg913.htm (Russian)

_____. "Romelii," http://judaica.kiev.ua/eg9/eg913.htm URL correct, but this item is not there.

Lukin, Benyamin. "Volodymyr Volyns'kyi," http://www.yivoencyclopedia.org

Muzychenko, V. "Viina tryvaie." *Novosti Khadashot*, http://vaadua.org/Hadashot%202011/Hadashot-06-2011/Had%2003-06-2011.html (Ukrainian)

"Rabbi Naftali Ha-COHEN family tree," http://www.loebtree.com/mahnl.html

"Rabbi Shlomo of Karlin," http://www.nehora.com/index.cfm?fuseaction=page.display&page__id=37&id=50&page=shlomokarlin.hetm&t=Rabbi%20Shlomo%20of%Karlin

"Raport zonderfiurera v ofitserskom zvanii E. Kumminga o ego sluzhebnoi poezdke v Sovetskii Soiuz v 1941 g. po zadaniu OKKh (otdel Frd. HeereOst IIC)," http://labas.livejournal.com/829546.html (Russian)

Reiner, Elchanan. "Yeshiva: The Yeshiva before 1800," http://www.yivoencyclopedia.org/article.aspx/Yeshiva/The_Yeshiva_before_1800

Slepoi, Alan. "Syn trekh narodov." http://pepovez.brinkster.net/html/son138.htm (Russian)

Sobolev, D. "Vozvrashchenie v Khazariiu," http://club.sunround.com/22/return.htm (Russian)

Stemkovs′kyi, V. "Istoriia i trahediia sela Zarichchia." *Volodymyrs′i ekspres*, April 28, 2011. (Ukrainian)

Tsivin, R. "Khronika odnoi zhizni, glava: 1946–1947 gg. Vladimir-Volynskii," http://www.proza.ru/2006/06/29-237 (Russian)

Ury, Scott. "Sabbath Rest," http://www.yivoencyclopedia.org/article.aspx/Sabbath_Rest

Van Gelder, L. "Woman Ahead of Her Time as a 19th-Century Rabbi," http://www.nytimes.com/1996/12/14/theater/woman-ahead-of-her-time-as-a-19th-century-rabbi.html

Willens, K. "Yiddish Theater," http://news.google.com/newspapers?nid=1891&dat+19970108&id=9r0fAAAAIBAJ&sjid=QNgEAAAAIBAJ&pg=1826,835646

"Wladimir-Wolynsk in Memory of the Jewish Community," http://yizkor.nypl.org/index.php?id-2483 (Hebrew, Yiddish)

Wunder, Meir. "Yehoshu'a ben Aleksander ha-Kohen," http://www.yivoencyclopedia.org/article.aspx/Yehoshua_ben_Aleksander_ha-Kohen

Books

Aronius. *Regesten zur Geschichte der Juden in fränkischen und deutsche Reiche bis zum Jahre 1273*. Berlin: Simion, 1902. (German)

Balaban, M. *Istoriia evreev v Rossii*, vol. 11. Moscow: Izd-vo T-va "Mir," 1914. (Russian)

Baliński, M., and T. Lipiński. *Starożytna Polska pod względem historycznym, jeograficznym i statystycznym*, 2d rev. & exp. ed., vol. 3. Warsaw: Orgelbrand, 1846. (Polish)

Bardakh, Ia. [Janusz Bardach], and Ketlin Glison [Kathleen Gleeson]. *Chelovek cheloveku volk: Vyzhivshii v GULAGe*. Moscow: Tekst, 2002. (Russian)

Buber, M. *Khasidskie istorii: pervye uchitelia* (Moscow: Mosty kul'tury; Jerusalem: Gesharim, 2006/5755). (Russian)

Deutsch, N. *The Maiden of Ludmir: A Jewish Holy Woman and Her World*. Berkeley: University of California Press, 2003.

Finberg, L., and V. Liubchenko, comps. *Narysy z istoriï ta kul'tury ievreïv Ukraïny*. Kyiv: Dukh i litera, 2005. (Ukrainian)

Firestone, T. *The Receiving: Reclaiming Jewish Women's Wisdom*. San Francisco: HarperSan Francisco, 2003.

Gutman, I. *Katastrofa i pamiat'*. Kyiv: Komplekttekhnika, 2008. (Ukrainian)

Hitler, A. *Reden und Proklamationen, 1932–1945*, commentaries by Max Domarus, vol. 2. Würzburg, 1962. (German)

Hrushevs'kyi, M. *Istoriia Ukraïny-Rusy*, vol. 5. Kyiv: Naukova dumka, 1994. (Ukrainian)

Isaievych, Ia., and F. Martyniuk. *Volodymyr-Volyns'kyi*. Lviv: Kameniar, 1998. (Ukrainian)

Kabanchyk, I., and O. Bohun, comps. *Mistsia skorboty: L'vivs'ka oblast'*. Lviv: Tsentr "Holokost" im. Ol. Shvartsa: Asotsiatsiia "Ukraïna-Izraïl'": LODO "Bnei-Brit Leopolis," 2003. (Ukrainian)

Kruglov, A. *Sbornik dokumentov i materialov ob unichtozhenii natsistami evreev Ukrainy v 1941–1944 godakh*. Kyiv: Institut iudaiki, 2002. (Russian)

Kuchynko, M. *Volodymyr seredn'ovichnyi*. Lutsk: Nadstyria, 2006. (Ukrainian)

_____., H. Okhrimenko, and V. Petrovych. *Istoriia mista Volodymyra-Volyns'koho z naidavnishykh chasiv do seredyny XX st.: u svitli sotsiotopohrafiï*. Lutsk: Volyns'kyi derzh. Universytet im. Lesi Ukraïnky, 2004. (Ukrainian)

Litopys rus′kyi, trans. Leonid Makhnovets′. Kyiv: Vyd-vo "Dnipro," 1989. Davn′orus′ki ta davni ukraïns′ki litopysy. (Ukrainian)

Margalit, M. *Childhood in Flames*. Tel Aviv, 2000. (Hebrew)

Marochkin, V. *Ukraïns′ke misto vid XV do seredyny XVII st.: Zvychaievo-pravova atrybutyka iak istorychnye dzherelo; Istorychna monohrafiia*. Toronto: Hypertext Plus, 1999. (Ukrainian)

Orenstein, H. *I Shall Live: Surviving against All Odds, 1939–1945*. New York: Beaufort Books, 1987.

Rabbi Shlomo of Karlin. *Shema Shlomo*. New York: Mir, n.d. (Hebrew)

Rosa, E. *Vospominaniia let, prozhytykh na Volyni*. Toronto, 1996. (Russian)

Sas, P., *Feodal′nye goroda Ukrainy v kontse XV–60-kh godakh XVI v.* Kyiv: Naukova dumka, 1989. (Russian)

Schiper, I. *Poczatki Zydow na ziemiach polskich i ruskich : od czasow najdawniejszych do r. 1350*. Tarnow: [s.n., 1917?] (Polish)

Shneer, A. *Plen: sovetskie voennoplennye v Germanii, 1941–1945*. Moscow: Mosty kul′tury; Jerusalem: Gesharim, 2005. (Russian)

Teodorovich, N. *Gorod Vladimir Volynskoi gubernii v sviazi s istoriei Volynskoi ierarkhii; Istoricheskii ocherk*. Pochaiv: Tipografiia Pochaevsko-Uspenskoi Lavry, 1893. (Russian)

Tsynkalovs′kyi, O. *Kniazhyi horod Volodymyr; Populiarno-naukovyi narys*. Lviv: Nakladom fondu "Uchitesia, braty moï," 1935. (Ukrainian)

_____. *Stara Volyn′ i Volyns′ke Polissia: Kraieznavchyi slovnyk vid naidavnishykh chasiv do 1914 r.*, vol. 1. Winnipeg: T-vo "Volyn′," 1984. (Ukrainian)

Index

A

Abramovych, Zrail, 17, 59
Agricultural training school, xxxiii, 85, 89–91, 101
Ahronova, Bohdana, 13
Aizen, Nisan, 98
Aizenberg family, 253
Aizenhart, children's camp councelor, 95
Akiba, Yossl, 41
Aktion, xl–xli
Alper, Golda Yakivna, 258
Alper, Moishe, 258
Alper, Samuil, 258
Alter Rebe, 27
Altvater, J., 222
"Amateurs" club, 106
American Jewish Joint Distribution Committee, (Joint) xxxiii, 82, 87
An-ski, Semen (Shloyme Zaynvl Rapoport), 45–46, 79
  Dybbuk, The, 46
Apeldman, Zev, 87
Ariel Singer, Nechama, 226, 229
Armia Krajowa, 158, 165, 197
aron ha-kodesh, 52, 56–57, 305
Asher, Rabbi, 31
Augustus II, King, xxx, 20
Avaticha, A., 269
Avigdor, Rabbi, 24

B

Ba'al Shem Tov, 27, 306
  Amud Hatefillah, 27
Babchuk, Dr., 89, 93
Babel, Isaac, 80
Babukh, Aron Nukhimovych, 137, 149, 156–157, 222
Bald, Mordechai Shlomo, 293
Bardach, Janusz (Natan) Markovich (Meirovich), xxxiii, 36, 106, 110, 114, 164, 171, 295–296
Bardach, Juliusz, 296
Bardach, Yakov Iuliovich, 296
Bardakh, Dr., 93
Bardakh, Ia. M., see Janusz Bardach
Barenkholts, Pesl, 95
Bar-Itzhak, Hayah, 36
Bass, Family (Eli, Pesl, Sarah, Shulamit) 219–221
Bass, Mykhail, xliv, 137, 189, 219–222, 281,
Batory, Stefan, King 10
Battle of Blue Waters, xxviii
Bazykin, Boris, 166
Bdanski, Asher Chaim, 58
Beit-Yaacov, 90, 104, 261,
Berberov, Henek, 226
Berberova, Mrs., 226
Berger, Esther, 175
Berger, Itshak, 175
Berger, Leon, 226
Berger, Rafi, 175, 217
Berger, Leon, 226
Bergman, Simcha, 126, 137
Bergman (Stein), Shoshana, 226
Betar youth organization, see Volodymyr-Volynsky
bet ha-midrash, 39–40, 57, 305
Bezalel, Ishaya ben, Rabbi, xxix
Bezalel, Yitshak ben, Rabbi, xxix, 19, 21–22, 25
Bima, 52, 56–57, 305

Birman, Dr., 89
Blokh, Dr., 246
Bohush, Hanna, 138, 189, 195
Boiarsky, Mikhel, 156-157
Boikes, Moshe, 88
Boim, Pesia, 97
Bokser, D., 89
Boleslaw the Pious, King, 7
Borenstein, Aaron, 226
Borenstein, Elia, 226
Borenstein, Klara, 226
Borenstein, Netel, 256
Borenstein, Pola, 256
Borenstein, Raia, 226
Botchan, Rachel, 46
Braune, Wilhelm, 168
Brekner, Mikhael, 87, 104-105
Broder, Feibl, 56
Browning, Christopher, xxxix
Buber, Martin, 27, 31
Bubis, Dr., 93, 110
Bubis, Itskhak, 89, 105
Budenshtein, Yaacov, 97

C
Casimir the Great, 7
Chaim ben Yitshak, Rabbi (Maharah), xxix, 6
Cheskis, Avrom, 296-297
Cholokhov, Serhii Dmytrovych, 72
Christianity, Christians, xxv-xxvi, xxviii-xxx, 2, 6, 8, 10-11, 16, 22, 59, 63-68, 77, 113, 124, 157, 210, 237, 240
Christian reconquest of Spain, 6
Church Union of Berestia (1596), 12
Clifton, John, 47
Cohen, Pepa [Paulina], 237, 240
Commissar Order of 6 June 1941, xxxviii
Committee of the Wolyn Center, 269
Committee of Volodymyr-Volynsky Natives, 268
Czartoryski, Aleksander, Prince, 59

D
Daluege, Kurt, xxxvi
Danylo of Halych, Prince, 5
David bar Khasdai, Rabbi, 4
Davydovych, Isaac, 59
Delburd, Roza, 165, 186
Desbois, Patrick, xl
Deutsch, Nathaniel, 35-36, 38n75, 41-42, 45, 46n81, 48n87, 66n117, 75, 301n6
Diachuk, Oleksandr, 224, 240-242
Diachuk, Pavlo, 224, 242
Diachuk, Solomeia, 224, 240-242
Diamant, Shmuel, 197
Diner, Meir, 56
Dluhach, Shloyme, 59
Dobryniuk, Paraskoviia Ivanivna, 203
Dov Ber from Mezhyrich, 26
Dubnow, Simon, 61
Dubnytsky, Mykhailo, 60
Dubralo, Isaac ben, 5
Dvorovska, Helena, 256

E
Ephraim ben Jacob of Bonn, 3
  Sefer Zekhirah, 3
Einsatzgruppen, xxxvii-xxxvii, 169
Eizenberg, Chana, 252-253
Eizenberg, Yosyf-Tzvi, 252-253
Elimelekh, Rabbi, 32
Elin, Yaacov, 87-88
Eretz Yisrael, 85, 100, 106, 305
Etrog, 265
Etz chaim, 256, 258, 260

F
Faivish, Meshulam, 24
Fedorivka, 18, 143
Feldman, Harry, xlv
Filarent, Leib, 109
Filatova, Halyna Serhiivna, xliv, 236-240

Fisiuk, Epistymiia (Ustymiia) Vakulivna, 224, 249
Fisiuk, Omelian Petrovych, 224, 249, 251
Flit, Pesach, 280, 282, 285
Flot, Zakhariia, 98
Frankfurt, Natan, 242
Frimer, Debora, 176
Frimer, Elke, 176
Frimer, Henya, 176
Frimer, Israel, 176
Frimer, Leah, 176
Frimer, Moshe, 176
Frimer, Pesach, 176
Fuchs, Motel, 158

G

Galiatovsky, Ioanikii, 63
Galicia-Volhynia, Principality of, xxviii
Garczynski, Leon, 215-216, 224
Garczynska, Zosia (Zofia), 215-216, 224
ghetto, 14, 55, 114, 117, 119, 121, 125, 131-135, 137, 139-140, 147-155, 160, 165-168, 171-176, 178-179, 182-185, 187-188, 191, 195-196, 210-213, 215, 220-221, 225, 230, 237-238, 244, 254, 256, 281-282, 287, 292, xl-xli
Ginsberg, Yaacov, 56
Golansky, Yaacov, 268
Goldberg, D., 88
Goldenberg, Karl-Yakutiel, 165
Goldenberg, Yehuda-Arie, Rabbi 123
Goldfarb, David, 156
Goldfarb, Rachel, 156
Goldshtern, Rabbi, 109
Golshtein family, 142-143, 145
Grinberg, Isaak, 243
Grossman, Itskhok-Isaac, 82
Grossman, Vasily, 204
Gruber, Shymshon, 242

H

Hagerman, Moshe, Rabbi 127
Ha Halutz youth organization, 100-101
Ha-Khaver (Comrade), xxxiii, 104
ha-Kohen, Yehoshua Ben Alexander, 22
ha-Levi Segal, Isaac ben Samuel, xxix, 22-23
  Siah Yitshak, 23
Ha-Levi Segal, Shelomo (Shemuel), Rabbi, 23, 33
ha-Nadib, Benjamin, Rabbi 3
Hannover, Natan, 61
Hanukah, 265, 306
Hapin, Leiba, 154
Hapko (née Sheptytska), Yevheniia Stepanivna, 247-248
Harari (Berger), Yaacov, 175-176, 217
Hasidism, xxxi, 25-27, 31, 35-36, 45, 55, 83, 306
Hebrew, 2, 7, 22-25, 29, 39, 70, 85, 87-90, 101, 103-104, 107, 170, 178, 204, 219, 223, 269, 272, 292, 296, 299
heder, 70, 104, 307
Heichal Yahaduth Wolyn (Beit Wolyn), 269-270, 274-275
Heist, M., 198
Heller, Asher, 84, 89
Heller, Yom-Tov Lipmann, xxix, 19, 23-24
Helmond, Shmuel Izrailevych, 297
Hemulka, Arie, 226
Herbert, B., 168
Hershtansky, Demian Iosyfovych, 297
Heydrich, Reinhard, xxxvi-xxxviii
Hladkova, Stepanyda Oleksiivna, 190
Hoffman, Miriam, 47
Horbachevsky, Petro, 293
Horodecky, Shmuel Abba, 36
Horowitz, Ya'akov Yitshaak, Rabbi 25, 35
Hraievsky, Stanislav, 59

Hrushka, Leibl, 88
Hrushevsky, Mykhailo, 16
Hynailo, Mykola, 293

I

Ihor Yaroslavych, Prince, 5
Ingber, Avraam, 87-88
Ingebar, Shoshana, 97
Interieur, Debora, 177-181
International Holocaust Remembrance Day, 227
Isaac ben Isaac, see Menahem Mendel
Ishaya ben Yitshak, Rabbi xxix, 19, 22
Islam, 6
Israelis, Dr., 99
Ivri, Ida, 226

J

Jabotinsky, Vladimir, 106, 128
Jagiello, King, 9
Jagiellon, Casimir IV, 10
Jagiellon, Alexander, Grand Prince, xxix, 10
Jewish Council (*Judenrat*), xxix, xl-xli, 121, 125-126, 125n25, 128, 130, 133-134, 137, 149, 179, 182, 212, 214, 220-
Jewish population of Volodymyr-Volynsky, 3-7, 66-68, 116, 295-300, xlii, xxvii-xxviii, xxxiii
  killed by Polish insurgents, 197
  life in twentieth century, 78-111
Jewish POWs, 190-191
Jewish printing houses, 59

K

Kabbalah, 25, 33, 307
Kaddish, 44, 271, 307
Kagan, Ruth Gan, Rabbi, 44-45
Kahals/kehila, 12-14, 19-20, 64-65, xxx
Kalfin, Robert, 47
Kam, Arie-Leib, 192
Kaminsky, Dr., 93
Kaplia, Vasyl, 17
Karduner, Wolf, 156
Karliner, see Shelomoh Gotlieb of Karlin
Karlin-Stolin dynasty, xxxi, 26, 35, 58
Karp, Beni, 97
Katz, Dr., 93
Kaufman, Chaim, 87
Kazimierz the Great, King, xxviii
Kazimirski, Ann, 55, 139, 181-185
Kazimirski, Henry, 93, 139, 184
Kazimirsky, Joshua, 181
Kazimirski family, 181
Keitelman, Marian, 244
Ketuvim (Writings), 6, 310
Khalemsky, Moisei, 107
Khigsh, Choren, 98
Khmelnytsky, Bohdan, xlvii, 60-63, 201
Khmelnytsky Uprising, 60-62
Khofen, Aron, 98
Khorunzhy, Yukhym Ustymovych, 189-190
kibbutz, 267
Kiper, Itsyk, 217
Kiper, Menashe, 217, 268, 277
Kipnis, Dr., 93
Kirgser, Moshe, 268
Klainer, Yehoshua, 87
Kleikhal, Jakub, 9
Kliger, David, 56
Kliger, Kakhat, 97
Klinmints, Chaim, 87-88
Kniazevsky, B. M., 77, 114
Koch, Erich, 122
Kochubes, Menachem (Mikhael), 268
Kohen, Bina, 97
Kohen, Bluma, 97
Kohen, Yakob, 125
Kofman, Chaim, 88
Kornfeld, Yaacov, 97
Korytnytsia, 201-203, 307
Kosher, 61, 67, 90, 307-308

Index

Kostiuk, Vasyl, 190
Kovalchuk, Halyna Oleksandrivna, 246
Kovalchuk, Oleksandr, xlv
Kovar, Mari, 255
Kovar, Wojtech, 255
Kozlovsky, Oleksandr Ivanovych, 246
Krall, Hanna, 25, 36, 45, 106
Krigser, Eva, 165, 185-186
Krigser, Moshe, xliv, 165, 185-187, 197, 277
Krigser, Tova, 185
Krigser, Joshua-Wolf, 185
Krigser family, 185
Kudysh, Leib, xli, 220
Kumming, E., 135-136
Kuproser, 89
Kurbski, Andrzej, Prince 13
Kyba, Yaroslav, 101
Kyivan Rus', Jews of, 2

L

Leizar, Nachim, 13
Lerer, Leib, 98
Leskovsky, I., 140
Lesyk, S. V., 281
Levit, Rachel, 243-244
Levit, Tuvia, 243-244
Levkovych, Fishel, xxx, 20
Liashchuk, Yefimiia, 254-255
Liashchuk, Yermolai, 254-255
Liberman, Rachel, 89
Libers, Aron-Moshe, 89, 98
Lipiński, Anatolii, 224
Lipińska, Iryna 224
Lipiński, family, 163-164, 231-233, 235-236
Lipińska, Kateryna Petrivna, 163, 224, 231-236, 257
Lipiński, Rostyslav, 224
Lipiński, Tymoteusz, 16n35
Liuksemburg, Anatolii Izrailevych, 297
Lizen, Aleksandr (Isroel Lizenberg), xl, 280

Lokachi, 13, 58, 90, 140, 216, 308
Lukin, Benyamin, 17n38, 19n43, 21, 62n105, 71n127, 78n134, 82, 301n1
Lutsk Congregation for Progressive Judaism, 289
Luzzatto, Shemu'el David, 23
Lysiuk, Nadia Dmytrivna, 199-201

M

Maariv (evening prayer), 57
Magid, 26, 40-41, 308
Maksymuk, S., 140
Malinowski, Jurek, 159
Manoakh ben Ya'akov, Rabbi xxix, 21
Margalit, Moshe, xliv, 121, 131, 135, 148, 166, 170, 198-199, 204-219, 268, 277, 289, 292
Margalit, Chaim, 205-209, 212-214
Margalit, Chana 205, 207
Margalit, Judah, 205, 207
Margalit Mordechai, 205, 207-209
Margalit, Sosia Rachel, 205
Margalit, Tali, 205, 207
matsevah, 34, 71-72, 75-77, 264, 308
Maziar, Fedir Mykhailovych, 202
Melech, cantor, 57
Melnytsia, village 141
"Memory of Babi Yar," Foundation, 227
Menachem Mendl, 58
Mendel, Moshe Goldberg, 58
Mendelson, Lipa, 58, 250, 252
Mendelson, Mordechai, 251-252
Miaskovska, Olha Pylypivna, 225, 239-240
Miaskovsky, Serhii Tykhonovych, 225, 239-240
Mibab, Peretz, 217
Mibab, Reuven, 217
Migdal, Freida, 226
Minyan, 57, 308
Mitsvah, 44, 308
Molotov-Ribbentrop Pact, 104, 116

Mordekhai of Chornobyl, Tsadik, 36–37, 40–41
Morgenshtern, Yaacov-David Rabbi, xl, 83, 109, 125
moshav, 267
Moshe, Rabbi, 24, 33
Moskaliuk, Mykola Vasyliovych, 147
Moyshe of Ludmir, 35
Mstyslav Iziaslavych, Prince 5
Muzychenko, Volodymyr, xxv–xxvi, xli, xlviii, 196, 288, 293
Muzykansky, Dr., 94, 197
Mykulychi Druhi, 143, 147, 188

N
Nadler, Allan, 35
National Democrats (NDs), 199, 308–309
Nazaruk, Halyna Zinoviivna, 249–252
Nazi anti-Jewish genocide, xxxiv–xxxvi
Nazi ideology, 114–115, 122
Nazis occupancy of Volodymyr-Volynsky, see Volodymyr-Volynsky, Nazi occupancy
Nestyruk, Herasym, 252–254
Nestyruk, Kyrylo, 252–254
Nestyruk, Marta, 252, 254
Nestyruk, Nastia, 253–254
Nestyruk, Potap, 252, 254
Nevi'im (the Prophets), 6, 310
Nifak (nee Liashchuk) Nadia, 254–255
NKVD (People's Commissariat for Internal Affairs), 110–111, 122–123, 131, 208, 245
Noach, Rabbi, 25, 35
Novak, Dr., 93
Nuger, Abram Petrovych, 297–299

O
Oberuk, Kasia, 222
Oberuk, Mykola, 222
Oderman, Israel, 93
OFLAG "Nord 365," 190–192
Ohlendorf, Otto, 169
Oitser, Dr., 93
Okon, Yosef, 88–89
"On Conferring State Awards of Ukraine" decree, 227
Operation Barbarossa, xxxvi–xxxvii, xxxix
Orenstein, Henry, 118n12, 128–129, 130n32, 138, 139n47, 149n61, 160, 163n71, 231–232, 235–236
Organization for Rehabilitation through Training (ORT), 104–105
orphanage, 20, 84, 92–96, 104
Ostrozky, Kostiantyn, Prince 17, 59
Otsaliuk (nee Diachuk), Maria Oleksandrivna, xliv, 224, 240–242
OUN (Organization of Ukrainian Nationalists), 166, 192

P
Palace of Wolyn Jews, 270, 272
Pasalsky, Vasyl, 157
Patuta, Volodymyr Oksentiiovych, 187–190
Paul of Aleppo, 63
"People's Kitchen," 92–93
Pekler family, 244
Peredun, Olha, 257–258
Peredun, Petro, 257–258
Peril, Chaim, 87
Perlov, Aaron, xxxi, 26,
Piatydni, xl, 44, 59, 72, 84, 119, 137–143, 146–148, 151–154, 167, 170, 173, 176, 187–190, 195–196, 203, 212, 215, 222, 230, 249–251, 271, 276, 279–293, 296
memorials, 251, 276, 279–288

Poalei-Zion Party, 98
Podlipski, Dr., 93
Podlis, 88
Poiva family, 142
Polishchuk, Klavdiia Danylivna, 224
Polish Committee of National Liberation, 268
Polish-Lithuanian Commonwealth, xxvii
Porytsk, 58–59, 90, 117, 186, 195, 220
Prokopiuk, Lidia, 176
Ptashnyk, Yosyp, 245
Pysets, Avraam, Rabbi 3–4

R

Raisfeld, Yosef, 217
Rapoport-Albert, Ada, xxxin2, xxxii
Rasch, Otto, 170
Reisfeld, Eliezer (Lazar), xliv, 149
Reiter, Yankel, 158
Rekunovych, M. V., 281
"Righteous Among the Nations," xliv, 223–230, 238, 242, 254–255, 258
"Righteous of Ukraine," 224, 238
Roh, Feivel, 255
Roh, Herschel, 252–253
Roh, Leah, 252–253, 255
Roiter, Avraam, 226
Roiter, Irka, 226
Roiter, Klara, 226
Rokhvarger, Beila, 226
Rokhvarger, Roza, 226
Roman Mstyskavych, Volhynian prince, 5
Rosa, E., 140, 141n53
Rosh Hodesh, 42, 57
Rozenhak, head of Poland's network of Tarbut schools, 88
Rozmarin, Aharon, 299
Rudnytsky, Andrii, 280, 282, 285
Ruthenian principalities, xxviii

S

Sabbath, 14, 19–20, 24, 28, 41, 67, 64n110, 182, 299, 309, 311
Sachkovych, Eska, 17
Sachkovych, Peisach, 17
Sahaniuk, P., 280
Savchenko, Yurii, 110
Savchuk family, 175
Savchuk, Savko, 175–176
Savych, Lev Mykolaiovych, 141, 147
Schiper, Ignacy, 4, 5n11
Schorr, Mojżesz, xxvii
seder, 108, 309
Segal, David ben Shemu'el ha-Levi, (Taz) 22–23
Ture zahav, 23
Segen, Yosef, 89
Semeniuk, Ivan Pylypovych, 155
Semitsky, Yanka, 89–90
Shachter-Shalomi, Rabbi Zalman, 44
Shampan, Azriel, 215–216
Shats, Shmuel, 97
Shavuot, 27, 57
Sheinebaum, M., 87–88
Sheinkestel, Pinchas, 87–89, 126
Shekhter, Dr., 93, 108, 110
Shelomoh Gotlieb of Karlin, xxxi, 26–35, 300
books written, 29–30
holiness of, 28–29, 32–33
Sheptytska, Maria Fomivna, 247–248
Sheptytsky, Stepan Antonovych, 247–248
Shimshon, Rabbi, 4
Shkolnik, David, xlv
Shlomo bar Yits[hak], 4
Shmoilovych, Itsko, 13, 59
Shmuel from Lutsk, cantor, 56
Shmukler, Itshak, 98
Shneer, Aaron, 190
Sholem Aleichem Library of Jewish Literature, 97
Shrah, Froim, 244

Shrah, Sarah, 244
Shraier, Israel, 98, 105
Shtern, Natan, 98, 104–105
shtibl, xxi, xxxi, 39, 55, 57, 69–70
Shulhan 'arukh, 12, 22–23, 34, 309
Shymanovych, Nachim, 59
Sigismund I, August, King, 10, 14
Sinai, Rabbi, 4
Singer, Rachel, 226
Singer, Rukhtsia, 226
Sinicki, Nachum, 89
Slepo, Alan, 257
Skolar, Yosef, 97
Smoliar, Yosyf, 215
Sobolev, Dennis, 3, 6n13
Sokhatsky, T., 140
Sokuler, 258
Soviet partisan movement, 165
St. Francis of Assisi, 30
Stahlecker, Franz Walter, xxxviii
Stampfer, Shaul, 62
Stanisław August, King, 20
Stein, Chenia, 226
Stein, Reizl, 226
Stemkovsky, Volodymyr Antonovych, 149, 159, 160n70
Stepaniuk, Yevdokii Ivanovych, 246
Stepasiuk, Matii, 189
Strojvons, Franciszek, 225, 243–245
Strojvons, Hanna, 225, 243–245
sub-kahals, 13, 61
Švitrigaila, Grand Duke , xxviii, 11
Symonenko, Vasyl, 270
synagogues, 5, 12–13, 15, 22–23, 28, 44, 47–58, 63–64, 69–70, 78, 82–83, 90, 111, 116, 132–133, 135, 201, 203, 205–206, 219, 258–259, 275, 291, xlvi–xlvii, xxix, xxxi

T
Tabak, Chaim-Zelig, 241–242
Tabak, Gitel, 240, 242
Tabak, Reizl, 241–242
Tabak, Semor, 242
tallit, 41, 80, 310
Talmud-Torah elementary religious school, xlvi, 70, 78, 84–86, 104, 219, 310
Tanakh, 6, 37, 299
Tarbut institutions, xxxiii, xlvi, 85–89, 91, 101, 104, 107, 135
Tarn, Alex, 46
 Dybbuk, The, 46
Tazhbuchevycheva, Svietliba, 13
tefillin, 41, 311
Topolia-Hertel, Matilda, 163–164, 233, 235
Torah, xlvii , 6, 12, 20, 23, 30, 36–37, 39, 41, 56–57, 70, 78, 84, 104, 206, 219, 263
Torbechko, Bernard, 244
TOZ (Towarzystwo Ochrony Zdrowia Ludnosìci Zydowskiej w Polsce), 92–94, 219, 310
Treaty of Versailles, 85
treyf, 61, 311
tsadeket, 26, 311
tsadik, 26–29, 32, 34–37, 40–41, 311
Tsaruk, Yakov 256
Tsaruk, Yaroslav (Ia.), 120n15, 129n31, 131n34, 141, 147, 149n60, 151, 153n65, 159, 164n72, 167, 168n82, 190n98, 223n1, 245n8, 286
tsedakah, 92, 310
Tsuker, Chaim, 171
Tsynkalovsky, Oleksander, 3, 65
Tsyvin, Roman, 170
Tulchyn, Dov Ber, 35
Türner, Günther, 258
Türner, Ludwig, 257–258

U
Union of Lublin (1569), 12
Unzer lebn (Our Life), xxxiii, 103–104

UPA (Ukrainian Insurgent Army), 166, 192–193
Ustyluh, 16, 58, 79, 90, 94, 117, 121, 134, 137, 141, 143, 146, 148, 160, 164, 185, 195–198, 202, 231, 254–255, 267, 270, 281, 285, 299
Uri Ben Pichas of Strelsk, 34

V

Va'ad Arba Aratsot (Council of Four Lands), xxx, 18–20, 24, 311
    Assembly of Regional Dayanim, 19
    Assembly of Regional Elders, 19
va'ad, 14, 18, 20, 24, 291, 311
Varma, Shaya, 192
Vasylkovych, Prince Volodymyr, 5
Vavrysevych, Mykhailo, 224–225, 227–229
Vavrysevych, Jr., Mykola, xliv, 224, 227–230, 236, 257
Vavrysevych, Maria, 225–228
Vavrysevych, Mykola Mykhailovych, xliv 224–230, 257
    Fascist Ghetto, The, 230
Veiler (Venger), xl , 125
Volodymyr Sviatoslavovych of Kyiv, Prince, xxvii–xxviii, 1
Volodymyr-Volynsky, xxvii, 295–300, 303,
    Akiba youth organization, 219, 259
    Austrians and Ukrainians in, xxvii, xxxii–xxxiii, xl–xlii
    émigrés from, 98–99, 267–273
    everyday Jewish artifacts, 263–266, 290
    fourteenth—sixteenth centuries, in economic conditions, 16–18
    organization of settlements, 14–16
    spiritual leaders, 20–26
    Hasidic dynasty of tsadiks in, xxxi, 34–35, 39
    history, xxvii–xxix, xxvii–xxviii, 1–2
    Jewish cemetery, 32, 66, 71–77, 129, 170, 196, 289, 308
    Jewish educational institutions, xxxiii, 70, 78, 83–92, 104, 107, 290
    Jewish hospital, 12, 66, 69, 78, 92, 97, 104
    Jewish pogroms and killings, xxxiv, xxxviii, 60–64, 79–80, 98, 148–150, 175–176, 183, 210–215, 221–222, 267
    liberation of (1944), xli , 170–171
    map prepared by O. Tsynkalovsky, 11
    monuments, xlvi, 131, 281–285, 288–291
    national composition of city and county of, 70
    Nazis occupancy,
    destruction of Jewish population, 120–170
    directives to Jews, 126–128
    food ration cards to Jews, 129
    ghetto Jews, 132–134
    Polish colonies near, 197
    privileges to Jewish settlers, 7–12
    safeguarding the memory, 289–293
    under Tatar rule, xxix
    taxation, 66–67
    traces of Jewish community, 258–262
    Zionist youth movements in, xxxiii
    Betar, xxxiii, 105–106, 305
    Ha-No'ar ha-Tsiyoni, xxxiii, 90, 106
    Ha-Shomer ha-Leumi (National Guard), xxxiii
    Ha-Shomer ha-Tsa'ir, xxxiii, 90, 92
    Ha-Tsofim (scouts), xxxiii, 90
Vorchyn, 169, 197–199
Vorobchuk, Stakh, 143
Vorzel, Esther, 254–255
Vozniuk, I. V., 55, 72, 118, 256

Vozniuk, Teklia Ustymivna, 156–157, 256
Vozniuk, Vasyl Mykhailovych, 156–157
Vytautas of Lithuania, Grand Duke, xxix, 8–9, 11

W

Warsaw Sejm (Diet), 20
Weinberg, Frida, 226
Weinboim, Abraham, 98
Weingarten, Rakhel, 95
Weinstock, Yosyf, 172
Weinstock-Zaar, Zippora (Feiga), xliv 172–174, 271
Weisgarten, Eliezer, 98
Weisman, Nachum, 198
Werbermacher, Khane-Rokhl (Maiden of Ludmir), xxxi–xxxii, 26, 35–47, 300
Westerheide, Wilhelm, 117, 131, 135, 137, 139, 141, 148, 168–169, 184–185, 210, 212, 218, 222
Wierzbowska, Maria, 183
Wilhelm, Shlomo, xxxi, 35
Willens, Kathy, 47

Y

Yad Vashem, 187, 190, 226, 233, 236, 242, 245, 254–255, 257, 266, 270
Yagel, Roman, 187
Yakira, Eliahu, 198, 245
Yakira, Irena (nee Ziental), 224, 243–245
Yakovovych, Avram, 13
Yakymiuk, Petro Semenovych, 146
Yalkut Wolyn (Volyn Almanac), 269, 270n6, 272n8
yeshiva, xxxii, 22, 24–25, 58, 70, 78, 90, 104, 312

Yevtoshuk, Liudmyla Stepanivna, 249–252
Yiddish language, xxxiii ,7, 11–13, 24, 45, 47, 85, 87, 103–104, 107, 154, 172n91, 177, 206, 216, 269, 272, 281, 292, 299
Yiddish-language periodicals, xxxiii, 103–104
Yiddish Theater (Folksbiene), 46, 47n84
Yom HaShoah-Holocaust Remembrance Day, 271–272
Yom Kippur, 31, 121, 210, 312
Yosef, Rabbi (from Hush Khalava), 4
Yushchenko, Viktor 277

Z

Zafram, Abram, 98
Zaichuk, N., 140
Zanvil, Rabbi, 19
Zarichchia, 143, 156–157, 159, 160n70, 189, 256
Zasadko, Olena, 246
Zasadko, Petro, 245–246
Zavydovych, Yankel, 151
Zetzik, the school principal, 88
Zeligzon, B. D., 282
Zelle, Johanna Eleonore, 137, 168, 212, 218
Zhornytsky, Ya. A., 281
Zhyntop, Zosia, 97
Ziental, Bronislawa, 225, 243–245
Ziental, (Yakira) Irena, 225, 243–245
Zilbert, Dora, 165
Zlatohorsky, Oleksii, 47
Zohar, Abigail, 44
Zohar, 28, 307, 312
Zuberman, Motel, 226
Zuberman, Tonia, 226
Zusia, Rabbi, 32
Zygmunt, August II, King, xxix–xxx
Zylinski, Mr. 186, 199

www.ingramcontent.com/pod-product-compliance
Lightning Source LLC
Chambersburg PA
CBHW061930220426
43662CB00012B/1854